SENSIBLE TAX REFORM

This book lays out a tax program that is well thought out, timely and holds the promise for a major transformation in how the American economy functions. In my work with companies across the economic spectrum, I see the misaligned incentives of the current system – creating suboptimal decisions in compensation, health care and retirement programs. That misalignment also encourages business decisions favoring debt rather than equity investments and, often, foreign investment rather than investments in the US - even when non-tax factors favor the US. Tax issues should not drive multi-billion dollar business decisions about where to invest and grow. This book suggests reforms that would eliminate misalignments and benefit the US economy and the US workforce.

The approach suggested here has numerous virtues:

- The system is clearer, more easily understood and far more free of incentives to "game the system" than what we live with now
- Businesses will have a more level playing field in the US and abroad – allowing decisions that reward the best product, the best service and the best ideas rather than rewarding tax management
- Individuals have an incentive to save and invest. Short-term consumption is no longer more advantageous than long-term saving. If taxes take away future value, people make short-term decisions. Preserving and growing value is simply a more logical approach – this book lays out a path to meet that objective

The US economy deserves a better tax system. We need a system that supports intelligent decisions by businesses and individuals. We need a system like this.

—**David A. Osterndorf**, Chief Actuary – Towers Watson
Member - Board of Actuaries, US Department of Defense
Medicare Eligible Retiree Health Care Fund

At a time when most Americans are discontented with the current tax system, there is a need for fresh ideas for overhauling the Internal Revenue Code. Many feel the current tax system is a drag on the economy because of its extreme complexity resulting in excessive costs of compliance to individuals and corporations and the enforcement problems associated with the Internal Revenue Service. There are many ideas for reform but most focus on simplifying the current tax code. Past experience in reforming the tax code has generally resulted in creative revisions to the code to satisfy the needs of special interest groups.

In ***Sensible Tax Reform***, Professor Korth has developed a unique plan that will eliminate most of the complications of our current system. His plan completely eliminates the corporate income tax, Social Security and Medicare taxes on both businesses and individuals, personal income taxes on all except the very wealthy and estate taxes. They will be replaced by a federal consumption tax and a tax on the personal income of those earning more than $1 million annually.

Korth's plan is revenue neutral and addresses the issue of transition to his proposed plan. ***Sensible Tax Reform*** offers a sophisticated proposal for tax reform and is consequently a must read for anyone interested in making our tax system simpler and more fair.

—**R. Austin Daily**, Ph.D., CPA
Professor of Accounting (retired)
Texas A&M University

In ***Sensible Tax Reform***, Dr. Christopher Korth has done more than take Occam's Razor to the behemoth we call the United States tax code. He has completely re-engineered it to more efficiently and effectively do the job it was designed to do -- support the legitimate work of government in a fair, efficient, and effective way.

Our current federal tax system requiring 77000 pages of documentation seems indefensible to me. So often when taxes are covered in the news media, we know in our guts we are being cheated. But the complexity of the system prevents us from knowing how. Dr. Korth has created a much simpler, and most exciting, much more transparent tax process that can be understood by everyone. The idea of transparency alone is enough to make lobbyists and tax attorneys quiver in their custom-made boots.

Dr. Korth moves much of the burden of taxation from production to consumption, providing a broad tax base with few exemptions. Implementing his vision in the face of powerful interest groups that greatly benefit from the complexity and inequality of our current tax system will be an enormously challenging task. It seems quixotic in its scope and ambition. Sancho, would you be good enough to fetch my sword?

—**Thomas Rienzo**, PhD,Business Information Systems
3325 Schneider Hall
Western Michigan University
Kalamazoo, MI 49008
269-387-5511
thomas.rienzo@wmich.edu
http://homepages.wmich.edu/~trienzo

SENSIBLE TAX REFORM

SIMPLE, JUST AND EFFECTIVE

CHRISTOPHER M. KORTH

New York

SENSIBLE TAX REFORM
SIMPLE, JUST AND EFFECTIVE

Published in New York, New York, by Morgan James Publishing. Morgan James and The Entrepreneurial Publisher are trademarks of Morgan James, LLC.
www.MorganJamesPublishing.com

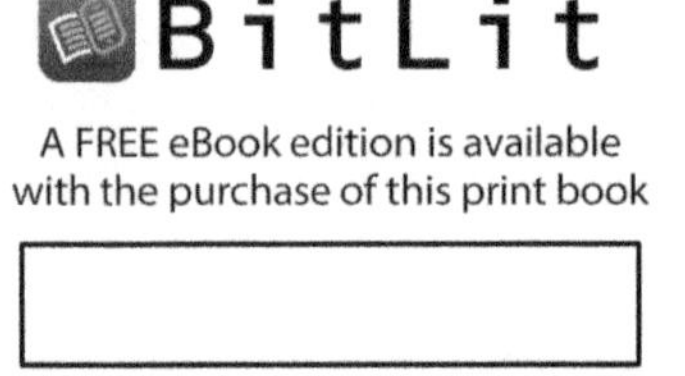

CLEARLY PRINT YOUR NAME IN THE BOX ABOVE

Instructions to claim your free eBook edition:
1. Download the BitLit app for Android or iOS
2. Write your name in UPPER CASE in the box
3. Use the BitLit app to submit a photo
4. Download your eBook to any device

ISBN 978-1-63047-086-9 paperback
ISBN 978-1-63047-087-6 eBook
ISBN 978-1-63047-088-3 hardcover
Library of Congress Control Number:
2013957755

Cover Design by:
Chris Treccani
www.3dogdesign.net

Interior Design by:
Bonnie Bushman
bonnie@caboodlegraphics.com

To the wonderful women in my life:

Shirley

Katie, Jennie, Bess & Sarah

CONTENTS

Preface xi

Part A The Problem—Our Current Tax Regime 1

Chapter 1 An Unbelievable Mess! 3

Chapter 2 The Burden of the American Tax System 16

Chapter 3 Taxes! Taxes! And More Taxes! 31

Chapter 4 Lies, Damn Lies & the Tax-Writing Process 46

Part B The Solution—*Sensible Tax Reform: Simple, Just and Effective* 59

Chapter 5 Tax Simplification, Justice and Effectiveness 61

Chapter 6 Federal Consumption Tax 85

Chapter 7 A Simple-and-Just Federal Tax on Very High Incomes 106

Part C The Impact of the *Sensible Tax Reform* Tax Plan 127

Chapter 8 ***Sensible Tax Reform*** and American Families 129

Chapter 9 ***Sensible Tax Reform*** for American Businesses 149

Chapter 10 ***Sensible Tax Reform*** for the American Government 169

Part D Making *Sensible Tax Reform* Work 187

Chapter 11 Transition to ***Sensible Tax Reform*** 189

Chapter 12 Is ***Sensible Tax Reform*** Right for America? 209

About the Author 219

Bibliography 221

Index 223

EXHIBITS

Exhibit 1-1: US Government Debt Held Abroad 12

Exhibit 2-1: Sources of Revenue for the Federal Government 20
Exhibit 2-2: Balance on Current Account 25

Exhibit 3-1: Total Tax Revenues (as a percent of GDP) 33

Exhibit 5-1: U.S. Government Revenues: 2012 65
Exhibit 5-2: Personal Taxes under our Current Tax System 69
Exhibit 5-3: Personal Taxes under ***Sensible Tax Reform*** 71
Exhibit 5-4: ***Sensible Tax Reform*** —Simple, Just & Effective 84

Exhibit 6-1a: Effective Tax Rates 92
Exhibit 6-1b: Effective Tax Rates 92
Exhibit 6-2: Income under the Current Tax System 96
Exhibit 6-3: Purchases and Savings under the Current Tax System 97
Exhibit 6-4: The ***STR*** Impact upon Income 98
Exhibit 6-5: The ***STR*** Impact upon Purchases 99
Exhibit 6-6: The ***STR*** Impact upon Total Savings 100
Exhibit 6-7: The ***STR*** Impact upon the Savings Rate 100

Exhibit 7-1: U.S. Government Revenues: 2012 108
Exhibit 7-2: Income and Taxes under the Current Tax System 108

Exhibit 7-3: Spending and Savings under the Current Tax System 110
Exhibit 7-4: Form 1040 HI: Income 115
Exhibit 7-5: Tax Brackets for Married Taxpayers Filing Jointly 117
Exhibit 7-6: Income Taxes Due under ***STR*** 118
Exhibit 7-7: Estate Taxes under our Current Tax System 121
Exhibit 7-8: Estate Taxes under ***STR*** 122

Exhibit 8-1: The ***STR*** Impact upon the Consumption of Low-Income Groups 132
Exhibit 8-2a: The ***STR*** Impact upon the Consumption of Middle-Income Groups 134
Exhibit 8-2b: The ***STR*** Impact upon the Savings of Middle-Income Groups 135
Exhibit 8-3a: The ***STR*** Impact upon the Consumption of High-Income Groups 136
Exhibit 8-3b: The ***STR*** Impact upon the Savings of High-Income Groups 137
Exhibit 8-4: FCT on the Purchase of Homes 144
Exhibit 8-5: FCT on the Purchase of Vehicles 146

Exhibit 9-1: Assets "Permanently Reinvested" Overseas (2012) 163

Exhibit 10-1: Balance of Trade (2011) 179
Exhibit 10-2: Major Foreign Holders of Treasury Securities (June 2013) 180
Exhibit 10-3: International Reserves (2012) 181

Exhibit 11-1: ***Sensible Tax Reform***: Personal Taxes—5-Year Transition 191
Exhibit 11-2: ***Sensible Tax Reform***: Corporate Taxes—5-Year Transition 196

PREFACE

America is at a crossroads in its history. We are confronting many serious economic, political and social problems that our government does *not* address and indeed often actually aggravates! Our government in Washington lacks strategic vision and ignores many critical issues that will only get worse by failing to confront them.

One of these critical problems, which affects not only our economy but also our political system and our very society, is the American federal system of taxation—income taxes, profit taxes, Social-Security taxes, Medicare taxes, and estate tax*es*. The US government has wrapped our families and our businesses in a smothering tax system that is:

- Unintelligible to any of us,
- Difficult to comply with,
- Very unfair to most Americans,
- Very expensive to each one of us,
- Imposed on all sectors of our economic life (our income, our expenditures, our assets and our savings), and which
- Distorts the integrity of our federal government.

Yet this is a situation which is within our power to correct—and quickly!

This book offers an innovative proposal for a sweeping, but simple and sensible, revision of the way in which the federal government taxes our country. Adoption of this proposal will increase the real income and wealth of virtually ALL Americans! The reader will find that the proposed system is:

- Clear and understandable,
- Simple to comply with,
- Just to all Americans, and
- That it will provide the basis for a strong economic boom that will create hundreds of thousands or even millions of jobs!

And because of its justice, balance and favorable impact upon the entire economy, this tax proposal will be very attractive to a wide range of Americans—moderates, conservatives and liberals alike. As a result, it will have a better chance of acceptance in Congress than any of the other proposals that are being promoted for serious tax reform.

Discussion of taxes, and especially tax reform, is not usually something that excites most readers. [In fact, it is usually effective reading for someone who is having trouble falling asleep!] However, the reader will find this book to be interesting, educational, thought provoking—and it may even change your life!

Chapters 1-4 examine the problem—the mess that is our current tax system. Chapters 5-7 are the core of the entire book; they explain the essence of ***Sensible Tax Reform—Simple, Just and Effective***. [A reader with a thorough knowledge of our current tax system and its many flaws or someone who simply wants to jump into the essence of this book could immediately read Chapters 5-7.] Chapters 8-10 examine in detail the impact of this tax proposal upon families, businesses and the government. The final two chapters, 11 and 12, discuss the process of transitioning to the proposed tax system and summarize why and how ***Sensible Tax Reform—Simple, Just and Effective*** is right for America—right now!

PART A

THE PROBLEM—OUR CURRENT TAX REGIME

Chapter 1: **An Unbelievable Mess!**
Chapter 2: **The Burden of the American Tax System**
Chapter 3: **Taxes! Taxes! and More Taxes!**
Chapter 4: **Lies, Damned Lies & the Tax-Writing Process**

CHAPTER 1

AN UNBELIEVABLE MESS!

We've got the best tax policy in the world.
—President George W. Bush

Everyone who has anything to do with the tax code agrees that it is an unbelievable mess!
—Paul H. O'Neill, U. S. Treasury Secretary under George W. Bush

Like almost everyone else, I hate taxes—especially our federal taxes:

- They are so complicated that I cannot understand them.
- The annual April 15 ritual of preparing my income taxes is something I view with dread.
- The design and complexity of the system makes it very unjust—so that only the wealthy can afford the tax experts who can help them take full advantage of tax loopholes.
- This complex, convoluted tax system is bad for our businesses and our economy.

- Our federal tax system makes it difficult for American companies to compete internationally, leading to:
    - o The off-shoring of hundreds of thousands of American jobs,
    - o Hundreds of billions of dollars of annual trade deficits and
    - o The need for our government and businesses to borrow *trillions* of dollars from foreign lenders, especially from foreign governments.
- And, our current federal tax system undermines not only the effectiveness but even the very integrity of both the White House and Congress.

More than 200 years ago, Benjamin Franklin quipped that *nothing in this world is certain but death and taxes*! That is still true today. However, Ben would not be so casual in his comment if he could see today's American federal tax system. President Bush might have had an optimistic view of our tax system but even his own Treasury secretary labeled it "an unbelievable mess." Indeed, our system is a fiasco—unfair, complicated and very damaging to our economy, our standard of living and even to our government. The tax system needs change—radical change!

Sensible but Fundamental Tax Reform

This book, ***Sensible Tax Reform—Simple, Just and Effective*** proposes a new federal tax system that will be:

- Simple—unlike our present system which is so complex that no one understands it.
- Just—in contrast to our current tax mess which is unfair to most taxpayers—poor, middle income and wealthy alike.
- Focused only upon collection of taxes—instead of our existing Internal Revenue Code that focuses as much upon offering numerous loopholes for the advancement of social and political goals as it does upon collecting taxes.
- Stimulating to our businesses—which will be so different from our current system that hurts our businesses, damages our entire economy and weakens us internationally.

In order to accomplish these goals, our new federal tax system must be radically different. We can no longer continue with the annual congressional ritual of merely "rearranging the deck chairs on the floundering Titanic" that is our tax system today.

Our Federal Tax System Is a Scandal!

Our current tax system here in the United States is more than a mess. No one really understands it—no one! *Do you know how much you actually pay each year in taxes*? Few of us, in fact, even know how many different types of taxes that we actually pay.

Fewer and fewer taxpayers can even prepare their own taxes without professional help. The Internal Revenue Service reports that almost two-thirds of all personal tax returns are prepared with the assistance of tax specialists. The tax system is an unbelievable mess for individuals, businesses, the entire economy, the government and even society.

How Big Is the Tax Mess?

In 2005, President Bush appointed a bi-partisan *Advisory Panel on Federal Tax Reform* to recommend ways to improve our federal tax system. The panel accurately summarized the case against our current federal tax system:

For millions of Americans, the annual rite of filing taxes has become a headache of burdensome record keeping, lengthy instructions, and complicated schedules, worksheets and forms—often requiring multiple computations that are neither logical nor intuitive. Not only is our tax system maddeningly complex, (but it also) penalizes work, discourages savings and investment, and hinders the competitiveness of American businesses. The tax code is riddled with tax provisions that treat similarly situated taxpayers differently and create perceptions of unfairness.[1]

Thus, the president's own commission notes that, for *individual taxpayers*, the federal tax code is:

- Burdensome;
- Maddeningly complex;
- Illogical;

- Riddled with provisions that treat some taxpayers better than others; and
- Perceived to be unfair.

It also:

- Penalizes work, and
- Discourages personal savings and investment.

For *businesses*, the report notes similar flaws of the current tax system:

- Burdensome, complicated and illogical;
- Discouraging corporate savings and investment; and also
- Hindering the competitiveness of American businesses.

The present situation of the U. S. federal tax code is intolerable! It is unjust! It becomes more and more unwieldy every year. *Every* observer of this existing system calls for significant changes. Virtually every politician (whether in Congress or the White House; whether Republican, Independent or Democrat) objects to its complexity—despite the fact that *they* are the source of those tax laws. Virtually every economist (whether conservative, moderate or liberal) complains about the system's inefficiency and ineffectiveness. Virtually every spokesman in society (whether business, labor, consumer or investor) berates the tax system for its injustice.

Taxes—a Necessary but Unavoidable Evil

Although we might resent taxes and our current tax system, it is obvious that they are unavoidable in a modern society. I accept them because they are necessary. Nevertheless, there is no need for the taxes to be so bewilderingly complex. It is infuriating that complying with the tax code is so difficult. [Remember how you feel as April 15 approaches each year and you prepare your taxes!] And, it is demoralizing to see that our tax system discourages prudent consumption and investment decisions, makes it difficult for the bulk of the population to provide for retirement, is manipulated to the advantage of special-interest groups (both individual and corporate) and is almost universally perceived to be unjust. I hate taxes! My wife hates taxes! My four kids hate taxes! In fact, I don't know any taxpayer who doesn't hate taxes! At best, they are a necessary, but unavoidable, evil.

The American tax system is in trouble. Indeed, it is broken! The first four chapters of this book will explore the extent, source and nature of the horrible tax system that has evolved over the years. The rest of the book will explain my proposed solution. Serious tax reform is badly needed, and needed now: ***Sensible Tax Reform—Simple, Just and Effective!***

Our Federal Tax System Is Incomprehensible!

Our current federal tax code, together with its supporting materials, is very big—more than 77,000 pages. How could we expect our congressmen or even tax accountants and tax lawyers to have read, let alone understand, such a mass of mess?!? [In contrast, the entire Bible contains less than 1400 pages. The Internal Revenue Code is as long as 55 Bibles!]

The size and complexity of the federal tax code is bad enough. However, the President's Tax Panel also observed how often it changes:

> Since the last major reform effort in 1986, there have been more than (15,000) changes to the tax code, many adding special provisions and targeted tax benefits, some of which expire in just a few years. These myriad changes decrease the stability, consistency and transparency of our current tax system *while making it drastically more complicated, unfair, and economically wasteful* (emphasis mine). Today, our tax system falls well short of the expectations of Americans that revenues needed for government should be raised in a manner that is simple, efficient, and fair.[2]

15,000 changes in only nineteen years! That averages almost 790 changes a year—*more than two changes per day*, seven days a week, fifty-two weeks per year for nineteen years!!!!

Seeking Tax Help

At least we might hope that tax accountants have mastered this labyrinth. It is after all their "bread and butter." Alas, it is not so. The American Institute of Certified Public Accountants (AICPA), the professional organization whose members include the foremost tax experts in the country, decries the complexity of our federal tax code. Even for tax experts, it is a nightmare!

For some years, Money Magazine periodically sent the tax information of a hypothetical family to more than forty tax accountants. Seldom did any of the experts get the return totally correct—and their estimates of the taxes owed could vary by thousands of dollars!

No wonder millions of taxpayers turn to the Internal Revenue Service for help in clarifying their confusion. Indeed, why didn't the CPAs in the above survey contact the IRS for clarification of any ambiguities? Perhaps it is because studies by the IRS itself have shown that more than 40% of all calls to the IRS yield wrong answers! What could be a more damning indictment of our tax system?

Even IRS commissioners, such as Shirley Peterson, acknowledge the craziness of our tax code:

> Eight decades of amendments (to the federal tax) code have produced a virtually impenetrable maze...The rules are unintelligible to most citizens...(And) the rules are equally mysterious to many government employees who are charged with administering and enforcing the law.[3]

The rules are "unintelligible" and change so often that there is ***no one*** who really understands our tax system:

- Corporations with highly-skilled tax accountants cannot understand it.
- CPAs and tax lawyers cannot understand it.
- IRS agents do not even understand it.
- Certainly no member of Congress understands the tax laws that he/she has helped to pass.

If none of these tax experts can understand this "virtually impenetrable maze," how can we "civilians" hope to understand? If we do not understand the system, we may well pay more taxes than are necessary because of our ignorance, caution and mistakes—which might also lead to government audits and possibly expensive penalties.

It is inexcusable that we are subjected to such excessive work and worry. Our current morass of federal taxes must end. It needs serious surgery. ***Sensible Tax Reform—Simple, Just and Effective*** is a comprehensive proposal for fundamental federal tax reform that is "simple, efficient, and fair" [President Bush's tax panel].

An Unmitigated Tax Mess

Our tax mess imposes unfair and unnecessary burdens for families, for businesses, for the American economy and even for our federal government.

A Mess for American Businesses

Companies pay income taxes and must also match the payroll-tax payments (Social Security and Medicare) of their employees. This is an especially heavy burden on labor-intensive industries (e.g., fast-food restaurants, grocery stores, department stores and many farms). Proprietorships, partnerships and small companies find it to be especially onerous.

Businesses actually pay much more in Social Security and Medicare taxes than they pay in income taxes. In FY 2012, businesses paid $242 billion in income taxes and $423 billion in payroll taxes—for total federal business taxes of $665 billion. 64%, almost two thirds, of the federal taxes paid by American businesses was Social Security and Medicare! In addition, tax-compliance expenses added another $150 billion of costs. [Compliance expenses cost companies two thirds as much as the income taxes that they pay.] Tax reform is needed to ease these burdens. Tax reform is especially needed in order to allow American companies to compete more effectively against their foreign competitors in both our export and import markets.

Embedded taxes: The firms from whom we buy our food, clothes, appliances and utilities have included (that is, embedded) all of their costs such as wages, supplies, interest payments, rents, etc. in the prices they charge. Included also are the costs of their payroll taxes as well as the implicit cost of income taxes. In a like manner, their suppliers have passed along embedded taxes to them and those taxes are also included in the prices that we pay. The cumulative 5-20% of embedded taxes significantly raises prices that we pay domestically. It also is included in the prices of both the exports of American companies and the goods and services that compete against imports.

Anything that can be done in the area of tax reform which will lower taxes on businesses will lead both to lower prices for us and to greater efficiency and competitiveness for American companies. That will save taxpayers hundreds of billions of dollars each year. We will be replacing many current federal taxes, several of which we do not even realize that we pay, with a new tax system which is transparent and easy to comprehend. As we shall see in later chapters, the elimination of these embedded taxes will be one of the key ways in which ***Sensible Tax Reform—Simple, Just and Effective***! will transform our economy!

A Mess for American Individuals and Families

Our federal tax system for individuals and families is actually a three-part system: Social Security and Medicare taxes, personal income taxes and the estate and gift taxes. Also, there are the numerous embedded taxes mentioned above.

Payroll taxes (i.e., Social Security and Medicare) are charged from the very first dollar earned, with no tax breaks of any sort. They are heavy burdens for not only the poor but also middle-class Americans. Up to an income of more than $65,000, most Americans pay more in Social Security and Medicare taxes than they do in income taxes. And, regardless of how poor someone is, payroll taxes are neither refundable nor even tax deductible.[4]

Individual taxpayers spend a substantial amount of time and money complying with our tax obligations (especially the April 15 ritual). Also, tax-related planning for retirement, healthcare and education imposes an additional heavy burden. Each of these is an important social goal that has been injected into the federal income tax. However, by including such "social engineering" in the income tax, both the taxes and social goals become more complicated and less satisfactory. These goals could, and should, be accomplished more transparently and honestly via other means.

The compliance and planning burden that the tax system imposes upon all income-taxpaying Americans is difficult, unjust, inefficient, wasteful and expensive. There is a better way—a much better way! ***Sensible Tax Reform—Simple, Just and Effective*** will show the way [Chapter 5].

A Mess for the American Economy

There is a heavy burden for individuals of trying to take advantage of the opportunities for saving taxes provided by retirement, health and educational accounts. Businesses similarly spend billions of dollars structuring investment decisions in order to benefit from tax angles. The Tax Foundation's estimates do not include any of these extra tax-related expenses. Nor does it include the $10 billion budget of the IRS, or the legal and accounting costs for individuals and companies that are involved in IRS audits and appeals to tax courts. Overall the tax-related costs exceed $260 billion annually. Most of that is wasted, non-productive expenditure that not only does not help the economy but also, as shall be shown, distorts and hurts our families, businesses and the overall economy.

Interest rates and debt: The way in which the tax laws reward or punish different types of income or expenses also has a very major impact upon the economy. For example, interest payments are generally tax-deductible for businesses and sometimes also for individuals (e.g., home mortgages). This tax deductibility of interest payments encourages both businesses and individuals to borrow more than they might otherwise be inclined to do. This is neither economically nor socially wise—as thousands of companies and millions of homeowners found in the 2007-2010 mortgage crisis and credit crunch. Also, lenders need to pay income taxes on most of their interest earnings, and therefore demand higher interest in order to cover their taxes on that income.

Americans borrow too much. Our companies borrow too much. And, our governments borrow too much. The United States has become the world's major borrower. This is true both domestically (where we borrow from ourselves) but also internationally, where we must rely upon the willingness of others (especially foreign governments) to lend to us.

International trade and debt: Our taxes make American producers much less competitive versus foreign competitors. Although most industrialized countries export more than they import, the United States does just the opposite. We import $700 billion dollars more of goods and services every year than we export. We spend like drunken sailors on leave! It costs us millions of jobs. It threatens the economic future of our country.

When we spend more abroad than we bring in, the difference must be financed from abroad. Such international financial irresponsibility can only last as long as other countries are willing to lend us the money with which to import from them. Our federal government owes more than four trillion dollars ($4,000,000,000,000) to foreign lenders. As Exhibit 1-1 illustrates, the US Government owes $1,276 billion to China and $1,083 billion to Japan and more than $120 billion to each of eleven other countries or groups as well! Most of those debts are held by the governments of those countries. And the total continues to grow rapidly—year after year, with absolutely no indication of slowing down.

Exhibit 1-1
US Government Debt Held Abroad[5]
(Billions; June 2013)

China	$1,276
Japan	$1,083
Caribbean banking centers	$291
Oil exporters	$257
Brazil	$254
Taiwan	$186
Switzerland	$180
Belgium	$176
United Kingdom	$163
Luxembourg	$151
Russia	$138
Hong Kong	$124
Ireland	$121

Like any debtor, the United States is at the mercy of its lenders. This heavy reliance upon borrowing from other governments, especially ones such as China with whom we have many current or potential strategic disputes, is economically risky and politically very awkward. It gives those governments financial leverage over the U.S. Government. ***Sensible Tax Reform—Simple, Just and Effective*** will help America internationally as well as domestically, by making American companies much more competitive in the world markets and by reducing America's need to rely upon foreign markets and governments for its money.

A Mess for the American Government

The international prestige and influence of the American government is directly related not only to its military strength but also to its economic strength. For many years after the second World War, the U.S. economy was not only the world's largest, but also the most dynamic, innovative and respected. That brought not only many economic advantages and the social benefits that went with it, but it provided our government a strong economic base and unsurpassed international prestige for its international activities.

That has changed drastically. The dollar is still the world's currency. However, many governments and companies are for the first time seeking alternatives to the dollar for pricing goods (such as oil), for maintaining international reserves and as a safe haven for investing funds during international tensions. The dollar's prestige has suffered significantly in recent years.

The U.S. economy is still by far the world's largest. However, it has lost its diversity. Millions of American jobs have been off-shored. Entire companies and complete industries have been lost to foreign countries. These factories and companies are still generally owned by American investors, which can be profitable. But, they are not creating many jobs in the U.S. Our economy is not only becoming rusted out, but its manufacturing sector is becoming hollowed out. Where are the good-paying jobs going to come from? Optimists note that America has repeatedly innovated and renovated the economy—automobiles, telecommunication, computers, software, etc. However, when that occurred, we still enjoyed a strong diverse economic base. Our economy has narrowed greatly.

American money and capital markets have long been the financial engine for the world economy—the largest, the most innovative and the most competitive. Now it is an object of scorn—selfish, blind to its own shortcomings, even stupid. It is widely perceived to be the source of the Great Recession of 2007-2010. The entire world has paid for its great excesses.

Although never a savings powerhouse, the American economy was able to fund most of its capital needs in years past. However, Americans have forgotten how to save. America (households, businesses and governments) is addicted to debt. Coupled with our failure to save, this has lead to massive, unhealthy and even dangerous reliance upon foreign lenders to fund our debt binges.

Conclusions

It is clear that there are many heavy penalties that we pay for our current system of federal taxes on income:

- The federal tax code is very complex and confusing.
- It changes constantly, often manipulated by our political leaders for merely political motives.
- It is very unjust to most Americans and American companies.
- Complying with it is difficult, time-consuming and expensive for both businesses and families.
- The intrusion of the government into our private lives through the tax system is excessive.
- Both individuals and companies have the incentive to try to "game" the system by trying to find loopholes in its complex features.
- When companies pay corporate income, Social-Security and Medicare taxes, the costs are added to (embedded in) their sales prices that make the producing companies less competitive and increases inflation.
- The anti-competitive effects of those taxes hurt our overall economy, hurt American companies and destroy American jobs.
- Embedded taxes hurt our international trade, seriously aggravate our trade deficits and lead to heavy borrowing from foreign lenders.

In Chapter 2, the burden of our tax system and the way in which it hurts our families, businesses and overall economy will be addressed. Chapter 3 will examine the complex nature of our taxes. Chapter 4 will explore the very complex, and often reprehensible, way in which tax laws are often written and passed.

Endnotes

1 President's Advisory Panel on Federal Tax Reform; *America Needs a Better Tax System; April 13,* 2005; p. 1

2 President's Advisory Panel on Federal Tax Reform; *America Needs a Better Tax System; April 13,* 2005; p. 1

3 Speech at Southern Methodist University, April 14, 1993

4 Although many of the poor qualify for the earned-income tax credit, which is designed primarily to offset payroll taxes

5 www.treasury.gov/resource-center

CHAPTER 2

THE BURDEN OF THE AMERICAN TAX SYSTEM

Taxes are the price we pay for a civilized society.
—Oliver Wendell Holmes, Jr.; US Supreme Court justice

As was seen in Chapter 1, our existing federal tax system is complex, unjust, burdensome, expensive and very ineffective. In this chapter, the real economic cost of this system will be examined.

Few people have any concept of how much he or she actually pays each year in taxes. We are taxed on income, purchases, transfers and property. We are taxed by all levels of government—federal, state and local. On the average, Americans pay about 25% of all their income in taxes.

The Direct Tax Cost to Individuals and Families

We will be focusing upon the five most visible and emotionally tinged of the federal taxes—the Social Security tax, Medicare tax, the personal income tax, the estate tax and the corporate income tax.

Social Security and Medicare Taxes

The basic income taxes on most individuals are the Social Security and Medicare taxes (the so-called payroll or employment taxes). They are charged on our wages and salaries from the very first dollar of earnings. Even workers below the poverty level, even those on welfare, must pay them! Unlike income and estate taxes, the rules governing Social Security and Medicare taxes are very simple: there are no exceptions, no exemptions, no exclusions, no deductions, and no credits. They are charged only on *earned* income, such as wages, salary, bonus, commissions and tips. However, dividends, interest, capital gains and other forms of *unearned* income, which are the sources of most of the income of most of the extremely wealthy, are *not* subject to these taxes.

The Social Security tax is 6.20% of wages & salaries—but only up to $113,700 per year (2013).

It is not collected on earnings above that level. Medicare is taxed at a 1.45% rate without a ceiling on earned income. [Thus, the payroll tax on wages and salaries is 7.65% up to $113,700 but only 1.45% (the Medicare tax alone) above that level.] Unearned income is charged neither Social Security nor Medicare taxes.

These are clearly taxes that Congress has deliberately designed to fall most heavily upon the poor and middle-income groups. Social Security and Medicare taxes are very *regressive* taxes—a heavy burden on the poor and middle classes, but having little impact upon the wealthy. *Indeed, most Americans pay more in Social Security and Medicare taxes than they do in federal income taxes!*

Personal Income Tax

The federal income-tax code is by far the most complicated of all of the tax laws on individuals. Numerous loopholes impose very different treatment of people at different *levels* of income and even different people at the same level of income but with different *sources* of income.

Unlike payroll and estate taxes, the income tax applies to all income levels. It involves a very complex array of exclusions, exemptions, deductions, credits, phase-ins, phase-outs and special tax rates for certain forms of income.

Individuals and families can be taxed on a wide array of income sources: wages, salaries and tips; dividends, interest, and capital gains; pensions, annuities and other retirement income; Social Security receipts; unemployment compensation; alimony received; personal business income, including farm income; awards and gambling winnings; income from trusts and estates; and many others.

The income tax is nominally progressive—charging higher tax rates for higher incomes, with eight different tax brackets—0%, 10%, 15%, 25%, 28%, 33%, 35% and 39.6%, with no ceiling on income. However, dividends and capital gains are taxed at only about half the rate that is applied to salaries, wages and other earned income—a maximum of 20% when the individual income tax rates are higher than that.

There are also numerous loopholes which only high-income taxpayers with sophisticated advisers are able to utilize. As a result, although the income tax is nominally progressive, it can be very regressive in terms of its actual effective impact upon taxpayers. Warren Buffett, one of the wealthiest Americans, famously challenged a large group of billionaires to prove that their secretaries do not pay a higher average tax than they do. Not one could do so! [Buffett acknowledged that his own average rate was only about 17%.] That makes no sense either economically or socially. Ours is a culture that has always prided itself upon being a *meritocracy*—one that encourages and rewards work. However, our federal tax system rewards wealth accumulation much more than it rewards work and success based upon personal effort.

If the income-tax codes simply focused upon the collection of taxes, it would still be incredibly complicated. However, presidents and Congress have distorted our tax laws in many ways in order to accomplish economic, political and social goals that have little or nothing to do with taxes: home ownership, charitable contributions, assisting with high medical costs, energy efficiency, retirement savings, etc., etc., etc. Some of the special provisions are designed to benefit the poor (e.g., the earned-income tax and child-care credits). Many more provisions primarily benefit the very wealthy who have the greatest opportunity to take advantage of such deductions (e.g., not many low and lower-middle income taxpayers have $1,000,000 mortgages, the interest on which is tax deductible) or can realize $500,000 of tax-free capital gains on the sale of homes.

Any of these may be desirable goals, but they are social or economic (or merely politically-expedient) goals and not directly related to our tax system. This adds immeasurably to the complexity, injustice, cost and inefficiency of the tax system. This "social engineering" needs to be completely eliminated from our tax system.

The United States is one of very few countries that tax the *foreign* income of their citizens. Individuals cannot avoid or generally even defer such taxes (although businesses can—and do—on a massive scale). The same tax rules generally apply to foreign income as for domestic income.

Estate and Gift Taxes

The fourth direct federal tax on individuals and families is the tax on estates and gifts. In terms of its tax impact, the estate tax is the exact opposite of the Social Security tax—it is progressive. A very generous provision excludes the first $5,250,000 (for 2013) of an estate from the tax, so that only the wealthy pay any estate tax. *More than 99% of all estates owe no tax at all!* For those that do owe taxes, the marginal tax rate is 40%, the highest rate of all of our federal taxes. However, the average rate paid is less than 16%. Like the income tax, the estate tax is very complex, penalizes those without the expertise to game the system, and treats similar estates very differently from one another. Like the federal income tax it is unfair—and a nightmare. It also needs to be changed.

Overall Tax Burden

Collectively, these four taxes are very heavy burdens upon taxpayers. Exhibit 2-1 details just how much the federal government actually collects in taxes ($2.4 trillion in 2012—the same as in 2006) and the source of those taxes (more than $1.1 trillion from personal income taxes, more than $240 billion in corporate income taxes, and $845 billion in Social Security and Medicare taxes. As this book will show, there is a simpler approach which would leave the federal government no worse off (i.e., with "tax neutrality") while individuals, businesses and the economy as a whole would be much better off.

The Direct Tax Cost to Businesses

Businesses also pay income (i.e., profit), Social Security and Medicare taxes. These burdens complicate the managing of business, add greatly to costs, increase prices, make our businesses much less competitive internationally and cost us hundreds of thousands of jobs.

Exhibit 2-1

Sources of Revenue for the Federal Government[6] (Billions)					
	1998	2002	2006	2012	% of 2012 Revenue
Personal income taxes	$828.6	$858.3	$1,043.9	$1,132.2	46.2%
Corporate income taxes	$188.7	$148.0	$353.9	$242.3	9.9%
Social Security & Medicare taxes	$571.8	$700.8	$837.8	$845.3	34.5%
Estate and gift taxes	$24.1	$26.5	$27.9	$14.0	0.6%
Excise taxes	$57.7	$67.0	$74.0	$79.1	3.2%
Import duties	$18.3	$18.6	$24.8	$30.3	1.2%
Other federal-government revenue	$32.8	$34.2	$44.9	$107.0	4.4%
Total USG Revenue	**$1,722.0**	**$1,853.4**	**$2,407.2**	**$2,450.2**	**100.0%**

Corporate Income Tax

Congress has also devised a complicated progressive tax on corporate income with a seemingly erratic pattern of nine rates: 0%, 15%, 25%, 34%, 39%, 34%, 35%, 38% and 35%. This convoluted structure is further complicated by such adjustments as deductions; accounting conventions for inventory pricing and depreciation; exclusions, credits and many other special loopholes. However, as Exhibit 2-1 shows, businesses actually pay only one fifth as much of the federal *income* taxes as individuals do.

Corporate Social Security and Medicare Taxes

Businesses (and most government and non-profits as well) must match, dollar for dollar, the Social Security and Medicare taxes that they withhold from their employees. For capital-intensive companies (e.g., utilities), these payroll taxes are not generally major burdens. However, for the millions of businesses that are labor intensive (e.g., restaurants, department stores, doctors, plumbers and accountants), the taxes can add substantially to total costs. Employers, private and government together, pay half (about $420 billion per year) of the entire Social Security and Medicare bills—a very heavy load. The self-employed pay an especially heavy burden since they must pay both as an employee and as a business—15.3% of their salaries, twice the level that employees pay.

The Tax Burden: The Cost of Compliance and Planning

Intaxification: The euphoria that a taxpayer feels from getting a tax refund, which lasts only until he realizes that it was his own money that he was getting back!
—Author unknown

The taxes that we pay are a heavy burden, but at least they pay for the services that the government provides. However, the *compliance* with our tax laws costs the American economy hundreds of billions of dollars while making no positive contributions. Most of the time and money spent on tax compliance is an actual drag on our economy. Millions of jobs are involved: accountants, lawyers, financial planners, tax-preparation services, IRS employees, corporate tax managers, etc. But the parts of their jobs that involve simply complying with or gaming our federal income tax system do not add to our economy. Most of these people have valuable skills. Significant and practical tax reform, ***Sensible Tax Reform—Simple, Just and Effective***, will free them to work on jobs that actually benefit our economy instead of burdening it. Let us allow them to put their skills to useful work.

Compliance and Planning Costs for Individuals and Families

Individual compliance costs: The annual April 15 nightmare of tax filing takes a huge amount of time and money for compliance, involves an extensive amount of record keeping and planning, and causes worry about government intrusions into our personal financial affairs and the possibility of IRS audits. The Tax Foundation has estimated[7] that individual taxpayers spend money and time valued in excess of $110 billion annually (2005) just complying with the record keeping, processing and filing of our federal income taxes.

Tax-filing season is the only time during the year when most taxpayers are really sensitive to how much taxes they pay. What may be especially painful is the twenty, forty, sixty hours or more that we spend working on our taxes. More than 60% of the taxpaying public seeks professional help to assist them to prepare their taxes. [Even 60% of those with incomes below the poverty level seek professional help to prepare their taxes!] Relative to income, the Tax Foundation found that the cost for the poor to comply with the tax obligations is far higher than any other group of taxpayers. Even our tax compliance is regressive.

Individual planning costs: Our tax burden also involves a major commitment of time and money in planning for retirement, for education and for healthcare accounts that can reduce or at least defer our income taxes. These are *indirect tax costs* that the Tax Foundation study does not even include but which undoubtedly total tens of billions of dollars more each year.

For example, Congress has created various programs tied to the income tax which are designed to encourage retirement savings: 401(k), 403(b), individual retirement accounts (IRA), Keogh, Roth IRAs, tax-sheltered annuities, etc. Contributions to these accounts are made with pre-tax income. The investments together with the investment profits from those accounts will not be taxed until many years in the future when the funds are withdrawn in retirement. Although these accounts were passed by Congress in order to improve our lives (a way of softening the impact of a burdensome federal tax system, for which Congress is also responsible), it still makes life a lot more complicated.

How much better would be a tax program that totally eliminates the need to make all of these tax-avoiding or deferring efforts! How much better would be a tax system that greatly increases families' after-tax income and thereby make it easier for them to save.

- We need a simple and just tax system.
- We need a tax system which focuses entirely upon taxes, without squeezing in social and political goals.
- We need a system which greatly increases our ability to save for retirement, education and healthcare.
- We need ***Sensible Tax Reform—Simple, Just and Effective***!

Compliance and Planning Costs for Businesses

Business compliance costs: Our tax system also imposes a very difficult compliance burden on businesses—a burden that affects us all greatly. Businesses must pay their own income, Social Security and Medicare taxes, but they must also collect, process and account for all of the income, Social Security and Medicare taxes which they deducted from their employees' wages and salaries. For many companies, the cost of complying with their tax burden is millions of dollars annually. [Citicorp's income tax report alone has been reported to exceeded 20,000 pages and General Electric's 57,000!!!]

The Tax Foundation estimates that the cost to businesses to comply with federal taxes exceeds $150 billion annually. Together with the $110 billion of individual tax-compliance costs, that total over a quarter of a trillion dollars! That is greater than the entire gross national product of Pakistan or the Philippines—every year!

An estimated *six billion hours* is spent by individuals and companies in complying with our federal taxes alone—collecting and filing data, processing it and preparing taxes.

> 6 billion hours per year represents a workforce of over 2,884,000 people: larger than the populations of Dallas.., Detroit…and Washington, D.C. *combined*; …more people than work in the auto.., computer manufacturing.., air(craft) manufacturing.. and the steel industry *combined*![8] [Emphasis mine]

Complying with the current tax system is an especially onerous and expensive task *for small businesses*. They often spend far more in tax compliance than they actually pay in taxes. That is insane! That makes establishing and successfully running a small business much more expensive and difficult than should be necessary—and greatly increases the probability of failure.

Millions of hours of management time are spent in trying to "game" the system: inventory valuation choices; depreciation schedules; credits; maneuvering expenses between domestic and foreign operations; deciding how to finance new investments; etc. Studies suggest that 20% or more of the time in planning new investments focuses upon the tax issue alone. That may be tax-efficient, but not economically efficient—indeed, it is a complete waste of economic resources.

The tax-deductibility of interest payments also encourages companies to borrow more than they otherwise would. That increases the companies' risk and susceptibility to bankruptcy in bad times.

However, American *companies* are able to defer such taxation by keeping the earnings of foreign subsidiaries abroad rather than bringing the taxes home. The amount kept abroad is estimated to be more than $2 trillion dollars!

The Tax Burden: The Damage to Our Economy

We now look at how these tax burdens hurt American companies and workers. It will also be shown how the taxes increase both our international trade deficit and the need for the American government and companies to borrow heavily abroad.

Imports Increased and Jobs "Off-shored"

In 2012, the U.S. imported $2.3 *trillion* from foreign countries—$6,300,000,000 *per day*! Our *trade deficit* (imports minus exports) exceeded $740 billion. The U.S. economy is like an import vacuum cleaner. This is something to be very worried about. Exhibit 2-2 illustrates just how extreme America's international economic performance is. The *balance on current account* measures how a country performs globally on its trade in goods and services, plus investment income and foreign aid. As can be seen, countries as diverse as Germany, China, Saudi Arabia, Russia, Japan and even Malaysia run healthy surpluses. On the other hand, countries like Turkey, Canada, the United Kingdom and the United States run large deficits—with the American deficit almost five times as large as the next most profligate country.

Exhibit 2-2
Balance on Current Account[9]
(2012; Billions)

Germany	$238
China	$193
Saudi Arabia	$165
Switzerland	$79
Kuwait	$79
Netherlands	$78
Norway	$72
Russian Federation	$71
Japan	$61
South Korea	$43
Malaysia	$19
Spain	($15)
Italy	($15)
South Africa	($24)
Turkey	($48)
Brazil	($54)
France	($57)
Canada	($62)
United Kingdom	($94)
United States	($440)

A deficit is not necessarily bad; indeed, it is very helpful for most developing countries. Even for the U.S., it need not be critical. It need not—but it is. It is not the deficit but its magnitude and the fact that it remains so large year after year. Those deficits are largely met by American borrowing from foreign countries—especially foreign governments such as Japan and China.

Self-imposed disadvantage: Imports contribute greatly to our standard of living and help to keep inflation in check. However, American producers are at a serious disadvantage versus imports. Countries, such as Germany and Japan where the basis for most taxation is a national sales tax, rebate those taxes to the exporters. When the imports arrive in the United States, they compete against domestic American producers who must pay significant Social Security and corporate profit taxes, both their own and the embedded taxes from their suppliers. American products are thus at *a serious tax disadvantage* even here in the U.S. We lose tens of billions of dollars of sales to foreign producers simply because of their lower taxes. The tax plan in this book will help to remedy that.

"Off-shoring": We have all read about the millions of American jobs that have been "off-shored" to foreign countries. American companies try to remain competitive by either setting up manufacturing plants abroad or contracting with foreign companies to produce goods and services abroad that we formerly produced here. Initially it was low-skill manufacturing jobs, but then higher and higher skills. For years more, we comforted ourselves with the fiction that, while that could happen in manufacturing, it would not occur in services. Since the turn of the century, however, we have seen a flood of American service jobs flowing to India and other countries—with no end in sight.

We cannot hope to match the low wages abroad. However, wages are not the only cost differential. Taxes are very important also. A tax-simplification-and-justice plan will save American companies almost a trillion dollars annually in reduced taxes and compliance and planning costs. They will be able to compete much more successfully against both imports and the allure of off-shoring.

Inadequate Exports

The annual trade deficit is as much a problem of inadequate exports as it is about *excessive imports*. American exporters perform relatively poorly against their foreign competitors. Even though the US economy is four times the size of Germany and 50% larger than the Chinese economies, they each export more than we do—and German labor is more expensive than is American labor. There are many reasons for this poor export performance. Many foreign countries do have significantly lower labor costs (although not Canada, Japan, Australia or most of Europe). Also, it is a fact that the typical American managers are uncomfortable in international markets and do not do as well as they should.

A third serious reason is that our tax system is a major obstacle to American exporters. Europe, as well as most of the rest of the world, has a very different tax system than we do here in the United States. The most important form of taxation in countries such as the United Kingdom, Germany, France, Italy, Japan and Australia is a form of national sales tax called a value-added tax (VAT). Corporate income taxes are generally a much smaller source of government tax revenues in those countries.

Tax rebates for exports: Very seldom do countries tax their own exports, since that would usually reduce exports, thereby hurting their own companies and workers. [Our founding fathers were very aware of this. As a result, it is against the U.S. Constitution for the American government to impose export tariffs!] However, we are effectively doing the same thing by our corporate income, Social Security and Medicare taxes that are embedded in our export prices—and thereby pricing ourselves out of the foreign markets. Those taxes cannot be rebated to the exporters.

When American exports are imported into countries such as France, which charges local customers the VAT on locally-produced goods and services, our exports are also charged the VAT. That is in addition to the embedded American tax burden that they carry. American exports are clearly at a significant cost disadvantage because of the tax burdens back here in the U.S. International law does not permit governments to rebate profit or payroll taxes back to exporters or to allow their export sales to be excluded from taxable earnings. American exports would be substantially greater if this embedded tax burden was not involved. ***Sensible Tax Reform*** will save thousands of American companies and hundreds of thousands of American jobs, if we act wisely—and soon.

Trade Deficit and International Debt—Both Out of Control

When the United States buys $740 billion more abroad than it sells each year, it must find a way to finance that trade deficit. The principal way in which this is done is for us to borrow abroad. The American Government has borrowed $1.3 trillion from the Government of China alone and an additional $1.1 trillion from the Government of Japan. Our federal government's total international debt was more than $5.6 trillion in mid-2013—and growing very rapidly year after year, with no end in sight! This is already equivalent to $18,000 per man, woman and child in the United States—$72,000 for a family of four.

This dangerous reliance upon foreign countries to finance our import extravagance should be a cause of concern for every citizen. *A great nation should not put itself at such risk*! If foreign lenders should become disillusioned with our profligate spending, rapidly-rising indebtedness and recurring threats of government default that threatens our credit rating, they might choose to finance less of our borrowing needs. In that event, we will pay a heavy price—our interest rates would rise, our economy could be pushed into recession, and unemployment would climb.

Perhaps even more importantly, if political tensions should increase, our economic and political exposures to both foreign-sourced oil and foreign-sourced loans could be used as weapons against us. [That is what happened in 1973-74 when oil prices were increased by Middle Eastern oil producers to punish the US and European governments that supported Israel during the Yom Kippur War!] We need to act now. The current tax system hurts the economy, hurts companies, destroys jobs, and threatens America's international power and independence. ***Sensible Tax Reform*** is the place to begin.

Our Federal Tax System Is a Major Obstacle to the American Dream

American Values

The United States is a country that was founded on solid moral and social values of freedom, opportunity, and a chance for everyone to progress if they are willing to try hard enough. There is no other country in the world today, indeed no other country in world history, which has offered so much to so many. This is a land where a Bill Gates or a Sam Walton can start with little or nothing but, through imagination and hard work, become fabulously successful.

We encourage our young people to follow the Horatio Alger vision of starting at the bottom, working hard, saving, becoming successful and giving their children a better future. We are a *meritocracy*—a society based upon merit. That is one of the things that has made us unique from the "old world" of Europe.

We are not an aristocracy, not a society based upon titles, inheritance, wealth or who your father was. It has never been necessary, nor should it ever become so, to have the right family name or connections to get a good education, to get the right job or to start a new business. However, there are very dangerous political currents that are seriously eroding the meritocratic nature of this country. Our current tax system, and the extensive efforts to distort that system for the benefit of the very wealthy few, threatens the very society and political system for which we have always stood!

Our Tax System Messes with our Values

The way in which our income-tax system has evolved interferes with all of these images:

- Often the harder you work, the more you are taxed on your earnings, while unearned income (e.g., dividends and capital gains) is taxed at much lower rates.
- The individual at the bottom of the economic ladder who is trying to improve him/herself is burdened with onerous Social Security and Medicare taxes, which are not even tax deductible.
- The tax system is perceived by all levels of society to be unjust. In many ways, it has been rigged to benefit the already-wealthy and big corporate interests that can afford the expert help that is necessary to take advantage of the special loopholes.

We must regain the values that have made America great! We must avoid government manipulation of our lives in ways that threaten our traditional values. Tax stupidity at the national level has caused many of the problems. Appropriately-chosen tax reform can help to remedy those problems and again maximize the opportunities for the most ambitious, hard working and entrepreneurial of our citizens to prosper. If America ever loses its uniqueness, ever ceases to remain the "land of opportunity," our days as one of the greatest nations in history will be numbered! The time for major tax reform is long overdue. My proposal to accomplish that reform will be examined in Chapters 5-7: ***Sensible Tax Reform—Simple, Just and Effective***!

Conclusions

The American federal system of income, estate, Social Security and Medicare taxes has been shown in this chapter to be a very heavy burden upon both families and companies. The taxes themselves are heavy enough. The compliance and planning that they require can often be an even heavier burden. On top of that, embedded taxes from companies further down the production chain are added to the overall taxation burden. Regardless of who pays those taxes and bears those expensive costs, they are passed on to the final customer. Thus, we consumers ultimately bear all of those numerous costs and distortions that impose a heavy weight on our economy. The next chapter will explore that bewildering matrix of taxes in detail.

Endnotes

6 *The Budget for the Fiscal Year 2013*, Office of Management and Budget, February 2012; Tables 2.1 and Table 2.5

7 *The Rising Cost of Complying with the Federal Income Tax*, J. Scott Moody et al. (December 2005); Special Report #138, The Tax Foundation, p.7

8 *The Rising cost of complying with the Federal Income Tax* J. Scott Moody et al. (December 2005); Special Report #138, The Tax Foundation, pp.10-11.

9 Central Intelligence Agency: *The World Factbook*

CHAPTER 3

TAXES! TAXES! AND MORE TAXES!

The political function of income taxes, which is served by their being complex, is to provide means whereby members of Congress who have anything whatever to do with taxation can raise campaign funds.
—Milton Friedman, Nobel laureate in economics

How Heavy Is the American Tax Burden?

The Burden of American Taxation

Our governments, both national and sub-national, are amazingly inventive in the ways in which they impose taxes on both individuals and businesses. On the federal level, we pay income and profit taxes, Social Security and Medicare taxes, estate and gift taxes, excise taxes, and import duties. On the state and local levels, we pay income taxes, sales taxes, real estate and other property taxes, gift, estate and inheritance taxes, and excise taxes. We pay more than a dozen different kinds of taxes.

Visible taxes: Some of the taxes are charged to us openly so that we can readily identify them. *Income, Social Security and Medicare taxes* are shown on our payroll receipts, and most of us are well aware of them. We can see when *sales taxes* are added to our grocery, restaurant and department store bills. We pay our *property taxes* either along with our monthly mortgage payments or in lump-sum payments twice per year. *Estate and inheritance taxes* are paid when someone dies. All of these are generally open and visible, even if it may be difficult to know the total of all of the taxes that we pay.

Invisible taxes: In Chapter 2, embedded taxes were discussed. They are part of the costs of what we pay and are difficult or even impossible to identify. Typically, we do not even think about *excise taxes* (for example, on gasoline, tobacco or alcohol) or *import duties* (which can be quite high on items such as clothing and shoes). They are embedded in the prices of those items when we shop and are not generally broken out from the listing of the base price. All of these taxes can add significantly to the price, but they are generally hidden from sight—embedded in the prices that we pay.

How Do American Taxes Compare to Other Countries?

Complaining about our taxes is as old as our days as a British colony before the American Revolutionary War. The flames of modern tax dissent are fanned constantly by radicals who oppose almost any taxation as being un-American

Our federal tax system is indeed very flawed. However, contrary to such extremist rants against all taxation, the American tax burden is among the lowest of any industrialized country in the world. Exhibit 3-1 is from the Organization of Economic Cooperation and Development (OECD) list of total taxes, both national and sub-national, for most of the major economies of the world. The American tax burden is the lowest of all of the industrial countries. Canada's tax level is a full 5% higher than ours while the British level is more than 10% higher and France's almost 20%! From the full OECD list of 34 countries, only a pair of developing countries in Latin America, Mexico and Chile, have lower taxes.

In proposing tax reform, it is critical that we have an accurate understanding of the facts. Too many of the arguments against our current tax system are emotional and based upon erroneous arguments. Our federal tax system has very serious flaws. Tax reform needs to focus on them—not on emotional fantasy. Even this book, while acknowledging the necessity for taxes and recognizing that

Exhibit 3-1
Total Tax Revenues[10]
(2011; as Percent of GDP)

United States	25.1%
Australia	25.6%
Korea	25.9%
Japan	27.6%
Canada	31.0%
Spain	31.6%
United Kingdom	35.5%
Germany	37.1%
Netherlands	38.7%
Italy	42.9%
France	44.3%

America's overall tax burden is among the lowest in the world, is based upon the author's own perception that the American federal tax system is unnecessarily and unfairly complicated and harmful to our economy. Serious tax reform is badly needed.

What is *Right* about Our Current Federal Tax System?

Although some critics will glibly say that there is nothing right about our current system, it does raise more than $2,500,000,000,000 (2012) to support the massive expenditures of the American Government. It successfully provides incentives to promote certain socially-approved goals (e.g., home ownership, charitable donations, retirement savings and energy efficiency). The elimination of these and other preferential treatments under the current tax system will need to offer very beneficial alternatives in order to avoid strong opposition from their supporters (for example, powerful groups including realtors, charities, retirees, Wall Street and the energy industry).

The current tax system succeeds in certain areas, but it is not the only tax system that could do so. All of the major alternative systems, whether income or sales-based, *promise* a better tax system—one that is simple, more just, more efficient and more effective than our current system. ***Sensible Tax Reform—Simple, Just and Effective*** actually accomplishes all of those goals.

What is *Wrong* about Our Current Federal Tax System?

All the Congress, all the accountants and tax lawyers, all the judges, and a convention of wizards cannot tell for sure what the income-tax law says!
—Walter B. Wriston, Chairman, Citicorp

Complexity

When the modern income-tax system was established in 1913, it was designed to be very simple and only applied to the very wealthy. However in the intervening years, the tax code has been revised tens of thousands of times. As was seen in Chapter 2, it has lost all pretext of simplicity. It now applies to most Americans, not just the wealthy, and exceeds 77,000 pages. Even with tax software, the Internet and books, when we are preparing our annual tax returns it is difficult not to feel that there is something wrong with such a complicated system. We worry: "Have I done this right?" "Have I missed any deductions or credits?" "Will I be audited by the IRS?" "Will I be penalized?"

There is something very wrong with a tax system that no one understands! Even if you really think that an income tax is the best form of tax system, you probably recognize that our existing tax system is not the right version. The accompanying box summarizes one particularly bad distortion of our current tax system—the very complex and contentious issue of the alternative minimum tax. It is one of the things that is very wrong with our tax system and an excellent example of "the law of unintended consequences." It is the result of very poor tax policy that we are currently forced to endure.

Deductions, Exemptions and Credits

All men and women may be created equal under American law. However, all are not equal economically and socially. There are wealthy and poor; married and single; small families and large; healthy and ill; homeowners and renters; high-tax states and low tax. Special provisions in the tax code have been designed to provide relief for each imbalance—differential tax rates for different incomes, and for the married and unmarried; deductions for mortgage interest and property taxes, for state income and sales taxes, large medical bills, as well as exemptions for every member of the family and numerous tax credits. All of these special provisions have been deemed necessary. However, the end result is our current income-tax system that is both unbelievably difficult and patently unjust.

Instability

It would be bad enough if this morass of tax rules remained stable, but our Federal Income Tax Code changes every year. There were major tax revisions in 1983, 1986, 1993, 1996, 2001, 2003 and 2005. Each of these produced very significant and often confusing changes. In addition, every year in-between also saw numerous changes. Many of these were necessary to correct or clarify conflicts, omissions or outright mistakes in the major revisions. However,

Alternative Minimum Tax (AMT)

Almost forty years ago, Congress imposed a supplemental income tax in response to the fact that hundreds of Americans were earning more than $1,000,000 (in 1970 dollars!) and paying no federal income taxes. They had been able to successfully use tax-free income and sophisticated tax shelters to avoid income taxes.

The AMT was widely supported, since it was targeted only at those who were perceived as unfairly (although legally) avoiding any taxes. Unfortunately, Congress did not see fit to index the AMT to inflation. As a result, while fewer than 20,000 people were subject to the AMT in 1970, now tens of millions of people, and not just the very wealthy, are scheduled to be hit by it every year.

In order to avoid that, Congress has needed to pass special legislation every year that has deferred for one more year the time when those millions of taxpayers would be hit by the AMT. But the law still fails to index it or permanently modify it so that this nightmare will not continue to hang over our heads year after year. *Sensible Tax Reform* will completely eliminate the AMT.

many others were the normal annual process of providing special loopholes for favored companies, industries or groups of taxpayers—and even individual taxpayers who received their own special loopholes. The result is our 77,000-page tax mess.

Bases for Taxation

Taxes can generally be broken down into five categories:

- Taxes on income
- Taxes on assets
- Taxes on transactions
- Taxes on people
- Taxes on production

Taxes on income

The most familiar forms of taxation, on both individuals and businesses, are income taxes. For individuals, there are taxes on *earned* income: wages, salaries, bonuses, commissions, tips, and executive stock options. There are also personal income taxes on *unearned* (or passive) income: interest, dividends and capital gains, as well as such miscellaneous sources of income as alimony, gambling winnings and lawsuits. Total income is adjusted for various deductions, exemptions and credits and the taxes due can be reduced by credits. [See the box below.]

Businesses pay taxes on income from operations, interest and dividend income, capital gains and lawsuits. They also pay Social Security and Medicare taxes on the compensation paid to their employees. Income taxes (personal plus corporate), including Social Security and Medicare taxes and estate taxes, are the principal sources of the U.S. Government's tax revenue [$2.3 trillion out of the total of $2.5 trillion in 2012.]

Taxes on Assets

Asset taxes basically fall into two groups: taxes on tangible or "real" property and taxes on intangible assets.

Real estate: Real-estate taxes are the most common form of property taxes. As any homeowner, farmer or owner of commercial property has experienced, an annual tax is imposed upon the assessed value of the property. Property taxes are usually local rather than state taxes. They are not imposed by our federal government.

In ages past, taxes within cities were often based upon some measure that was easier to determine than the value of the property. One of these taxes was based upon the amount of footage that a property had on the street (thereby

Deductions versus Credits

All tax-reform proposals, past and present, address the concepts of deductions and credits. Although most people confuse them, the distinction is simple—and very important.

In a simplistic sense, the taxation process is:

(1) Your total income = your taxable income
(2) (minus) your taxes due [i.e., the government's share]
(3) = Your disposable income.

In practice, the process is far from simple:

(1) Your total income
(2) (minus) your deductions, exemptions and exclusions
(3) = Your taxable income
(4) (minus) your taxes due [i.e., the government's share]
(5) (plus) your tax credits
(6) = Your disposable income.

Deductions, exemptions and exclusions are subtracted from income. They reduce the total of income that is subject to taxes and therefore also reduce your taxes. Deductions are helpful.

Credits are subtracted not from the taxable income but from the actual taxes due. They reduce the amount of taxes that you must pay. Credits are very, very helpful!

encouraging the very narrow houses that are common in old communities, such as Georgetown in Washington). Even earlier, taxes were sometimes based upon the number of windows that a house had (the window tax), since those luxuries could only be afforded by the well-to-do.

Some localities also tax other major "real" assets, such as automobiles, boats, recreational vehicles, motor homes, airplanes, etc.

Intangible assets: *Intangible* assets are financial assets such as stocks, certificates of deposit and bonds. Many states once imposed intangible taxes, but only a few still do. Estate taxes and gift taxes are imposed upon both real and intangible assets, such as homes and stocks.

Taxes on Transactions

Sales tax: Transaction taxes are the most numerous and varied of the five groups of taxes.

The most familiar form of transaction tax to most of us is the sales tax (also called a consumption, purchase or expenditure tax). In the United States, sales taxes are only assessed by states and other municipalities, not by the federal government. Such taxes are usually calculated as a percentage of the amount spent. Other important varieties of transactions taxes are the value-added tax (which is used in almost all countries other than the United States), import duties, tourist taxes and excise taxes. These are described in the accompanying box.

Tobin tax: Those other transaction taxes are applied to the purchase of tangibles—goods and services. In the early 1970s the British economist, James Tobin, proposed a tax on an intangible asset—the purchase and sale of foreign exchange. Because of the relatively large amount of such transactions, a very small tax could raise income as well as assist Tobin's other goal—to deter the relatively high degree of speculation in those markets. His proposal was widely debated but was not implemented.

However only a few years ago, the European Union approved, but has not yet implemented, a Tobin-type tax on stock and bond trading. A tax of only a small fraction of 1% could raise billions of euros in taxes yearly. However, there is a very major obstacle to such a tax: Unless all of the major financial markets (especially the United States) cooperated, it would be very easy for trading to move to untaxed markets.

Other Forms of Transactions Taxes

Value-added tax (VAT): In Europe and many other industrialized countries of the world, the principal form of taxation is a very different form of transaction tax—the VAT. Unlike the sales tax, which is collected only from the final customer, the VAT is paid at every stage of production. Each producer pays taxes upon the increase in value that it has produced (i.e., the "value added" at that stage of production). However, the final customer is ultimately charged for all of the VATs and the interim taxes are rebated back to the producers. Thus, once again it is the customer, not the producers, who ultimately bears the brunt of the tax.

Excise taxes: Not all transaction taxes are based upon value. For example, an excise tax is usually a flat tax paid upon some measure other than value. Gasoline and alcohol taxes are based upon volume, such as gallons or liters. Cigarette taxes are calculated per pack or carton. The excise tax is not usually affected by price.

Import duties: These are transaction taxes on goods that are imported into a country. They can be applied either as a percentage of value or upon some non-value measure, such as per unit, per volume (e.g., barrel of oil), weight, etc. During the early 1930s, Congress displayed its infamous lack of economic wisdom by raising the average import duty to more than 80%!!!! Fortunately for us, almost seventy years of international negotiations has helped to reduce the average import tariff to less than 4%. However, for a few classes of goods, such as shoes and apparel, the US tariffs can still be more than 20%!

Tourist taxes: Major cities such as New York and Chicago and vacation destinations sometimes levy special transfer taxes on restaurants, hotels, parking and/or rental cars. As with sales or VAT taxes, these are based upon value.

Taxes on People

A simple per capita tax is one of the very oldest forms of taxation. It is usually a fixed amount that is charged to every one who is covered, without any distinction as to income or wealth. It is clearly a very regressive tax. Poll taxes or head taxes or occupancy taxes might be charged on each voter or each member of a household. Alternatively, there might only be one charge per household, rather than per individual.

Another form of per capita tax is the occupation tax, which was common in ages past. Unlike the other per capita taxes, the occupation tax can differentiate between professions (e.g., doctors would be charged more than waitresses). All people in each category would pay the same fixed amount. Head and occupation taxes are generally collected every year. They are not used by the United States Government, nor are they very common at the state and local level.

A different type of per capita tax that is common today is the tourist (or traveler) tax, which some countries and regions impose. For example, Alaska approved imposed a $50 per passenger tax upon tourists arriving on cruise ships. Similar taxes are charged at many airports or upon entering or leaving some countries. Such tourist taxes are imposed every time someone falls subject to it, such as any time that they fly into or out of a particular airport.

Taxes on production

Some countries charge taxes upon the output of production. This is usually based upon some valuable mineral, such as oil, gold or diamonds. Other countries tax the pollution that is caused by production (for example, a carbon tax).

The Impact of Taxes

When proposals are made regarding designing or reforming tax systems on individuals, whether income, Social Security and Medicare or estate taxes, one of the most complicated issues is the social question of *whom* the tax burden falls upon most heavily. Some taxes fall more heavily upon lower-income groups. Other taxes fall more heavily upon upper-income groups.

Regressive Taxes

A tax that falls more heavily upon lower-income groups is called a regressive tax. Our present system, in which families at the poverty level must pay 7.65% in Social Security and Medicare taxes, is quite regressive on the tax side. The Social-Security tax is only paid upon the first $113,700 of earned income (2013). Thus, the poor and lower middle class bear the full brunt of those taxes on almost all of their income. [Although the taxation itself is regressive, it can also be argued that the overall Social-Security program is not, since the poor and middle classes generally receive a higher payoff relative to the wealthy when they collect benefits.]

However, the executive earning $5,000,000 per year or the professional athlete earning $20,000,000 only pays the tax on a small fraction of their earnings. The wealthy socialite living upon interest and capital gains, trust income or loans pays no Social Security or Medicare taxes at all since they have no earned income.

Warren Buffet, one of America's wealthiest men, has acknowledged publicly that with tens of millions of annual income he pays less than 17% in federal taxes—a lower rate than his secretary! Likewise, Mitt Romney, during his presidential campaign, admitted that he regularly pays less than 15% on millions of dollars of annual income.

Buffett was not bragging. He was holding his own personal situation up as an example of how unjust the American federal tax system is. Indeed, a report from the IRS (May 2013)[11] analyzing the 400 taxpayers with the highest incomes in the United States (minimum annual income of the 400: $109 million—a very exclusive club!) found that their average tax was only 18.1% of adjusted gross income. Millions of less-fortunate Americans paid much higher tax rates. Most of the major tax-reform proposals that are circulating in Washington recognize this regressive nature of our current system and have included exemptions to help the poor.

Other regressive taxes include import duties upon clothing and shoes, as well as excise taxes upon gasoline, tobacco and alcohol. Consumption of such products is typically a much smaller part of the income of the wealthy than of the poor and middle classes.

Progressive Taxes

A tax system that taxes higher-income groups at higher rates than low-income is called a progressive tax system. The federal income and estate-tax systems, as well as the corporate income tax, are progressive. As was noted in Chapter 2, the personal income tax on an individual or family is an irregular but consistent progression: 0%, 10%, 15%, 25%, 28%, 33%, 35% and 39.6%. The progression of corporate income tax rates is somewhat erratic: 0%, 15%, 25%, 34%, 39%, 34%, 35%, 38% and 35%.

The *estate tax* currently ranges from 18% to 40%, but because of a generous exclusion of $5,250,000, is effectively charged at a flat rate of 40% (2013). Only the wealthiest ¾ of 1% pay any estate tax at all: of the roughly 2.3 million deaths each year in this country, fewer than 1500 paid *any* estate taxes. And their average tax in recent years has only been about 15-16%. Thus, although our estate-tax system is nominally very progressive and widely demonized by extremists as an oppressive "death tax," it is in fact much more moderate.

Neutral Taxes

The theoretical ideal for a tax system would be a *neutral tax*—one that falls equitably upon all groups. Unfortunately, while it may be possible to theorize about a neutral tax, it is impossible to design one. The core problem is that we cannot all agree upon the real meaning of concepts such as equitable, just or neutral. Low-income families spend all of their income and are able to save very little. The wealthy, on the other hand, are fortunate enough to not only live a very comfortable lifestyle but also to save a considerable amount of their income; most personal savings is naturally done by high-income families.

What may seem equitable and just to the wealthy (e.g., being able to keep as much as possible of what they have earned or inherited) is quite different from what might be perceived as equitable and just to those with low incomes and no inheritance (e.g., having the burden of Social Security and Medicare taxes removed, since those are much heavier burdens on the poor than are income taxes).

Our current income-tax system is basically progressive with regards to earned income (i.e., wages, salaries, bonuses, commissions, tips). But it is regressive with regards to dividends and capital gains (received primarily by the upper-middle and high-income groups), since they are taxed at a maximum rate of only 20% (which is much lower than the 25% tax on couples with taxable income of only $36,250).

Our income tax system is simply far too complicated and unjust. Although absolute tax neutrality is not possible, much better can be done than what we currently have. Radical change is needed: ***Sensible Tax Reform—Simple, Just and Effective***! It will address all of those inequities by treating everyone the same.

A Call for Reform

Opposition to the current American federal income-tax system spans the political spectrum. Our current system is faulted for many reasons: its complexity; the financial burden and compliance headaches it imposes; the unjust way in which it falls disproportionately upon the poor and middle classes; the use of the tax code to favor preferred groups of taxpayers (whether low, middle or upper income) or types of expenditure (e.g., environmentally-friendly purchases or investments in retirement accounts); and the inherently suspicious system of tax lobbyists being able to manipulate our tax system for the special treatment of their clients (both corporate and wealthy individuals).

The federal tax code uses deductions, exclusions, exemptions and credits to reduce taxes. It taxes wages, salaries, bonuses, tips, interest and dividend receipts, capital gains, profits, alimony, rental income, pensions and Social Security benefits, even unemployment benefits. The code applies different tax rates to different levels of income, forms of income (wages vs. capital gains) and the length of time that an investment has been held (short-term vs. long-term capital gains). Major tax reform is necessary to create a new tax system that is simple, just and effective.

Tax Reforms

Tax reform is not a new notion. It has been actively promoted by both liberals and conservatives, both Republicans and Democrats, for many years! The flat income tax, which was the central feature of very conservative Steve Forbes' two Republican presidential bids in the late 1990s, was introduced by the very liberal Jerry Brown as a key element of his Democratic presidential bid in 1990. Similarly, President George W. Bush's Advisory Panel on Tax Reform, followed by the Domenici-Rivlin Task Force, President Obama's Economic Recovery Advisory Board (PERAB) and the Simpson-Bowles Commission all offered serious, carefully-reasoned tax-reform proposals. Unfortunately, all of their recommendations have fallen on deaf ears in the White House and Congress.

In addition to these formal political pushes for significant tax reform, private-sector organizations have been promoting reform from the "grass-roots level." Americans for Fair Taxation, Citizens for Tax Justice, the Tax Foundation, and the National Taxpayers Union are only a few of the numerous organizations that very strongly support major surgery to our tax system.

Of course, there is wide variation to the proposals that these different groups and individuals propose. Some strongly espouse a particular reform (e.g., the flat income tax, a value-added tax or a federal consumption tax). Others are more open to any of several reforms. Some even seem to choose ABCITS (**A**ny **B**ut the **C**urrent **I**ncome-**T**ax **S**ystem).

Individuals and Reform

Major tax reform has been an important part of most presidential campaigns for the past generation. Indeed, each new president has overseen significant tax changes and even reform. However, reform has *always* led to greater complexity—and confusion. [President Reagan's major tax program, the Tax Reform Act of 1986 that had claimed to simplify the tax code, was so complicated that wags dubbed it the "Accountants and Lawyers Employment Act of 1986."] Most taxpayers have become numbed by all of the rhetoric and changes. However, more and more taxpayers have become frustrated enough to actively support not just major, but even radical, change to our system.

Conclusions

No reform will occur until the grass-roots indignation about the current tax system boils over. At the present time, it merely simmers. This book will offer a unique proposal that will be very just and simple and which will offer strong impetus for strengthening the American economy, both domestically and globally. It aims to turn up the heat from simmer to boil!

Chapter 4 will complete Part I of this book with a discussion of the process by which tax laws are written and enacted.

Endnotes

10 *Total Tax Revenue*, OECD, October 25, 2012

11 www.irs.gov/pub/irs-soi/09intop400.pdf

CHAPTER 4

LIES, DAMN LIES & THE TAX-WRITING PROCESS

The less that people know about how laws and sausage are made, the better they will sleep at night.
—Otto von Bismarck, German chancellor

No one who has ever witnessed lobbyists' perennial infestation of Capitol Hill can ever again confuse the making of tax laws with the making of sausages: at least when you make sausage, you know that the pigs won't be coming back!
—J. Mark Iwry, former U.S. Treasury official

In the first three chapters, we have seen how complicated, ineffective and unjust the tax system is under which we live. In this chapter, first the process by which Congress and the president created and continuously changed these laws will be examined. Then the "gaming" of the tax system by the tax lobbyists and their patrons (the wealthy, the powerful and large companies) will be explored.

Congress, the President and the Tax Mess

The U. S. Constitution did not give Congress and the president the authority to impose income taxes. An income tax was introduced during our Civil War and re-created after the war. However, it was declared unconstitutional by the Supreme Court. The passage of the 16th Amendment in 1913 overcame that obstacle. At that time, a very small number of the extremely wealthy were rapidly accumulating and flaunting their wealth in the face of great poverty. The amendment was seen, by the American people and by a *Republican* president and a *Republican* Congress, both as a means to raise needed funds and also to insure that the very wealthy were sharing the costs with the rest of the country.

The authority to tax greatly increased the power of the president and Congress. The control of the "federal purse" permanently enlarged government. That had been foreseen. What had not been foreseen, however, was the corrupting influence that it was to have upon our political processes. As Lord Acton said long ago, "*All power corrupts and absolute power corrupts absolutely*!"

The leadership of our government became addicted to almost unlimited control of the taxation and spending in the federal budget. That addiction is deeply entrenched today. President Reagan once colorfully quipped that "*government is like a baby's alimentary canal, with a happy appetite at one end and no responsibility at the other*!" Indeed, the government has learned to spend money very easily ("happy appetite at one end") without much self control when it comes to financing ("no responsibility at the other").

The two political parties characteristically blame and label each other as either "borrow and spend Republicans" or "tax and spend Democrats." In either form, we the American taxpayers must pay the bill—either in higher taxes, higher debt (which will be passed on to our children) or poorer government services.

Tax Lobbyists

With the passage of the 16th Amendment and the legalization of federal income taxes, the private sector realized that it could gain handsome rewards if it could influence either the design or application of the tax itself. The *tax lobbyist* was born! As the economy grew so also did the incentives for the tax lobbyists. The potential reward for large companies, the wealthy and other powerful groups can mean not just millions of dollars of benefits to their clients, but even billions. Their influence has grown to where they are one of the largest industries in Washington.

A Political Sickness

The potential reward made the expenditure of millions of dollars as political "contributions" a worthwhile investment for tax lobbyists on behalf of their wealthy and powerful clients. The result has been the growth of a symbiotic relationship between politicians, who anxiously seek the funds to finance their perennial re-election campaigns, and cash-rich and aggressive tax lobbyists who are not only willing, but very anxious, to pay. The result has changed Washington dramatically—and very much for the worse.

It once took tens of millions of dollars for a candidate to run for president. Then it became hundreds of millions. Now it is billions of dollars! It often takes more than $10 million now just to run for a House seat. That massive infusion of money does not come from mainstream America. No, it comes from companies, organizations and wealthy individuals who obviously think that their money is well spent. However, it is very often not for the overall benefit of the American economy or of the American people! Those deals not only complicate our tax system but also actually tilt the entire system to the advantage of the special-interest groups at the expense of the rest of us—the lower and middle-income groups and even of the "merely rich."

As Bismarck observed, we would sleep better not knowing how laws are made—however, we would certainly not be better off. Eternal vigilance is not only the price of liberty, it is also the price of keeping Washington working in our interest, rather than just its own. The scandals that brought the downfall of the lobbyist, Jack Abramoff, together with the resignations and imprisonment of several prominent congressmen in 2006 illustrated that this interaction between lobbyist and politicians can cross the border between what is ethical and what is illegal.

Selling Political Influence?

Frequently, the lobbyists even write the tax legislation itself. And that is legal! Our congressmen either do not want to take the time to write such legislation themselves or cannot do it since they often do not even seem to understand the tax legislation they are sponsoring! What results are cynical manipulations of a system that is far too complex, inefficient and susceptible to these types of political games for the benefit of the favored few but to the detriment of the rest of us.

To politicians, the ability to change taxes for the benefit of their contributors is one of the strongest, and potentially one of the most corrupting, tools available to them. The tax-writing committees of the two houses of Congress, the Senate Finance Committee and the House Ways and Means Committee, are among the most powerful units of Congress—and therefore among the most desirable committees for congressmen. John Linder, a member of the latter but a strong proponent of tax reform and simplification, said that, when major tax reform is passed, his committee will lose most of its appeal, so he will leave it. Although he has since retired from Congress, his honesty and forthrightness were refreshing.

Taxation by Representation—for Whom?

Almost every time we pass a tax bill, we make the code more complex, increase the burden on the taxpayer, and make it harder to enforce!
—Trent Lott, former Senate Majority Leader

The president (every president) and the Congress (every Congress) add to the complexity of the tax system every year. Their efforts *never simplify* the system.

Despite almost universal detestation of our tax code, bitter resentment against the Administration and Congress that have given us this system, and great bitterness against the most visible agent of the system (the Internal Revenue Service), the native good will of most Americans assumes that our government is sincerely working on our behalf. Yes, we would like to believe that all of the tax manipulations, however confusing, are done for our country's benefit. However, there is far too much evidence that this monstrous tax code is deliberately manipulated to benefit the clients of tax-lobbyists! That unholy alliance costs the country dearly. And remember: When special-interest groups get these tax breaks, it increases the federal government's deficit and increases the tax burden on the rest of us! WE pay those bills—sooner or later!

A Tax System or Social-Improvement Program?

Our federal tax systems were designed primarily to raise money for the federal government. Properly designed, a truly simple income-based tax system could work, although with potential problems of justice and effectiveness. However, the wealthy and powerful and their lobbyist-agents found ways to manipulate the tax systems to their advantages. What resulted is the 77,000-page monstrosity that we have now—which meets none of *the standards of good taxation: simplicity, justice and effectiveness.*

Not all of the complexity and manipulation has been for narrow selfish purposes. Some of the complexity has resulted from generally honest efforts to use the code for pursuing social-improvement programs such as home ownership, charitable donations, education, retirement savings, etc. Few would deny the desirability of such programs to society and to the economy. While that motivation may be commendable, it greatly complicates our tax system and reduces its effectiveness.

The more complicated and heavy that the tax burden became, the more attractive it became for different types of expenditure or different groups of people to receive special treatment in order to reduce the various tax burdens. Exclusions, deductions, exemptions, credits and special tax rates can all serve valid purposes, are broadly supported, and are very widely used to bend the tax system to encourage desirable behavior.

Exclusions from Taxable Income

Not all income is taxable. The interest from municipal bonds is excluded. Most life insurance benefits are exempt. Also, the first $250,000 of capital gains from the sale of a primary residence ($500,000 for a married couple) is not subject to federal taxation. Thus, total income minus excluded income equals taxable income.

Deductions from Income

After taxable income is determined, deductions are subtracted. Some of the most common are special tax-deferred investment accounts: retirement [e.g., 401(k)s and IRAs (individual retirement accounts)]; education [such as 529 College Savings Plans or Cloverdell accounts], and health-savings accounts.

Other deductions include alimony paid; certain educator and student expenses; property taxes; state and local income taxes or sales taxes; charitable contributions and casualty losses; and standard deductions. Congress has created dozens of deductions from total income, if you qualify—and if you know the special rules in order to qualify. The tax rate is then charged against this net taxable income.

Credits against Taxes

Tax credits reduce the actual taxes that are due. Credits are much nicer than dividends since they reduce the taxes that you owe, dollar for dollar. There are also dozens of tax credits, something for almost everyone: child and dependent-care expenses; care for the elderly or disabled; retirement-savings contributions; education; adoption; foreign taxes paid; qualified hybrid-electric vehicle; renewable energy; earned-income credit; and many others.

Special Tax Rates

After many years of an aggressive (and expensive) assault against the traditional system of equal treatment of all sources of taxable income, lobbyists and their wealthy sponsors finally got their way: the tax rate on dividends and capital gains was cut to less than half of the maximum tax rates on earned income—a very sweetheart deal for wealthy investors.

Thus, those who are gainfully employed (earned income) may pay as much as a 39.6% tax rate while dividends and capital gains pay a maximum of only 20%. That one change has been estimated to save the Walton family, with dividends on their Wal-Mart stock exceeding $3,000,000,000 annually, more than $500,000,000 per year in lower taxes.

A worker with taxable income of $36,250 can be paying a significantly higher tax rate (25%) than someone with an income of $1 million, $40 million or even $200 million of dividends and capital gains. To add insult to injury, the preferential 20% rate does not extend to the majority of taxpayers. Investments in tax-sheltered accounts, such as 401(k)s, 403(b)s, IRAs, etc., where most Americans have the bulk of their financial investments, do not benefit from the lower tax rate on dividends and capital gains.

The special tax rate was deliberately designed for those wealthy enough to *not* need tax-sheltered accounts. If the designers of this welfare-for-the-rich loophole had honestly intended to eliminate the double taxation of dividends and to encourage productive investments by reducing the tax on capital gains, they would have applied the special rates to all individuals. In the case of dividends, it would have made more sense if corporate dividend payments had been made tax deductible for the companies, while continuing to tax those receiving the dividends. It would strongly encourage companies to pay higher dividends, would lower the financing costs for the companies, would stimulate the stock market and would tax all investors equally.

The absurdity of the intent of the special 20% rate on capital gains is shown by its application to the profit sharing of hedge funds and private-equity funds. A capital gain is the appreciation in value of an asset over and above what the taxpayer paid for it. However, the managers of these funds have been able to get their share of profits (sometimes more than $1 billion in a single year) to be renamed with the innocuous term of "carried interest" and to be taxed as capital gains. What a farce! More favoritism. More unfairness. More lies!

Tax-Favored Incentives

All of those tax-favored incentives are now well entrenched in our income-tax system. We do want to encourage savings. We do want to encourage home ownership. We do want to make healthcare more affordable. We do want to encourage charity. However, they are all part of the complexity of a tax system that has become a vehicle for promoting social programs (and for political back-scratching).

We pay a very high price in cost, complexity and inefficiency for what our tax system has become. Our lawmakers inevitably claim that they are making the system simpler and helping the economy—lies, lies and more lies! Initial tax proposals may start out with true simplification as one of their goals. However, once the proposal gets into the political grinder, the result will inevitably be legislative sausage.

However, the tax-reform proposal that will be discussed in the next three chapters, ***Sensible Tax Reform—Simple, Just and Effective***, will demonstrate a better way! It will be much simpler, much more just and much more economically effective than our current federal tax systems.

Gaming the Tax System

We don't pay taxes. Only the little people pay taxes!
—Leona Helmsley, the billionaire hotel heiress and convicted tax felon, widely known as the "queen of mean"

Our federal lawmakers have created a tax system that is bad for everyone except the lawmakers themselves, for the wealthy tax-avoiding companies and individuals, and for the tax lobbyists, lawyers, accountants and financial advisors who specialize in gaming the system. Yet, even some important organizations representing these groups, such as the American Institute of Certified Public Accountants, condemn the complexity of the tax systems.

Convoluted Tax Maneuvers

The true gaming of our federal income-tax systems is not found in the basic treatment of deductions, which are available to everyone, or even in the favoritism of various credits and the preferential tax rates on dividends and capital gains. The extreme "gamers" are those who distort the system and seek special privileges which are available to only the very few. This privileged group is comprised of the few who know the special loopholes, can afford the financial, legal and accounting expertise to identify the special opportunities, who can afford to create the special vehicles that will give them massive advantages which are not available to 99% of the taxpayers, and who actually are often able to create their own special loopholes through their political influence (e.g., many of the "earmarks" which became such a scandal in Washington—though the capacity to create earmarks has been significantly reduced, the negative effects of past earmarks are still with us).

On the surface, that might appear to be a legitimate part of our democratic system. However, those results often cost the American government *billions in lost tax revenues.* These are not billions lost to illegal Mafia activities and drug smugglers, but billions lost because our legally-elected officials create special loopholes to benefit a small group of very wealthy individuals, large companies or other power groups. Sometimes these loopholes benefit a single company or family. This is a "*reverse Robin-Hood system*"—steal from the poor to further enrich the already very rich.

Gaming by Individuals

There are also many convoluted efforts devised by clever tax lawyers and / or accountants to create unique investment vehicles to give special wealthy clients ways to avoid taxes that are not open to the rest of us. Some are just legal enough to be accepted by tax courts. Many of these prove to be improper or even *illegal*[12]. The law is so complicated and contradictory that new ideas crop up every year. Some law firms have even applied for and received patents on tax-avoidance schemes that they have been able to carve out of our Internal Revenue Code. They will presumably make such unique scams available only to select customers. That makes an absolute mockery of our already very distorted and unfair tax system.

When Sam Walton (the founder of Wal-Mart) died, the bulk of his estate was 40% of the stock of Wal-Mart, then worth more than $27,000,000,000 (now worth more than $130 billion). Capital gains had never been paid on that wealth accumulation. And, because of clever estate planning, Walton's estate also paid no taxes. Now twenty years later, neither that estate nor the heirs have paid any capital gains taxes, any estate taxes or any inheritance taxes. In fairness, the wealth should not be taxed twice by the federal government. However, in fairness, it should be taxed once—if the capital gains or other income has never been taxed, then it should be taxed in the estate or when inherited. [Many critics of estate taxes blandly claim that the wealth has already been taxed. They either do not know their facts or are deliberately misleading the public. More lies!]

I do not begrudge the Waltons their good fortune (the result of what some pundit referred to as "winning the sperm lottery"—being fortunate in who they "chose" as their father). As U.S. Supreme Court Justice Learned Hand stated, "*Over and over, our courts have said that there is nothing sinister in so arranging one's affairs so as to make taxes as low as possible.*" We all have the right to minimize our tax obligations. That applies to both income and estate taxes. However, the tax rules should not be twisted for the advantage only of the wealthy and powerful. If the wealth of an estate has never been taxed (e.g., as capital gains), then it should be taxed when transferred to heirs.

Gaming by Companies

Corporations are just as aggressive as individuals in using sophisticated planning and eliciting very favorable tax loopholes to game the system for their own benefit. About ten years ago, a small number of mostly very large American corporations received one of the most outrageous tax scams ever approved by Congress and the White House. The companies had accumulated massive profits abroad from either their foreign operations or from *shifting profit from their American operations in order to avoid American profit taxes.* Lawmakers allowed the companies to bring home $300 billion dollars of accumulated earnings and pay only 5.2% in income taxes! Pfizer, the pharmaceutical giant, alone repatriated more than $37,000,000,000. [Even many families and individuals near the poverty level pay 10%!] Supporters say that this was fair and good for the country. It was neither—it was patently unfair! More lies! Subsequent economic studies, by both conservative and liberal researchers, confirm that there were very few benefits and a lot of tax loss from this legal scam.

Legal Crime: Such favoritism and preferential treatment is inexcusable. It may be technically legal, but it is morally, socially and economically wrong! Only politically can it be viewed as justifiable. Our tax system should not be so open to influence buying. Why should special-interest groups receive advantages that are not available to the rest of Americans? It is unconscionable that managers of hedge funds and private-equity funds should be able to receive billions of dollars of profit sharing and have it taxed as capital gains. All taxpayers should be subject to the same rules, and the rules should be simple. The playing field should be leveled.

I am not against reducing taxes on companies. Indeed, my tax program involves eliminating most federal taxes from businesses, which will make American companies much more competitive and also eliminate the incentives to move American-generated profits abroad. I am also not against reducing the taxes on the wealthy. Most high-income and wealthy individuals will pay lower taxes under my proposal. What I do oppose is the way in which privileged groups can "game" the current tax system to the disadvantage of the poor and middle-income groups in this country. The current federal tax system is not level for all taxpayers. And the tax code should not be allowed to be manipulated in secret. That is legal crime!

We need to get rid of the current federal tax system and replace it with a one that is much simpler, more just, economically much better for our country and where all taxpayers are subject to the same rules. However, until we do, phony tax gimmicks (e.g., the profits of private equity funds that are taxed at 20% as capital gains instead of as ordinary income which it really is) and convoluted loopholes need to be eliminated and violators of the rules severely punished. Complexity of the system is what makes such practices possible. With a truly simple system, the playing field will be leveled.

No Free Lunch

Remember that with these special sweetheart tax deals "there is no free lunch." That federal subsidy to wealthy families and big businesses (which they will typically receive every year—year after year!) is money that the U. S. Treasury will not receive. There are only three possible ways in which that can be handled by the government:

(1) The taxes paid by the rest of us will *not* be reduced (or might even be increased)
(2) Government services (e.g., port security, education and medical research) will be cut so that the special tax benefits can be offered to the privileged few. Or
(3) Our national debt will rise even higher—every year[13].

The United States Government, while it can continuously run moderate deficits, cannot continue to run such massive deficits. The day of reckoning is coming.

The Federal Tax Code Is Really a Fantastic System!

Fantastic: (1) "very odd or queer; strange and wild in shape or manner"
(2) "very fanciful; capricious; eccentric; irrational"
—World Book Dictionary

There is almost universal agreement in the U.S. that the current American federal tax system, which is based primarily upon taxes on income, is terminally flawed. Our tax code is incomprehensible. It is confusing. It is very expensive. It is very inefficient. It is very unfair. It is fantastic!

However, this "fantasy" is unnecessary. Let us now consider a radical, but very sensible, proposal for reform—one which offers not only much greater fairness in our tax system but also much, much greater simplicity and will give a strong and permanent economic boost to the American economy. It is also a proposal that can appeal to all parts of the political, economic and social spectrums.

The current system is very costly and inefficient. ***Sensible Tax Reform—Simple, Just and Effective***, the proposal to be outlined in the next three chapters, will bring rationality and decency back to the relationship between Congress and the American people. It will level the playing field in taxation. It will make our lives simpler, increase our real income and make American companies much more competitive, providing a strtong stimulus to the U.S. economy, creating hundreds of thousands of well-paying jobs and helping to significantly reduce the horrendous budget and international trade deficits of recent years.

Individuals will no longer need to limit their investments to highly restrictive 401(k)s, etc. Our investment and tax planning will be much easier and less expensive for low-income, middle-income and high-income taxpayers alike. In fact, most of us will never again need to worry about tax planning at all.

Endnotes

12 In 2007, Merck had to pay $2.3 billion of unpaid taxes and penalties for illegally hiding profits abroad.

13 The U.S. Government already pays more than $300,000,000,000 in interest annually on the *existing federal debt of more than $16 trillion* (which is more than $50,000 for every man, woman and child in America—$200,000 for the typical family of four!). That is equivalent to 100% of America's gross domestic product—the highest level since the 2d World War era and three times what it was at the end of the Vietnam War!

PART B

THE SOLUTION—
SENSIBLE TAX REFORM: SIMPLE, JUST AND EFFECTIVE

Chapter 5: **Tax Simplification, Justice and Effectiveness**

Chapter 6: **A Federal Consumption Tax**

Chapter 7: **A Simple-and Just Federal Tax on Very High Incomes**

CHAPTER 5

TAX SIMPLIFICATION, JUSTICE AND EFFECTIVENESS

The income tax...can be likened to a dirty industrial smelter that does an efficient job, but pollutes the air, poisons the streams, and kills the forests.
—Charles Adams, tax historian

The first four chapters examined our existing federal tax code, which is incredibly complicated, unjust and very damaging to the entire American economy. It hurts both families and businesses, discourages savings and encourages the excessive use of debt. It significantly increases our international trade deficit, drives American companies overseas, and costs millions of American jobs.

Our existing federal tax system has harmed us for too long. We can no longer afford it. The United States needs new fiscal vision and leadership. We need a completely new tax system: ***Sensible Tax Reform—Simple, Just and Effective***. It will introduce a new tax system that is:

- *Simple* to understand, transparent and easy to comply with;
- *Just* to all taxpayers with the same rules applying to everyone; and
- *Reinvigorating to our economy*, creating millions of new jobs.

This chapter will introduce a new federal tax system that will attain those three goals while remedying most of the deficiencies of our current Internal Revenue Code: This proposal will offer sweeping reform of our federal tax system:

- ***STR*** will eliminate most of our existing federal taxes:
  - An end to the corporate income tax
  - An end to the collection of Social Security and Medicare taxes—for both individuals and businesses
  - An end to the estate tax and
  - An end to personal income taxes for 99% of Americans.
- ***STR*** will introduce
  - A federal retail consumption tax and
  - A very simple tax on very high incomes.

77,000 pages of incredibly complicated tax code will be replaced by a few thousand pages of simple, easy to understand and transparent text. 148 million personal tax returns will no longer need to be filed each year. Businesses will be effectively "untaxed." Tax reporting and filing by both individuals and businesses will be minimized.

This chapter will present an overview of ***Sensible Tax Reform***. Chapter 6 will examine the federal consumption tax in detail. Chapter 7 will do the same for the tax on very high incomes.

A Sensible Tax-Reform Proposal

Almost all taxes on production fall finally on the consumer.
—David Ricardo, 19th Century British economist]

An End to Politics as Usual

There is no shortage of tax-reform proposals being offered in America today: income taxes, consumption taxes, transactions taxes, excise taxes, carbon taxes, turnover taxes, import duties, etc., etc. However, most of the proposals coming out of Washington in recent years have been little more than "politics as usual."

They are plans that serve to further distort our current 77,000-page federal tax system—which is already the most complicated and one of the most unjust and ineffective tax systems in the entire world.

Our current federal tax system is a failure and must be thoroughly changed. Einstein once said: *Insanity is doing the same thing over and over—and expecting different results!* Continuing to pursue our current tax policies will simply lead us further down the road to economic, social and political troubles—a continuation of the fiscal insanity that causes so much harm to American families, businesses and the overall economy.

A Selfish Bequest to our Children

Unfortunately, Congress and the White House have shown repeatedly over many years that, left to their own devices, they lack the vision, intelligence and courage needed to make the tough choices to replace our very damaging tax system. For much too long, the burdens of our government's economic failures, especially our $17 trillion national debt, have been pushed off to future generations. It is modern America's selfish bequest to our children.

If America is ever to attain a simple tax code that treats everyone equally and is designed to help the economy, *we American voters must demand* that the White House and Congress begin to think strategically about what is good for *all* of the United States and *all* Americans.

Fundamental Federal Tax Reform

Sensible Tax Reform—Simple, Just and Effective provides a vision for *comprehensive reform* of our federal tax system *for both individuals and businesses.* It is aggressive and ambitious—even revolutionary. It is also a call for the bold leadership that will be necessary to implement it.

STR is a proposal for a major reform of the federal income, Social Security, Medicare and estate-tax systems whose flaws have been addressed in the preceding chapters. It is designed to:

- Be *simple,* consistent, easy to understand, and easy to implement;
- Be *transparent* and *very difficult for politicians to manipulate secretly*;
- Be *just* to all Americans—*treating all taxpayers alike*;

- *Benefit all social and economic groups*;
- *Remove heavy tax burdens from businesses*, large and small, so they can innovate, grow and compete much more successfully in foreign markets and against the surge of imports;
- Stimulate a rapid *economic resurgence* that will *create millions of jobs*;
- *Raise the standard of living* of the vast majority of all Americans;
- Be *tax neutral*, so that the federal government should receive about the same annual tax revenue as is projected with our current tax system; and
- Be *moderate both economically and politically*, so as to *attract wide-based political support*, which will be necessary for the proposal to become law.

Is it reasonable to expect that a single tax reform can improve all of the above problems? Yes. ***Sensible Tax Reform—Simple, Just and Effective*** will deliver exactly what it promises: *simplicity, justice and economic effectiveness*—for both businesses and families. It can dramatically strengthen our economy and bring important social and political benefits as well. However, that will only occur if the American people demand that change. Popular enthusiasm and nationwide support is necessary to *bring fiscal responsibility back to America*.

Existing Federal Taxes

In 2012, the American Government collected more than $2,448 billion of taxes [Exhibit 5-1, Column 4]. $664 billion of the taxes or 27% of the total [Column 2] came primarily from corporations. However, only $242 billion came from taxes on corporate *profits*. Almost twice as much, $422 billion, was business payment of Social Security and Medicare taxes on compensation paid to employees. *Thus, less than 10% of federal tax revenues comes from corporate income taxe*s. And, more than two-thirds of the total revenue of the federal government, almost $1,700 billion [Column 1], came from individuals. That is two and a half times as much as the total taxes paid by businesses.

Exhibit 5-1
U.S. Government Revenues: 2012[14]
(in billions)

	(1)	(2)	(3)	(4)	(5)
	Individuals	Corporations	Other	Total	
Income Taxes	$1,132	$242		$1,374	56.1%
Social Security & Medicare	$422	$422		$844	34.5%
Estate and Gift Taxes	$14			$14	0.6%
Excise taxes	$79			$79	3.2%
Import duties	$30			$30	1.2%
Miscellaneous			$107	$107	4.4%
Total	$1,677	$664	$107	$2,448	
Share of taxes	68.5%	27.1%	4.4%		100.0%

Source: ***The Budget for the Fiscal Year 2014,***
Office of Management and Budget, February 2013; Table 2.1 and 2.5

Income taxes, both individual and corporate [Row 1], account for more than 56% of federal revenues. Social Security and Medicare taxes, paid equally by both employees and their employers, are the second most important source (34.5%) of all federal taxes [Row 2]. Other federal revenues (estate and gift taxes, excise taxes, import duties and miscellaneous) together account for less than 10% of the total.

Tax Reform—Not Social Policy

Among the many flaws of our current federal tax system is the wide array of social, economic and political goals with which it is littered. While that may be *good political policy*, it is *very bad economic and social policy*. And, it is certainly *terrible tax policy*. If the government wishes to pursue non-tax goals (such as encouraging investment, job creation, home ownership or energy-saving investments), that can be accomplished by means other than distorting and corrupting our tax system.

Sensible Tax Reform—Simple, Just and Effective focuses upon tax reform alone—*federal* tax reform. [It does not target state and local taxes.] As indicated above, it will eliminate most of the existing taxes as well as the vast array of loopholes that curse our current tax system. *Simplicity, justice* and *economic effectiveness* are the core elements of this plan.

Fundamental Tax Reform Will Not Be Easy

Sensible Tax Reform is not a proposal for simply modifying our existing federal tax system—not merely more "politics as usual." It is call for *an ambitious redesign of most of the entire currently-existing federal tax system.* The implications of these changes will be very significant—for everyone. They will be changes that will greatly benefit most individuals and businesses as well as the overall American economy. The ***STR*** proposal is ambitious. It is audacious. The manner in which we are taxed will change significantly—and *most of us will be paying less, often much less, in taxes.* How Americans save and spend will change greatly:

- *Individuals* will have much greater capacity to save for retirement, for buying a home, for starting a business, for putting our kids through college.
- How our *businesses* operate and finance themselves will also change greatly, since they will not be paying any federal income taxes.
- And, how our *federal government* operates will change—very much for the better, including the elimination of thousands of tax lobbyists and the billions of dollars of their political influence.

The current monstrosity known as the Internal Revenue Code has taken 100 years to create. As much as we might hate it, as unjust as it is, and as bad as it is for the American economy, *we are accustomed to it.*

There will be strong opposition from many who worry about change. That will include those individuals and businesses that disproportionately benefit from some of the special provisions that they have been able to exploit. And it will certainly include tax lobbyists. However, opponents will also include some of those individuals and businesses (especially small businesses, which are not able to reap all of the benefits of our current system that primarily benefit much larger companies) who, despite how much they might despise the current tax system and even despite the fact that it may have hurt them badly, are simply afraid of serious proposed change—"better the devil you know than one you don't know!"

In examining ***STR***, it is critically important that we each carefully consider its overall impact upon us individually and upon the entire United States. Therefore, as you evaluate the following proposal, ask yourself:

- Are the substantial *benefits* from a fundamentally different system worth giving up our existing complicated, unjust, damaging and hated, *but very familiar*, tax system?
- Would *you* support a tax system that would *increase your income and wealth* while simultaneously providing a *strong, long-term boost to the American economy* even though it will *significantly change the way in which you spend and save*?
- Are the *sacrifices* involved in adjusting to a very different tax system worth the results?

Fundamental Reform of Federal Taxes on *Individuals*

STR will involve an almost total redesign of the federal taxes on individuals and families. Personal income taxes, Social Security and Medicare taxes, and estate taxes will all be completely changed. This section will first review our existing federal taxes. Then, the changes that ***Sensible Tax Reform*** will introduce will be examined.

Taxes on Individuals under our *Current* Tax System

There are four principal federal taxes that are charged to individuals: Social Security, Medicare, income and estate taxes.

Social Security and Medicare taxes on individuals: The so-called "payroll taxes" cost individuals in the United States more than $420 billion in 2012. For millions of taxpayers, the Social Security and Medicare taxes are the *only* federal income taxes that they pay. Some critics erroneously interpret that to mean that those employees do not pay *any* federal *income* taxes. Those observers fail to understand that payroll taxes (7.65%) are part of income taxes. In addition, matching payroll taxes that are paid by employers on their employees' income are also part of the compensation paid by employers to their employees. Thus, the basic tax rate paid by even the poorest workers is actually a total of 15.3% of their income on Social Security and Medicare taxes alone. Two thirds of Americans, including virtually all lower-income and even most middle-income taxpayers, pay more in payroll taxes than they do in income taxes!

Personal income taxes: As was shown in Exhibit 5-1, the personal income tax ($1,132 billion in 2012) is by far the largest single source of federal tax revenue. It is also the most complicated of all parts of the Internal Revenue Code. The incredible conglomeration of deductions, credits, special tax rates, exclusions, exemptions, marriage penalty, alternative minimum tax, phase ins, phase outs, and numerous other loopholes and burdens makes this part of the tax code an unmitigated nightmare—and the part that changes most frequently.

Withholding taxes for individuals: Ever since World War II, when income taxes first became almost universal for American employees, income as well as Social Security taxes have been withheld from wages and salaries. This system gets tax revenues to the federal government earlier, and it also made sure that the taxes would be paid. When Medicare was introduced in the 1960s, those payroll taxes were withheld too. The net effect is that a significant amount of an individual's earnings never reach his or her pocket

Wealth-transfer taxes: The federal estate tax is a tax on the transfer of wealth from one generation to another. In the US, it is levied on the estate of the deceased, not on the heirs. It is thus imposed *before* the wealth is distributed.

Our wealth-transfer system is a very poorly designed and unjust tax. It has few defenders. It is very complex and riddled with loopholes. Often only those who can afford expensive tax counseling even know what special opportunities exist under the estate-tax law. Yet, the loopholes are so extensive that less than 1/10 of 1% of estates (only about one out of every 1500 estates) pays any estate tax at all! 99.9% of estates pay *none* of the so-called "death tax" that dishonest critics have convinced Americans will ruin their estates and the lives of their heirs.

In addition, a highly-orchestrated marketing campaign claims that thousands of small businesses and small farms are devastated by the estate tax. Those claims are complete fiction—totally dishonest. Those who make these claims can never seem to find real examples to back up their phony and deliberately misleading claims. The fact is that our estate-tax rules offer extensive protections for small businesses and farms.

Although only big estates pay any estate taxes now and although small businesses and family farms are already well protected, the marginal estate-tax rate is generally 40%, the highest tax rate paid by individuals. In order to avoid or reduce the tax, millions of Americans engage in expensive and often very inefficient estate planning. That can be a very great waste of family wealth. Families that do not know how to "game" the estate-tax system can end up paying far too many taxes. Indeed, the super-wealthy today often pay much lower estate-tax rates than do the merely "very wealthy." [As noted earlier, the tax code can be unjust even to the very wealthy.]

Federal taxes paid by individuals: Exhibit 5-2 shows the impact of federal payroll (i.e., Social Security & Medicare) and income taxes upon individuals with a wide range of incomes. Columns 2 through 5 show *estimated* payroll taxes (not including the employer's matching share), income taxes, total taxes paid and average taxes paid at various income levels. Column 6 shows the after-tax income under our current tax system.

Exhibit 5-2

Personal Taxes under our *Current Tax System*

(1)	(2)	(3)	(4)	(5)	(6)
Total	Estimated Income-Based Taxes				Net
Income	Payroll Taxes	Income Taxes	Total Taxes	Average Tax Now	Income Now
$20,000	$1,530	$0	$1,530	7.70%	$18,470
$30,000	$2,295	$800	$3,095	10.30%	$26,905
$60,000	$4,590	$3,200	$7,790	13.00%	$52,210
$100,000	$7,650	$10,000	$17,650	17.70%	$82,350
$250,000	$10,000	$45,000	$55,000	22.00%	$195,000
$500,000	$14,000	$125,000	$139,000	27.80%	$361,000
$750,000	$18,000	$200,000	$218,000	29.10%	$532,000
$1,000,000	$22,000	$275,000	$297,000	29.70%	$703,000

Taxes on Individuals under *Sensible Tax Reform*

Under ***Sensible Tax Reform—Simple, Just and Effective***, *there will be no deductions from income for federal taxes*. In Exhibit 5-2, total taxes [Column 4] are the amount of taxes that ***STR*** will eliminate at various levels of income. Total income [Column 1] will be the amount of net income that individuals will have available, rather than today's take-home [Column 6].

Social Security and Medicare taxes: *Payroll taxes will be totally eliminated* under ***Sensible Tax Reform***. Note that the taxes, but not the safety nets that they provide, would be eliminated. *Both the Social Security and Medicare programs would be fully protected*. However, the *funding* for both programs will come from the general federal budget rather than directly from payroll taxes on workers and their employers. The entire American economy would support the systems.

This will involve a radical change in how these programs, especially Social Security, are financed. Our economy has changed drastically since Social Security was introduced 75 years ago in the 1930s. Both programs are under severe financial strain. The time has come to re-examine their funding.

Sensible Tax Reform will remove this burden from all employees. It will *end federal tax withholding completely*, since payroll taxes will no longer be due and few individuals will pay any income taxes.

Personal income taxes: Under ***STR***, *most personal income taxes will be completely eliminated*:

- All taxpayers will be subject to exactly the same tax regulations.
- All income (wages, salaries, bonuses, interest, dividends, capital gains, inheritance and all other sources of personal income) will be subject to the same tax rules and tax rates.
- All existing tax deductions, credits, preferential tax rates, as well as all other tax loopholes, will be eliminated.
- A single large annual income-tax exclusion will protect 99% of Americans from paying any *income* taxes.
- No personal-income taxes will be withheld from any of our incomes.
- No *Social Security and Medicare taxes* will be collected.

- Our *annual burden of complying* with the federal personal income tax (the annual April 15 nightmare as well as most of the record keeping that it requires) will be gone.
- *The alternative minimum tax* will no longer exist. And,
- All relevant parts of the new tax system will be *indexed for inflation.*

Sensible Tax Reform will *totally change how the American government taxes individuals.* Indeed, it will *completely eliminate income taxation for most Americans* and create a very simple system for the few who will still need to pay. Our *real incomes* will rise significantly.

As can be seen in Exhibit 5-3 below, payroll taxes [Column 2] and income taxes [Column 3] would both be $0 under ***STR*** for all of the income levels up to $1 million (the level of the annual personal-income exclusion). Column 5 shows the percentage increase in take-home income from the elimination of those payroll and income taxes alone. Although these changes would benefit all income groups, the greatest benefits would disproportionately favor the highest-income taxpayers, since they pay the greatest share of income taxes.

Exhibit 5-3

Personal Taxes under *Sensible Tax Reform*

(1)	(2)	(3)	(4)	(5)
Total	Income-Based Taxes		Current	Increase
Income	Payroll	Income	After-Tax	in
	Taxes	Taxes	Income	Income
$20,000	$0	$0	$18,470	8.30%
$30,000	$0	$0	$26,905	11.50%
$60,000	$0	$0	$52,210	14.90%
$100,000	$0	$0	$82,350	21.40%
$250,000	$0	$0	$195,000	28.20%
$500,000	$0	$0	$361,000	38.50%
$750,000	$0	$0	$532,000	41.00%
$1,000,000	$0	$0	$703,000	42.30%

However, there are other benefits from ***STR***, which will be described below and in Chapter 6, which will insure that the lower income groups will benefit greatly.

No tax deductions or credits? The question is often asked with regard to ***STR***: "Why do I need to give up mortgage interest and property tax deductions?" The answer, of course, is: "Deductions from what? There will be no need for deductions, or even credits, if you will not be paying any income taxes!"

No tax refunds? Many taxpayers say that, however much they may resent our current tax system, they enjoy receiving an income-tax refund every year. Would they still be getting a refund under ***Sensible Tax Reform***? The response to that is: "A refund of what?" You now get a refund because *you overpaid your taxes*. [An unknown pundit has coined the term *intaxification* to describe the short-lived euphoria that a taxpayer feels when he or she receives a tax refund. The euphoria quickly dissipates when the realization sinks in that *it is their own money that they are getting back*—a loan that they had made to the government at 0% interest!] There will be no withholding of taxes and no overpayment of taxes. You will not need a refund, since you will never again need to pay any taxes.

Estate taxes: Under ***STR***, *estates* will pay no taxes. However, since *the majority of the wealth in these estates has never been taxed* (even with estates totaling hundreds of millions or billions of dollars), the wealth-transfer tax will be charged to the heirs, if appropriate. [Charitable donations from estates will not be taxed.]

Instead of the estate of the deceased being taxed, *the inheritance will be taxed* to the heirs (which is what many states already do). The inheritance income will be combined with all other sources of income of the heirs (wages, salaries, dividends, capital gains, etc.) and be taxed as part of total personal income, as described above.

Since the *estate* will not have been taxed first, the net effect of taxing the inheritors rather than the estate will generally be the receipt of *substantially larger bequests* and a *reduction in the taxes paid* versus our current estate-tax system. Even most heirs who must pay the income tax will pay a much lower tax rate than the 40% marginal rate that is applied to *estates* today. [The taxation of very high incomes, including the inheritance, will be the topic of Chapter 7.]

Fundamental Reform of Federal Taxes on *Businesses*

As with taxes on individuals, ***Sensible Tax Reform—Simple, Just and Effective*** will totally change the system of federal taxes paid by businesses. In fact, *businesses in the United States will pay almost no federal taxes.* ***STR*** will eliminate both corporate income taxes and the business share of Social Security and Medicare taxes.

Federal Taxes on Business Today

Federal business taxes in the United States are almost as complicated as are taxes on individuals. The two primary taxes are corporate income and payroll taxes.

Corporate income taxes: The federal government collected more than $240 billion in corporate income taxes in 2012. Taxes on business profits are very complex, very expensive to administer and can differ significantly between industries and even between different companies in the same industry. This has created many negative impacts for our economy:

- *Compliance costs* can be very high: General Electric alone has more than 1,000 tax accountants who produce a federal tax return of more than 57,000 pages. [Does anyone believe that the IRS actually reads all of that?] That is very costly and nonproductive.
- Taxes affect *how businesses finance* their operations. Since all interest that is paid by businesses is tax deductible, the Internal Revenue Code actually encourages companies to *borrow more* than they otherwise would. They thus get saddled with expensive debt obligations for years to come. That can be very dangerous in a recession.
- Taxes *affect where our companies locate their production and where they hire their workers.* Thousands of factories and millions of jobs have been "off-shored," with tax avoidance being an important motivation.
- Taxes affect where American businesses "earn" their profits and where they keep their profits: Using loopholes in our current federal tax system, American businesses have amassed more than $1.9 trillion of untaxed income outside the country in order to avoid income taxes here.

Social Security and Medicare taxes: Businesses in the United States must pay Social Security and Medicare taxes upon the wages of their workers. The business share is generally equal to those same taxes paid by the employees (7.65%). As was shown in Exhibit 5-1, businesses' share of these taxes was $422 billion in 2012. That is 75% more than the amount of corporate income taxes—a very heavy tax burden.

Proprietorships and other small businesses fare even worse. The *self-employment tax* which they must pay combines both the individual's and the business' share of the payroll taxes. That totals 15.30%. That is a very heavy tax—especially on start-up businesses that may not be earning any or not very much profit but still must pay that 15.30%.

Whose tax burden? It is important to remember that taxes are expenses for businesses—as are wages and the cost of supplies. Businesses pass *all* of their costs, including the taxes and tax-related expenses to others, either to their customers in higher prices, to their employees in lower wages or to shareholders in lower profits. *Businesses do not actually pay any taxes.* Businesses merely serve as an alternative way for the government to collect taxes from us—a very inefficient, expensive and damaging way.

International competitiveness: Our existing tax system is a major factor in America's poor international economic performance. American exports of goods are $400-$700 billion a year *less than* our imports—a trade deficit that has been as high as $2 billion *per day*! Many of those imports are goods which American producers could provide—and indeed did produce until relatively recently. American businesses are being undersold by foreign companies. A major reason is *the much higher tax burden that is borne by American companies when they compete internationally.*

In general, foreign businesses pay *more taxes* overall than do American businesses. However, most major foreign governments rely primarily upon a form of national consumption tax called a *value-added tax*. VATs, like all sales taxes, are charged to domestic buyers but not to foreign buyers. When companies in Europe, Asia or Latin America export goods, the exporter receives a *rebate* of all VATs that have been paid on those exports. That significantly reduces the price of their exports—often by 10%, 15% or even more.

On the other hand, in the United States, much of the federal income and Social Security taxes paid by American businesses ($664 billion in 2012) are *embedded in the prices* of all American-made goods, whether consumed in the United States or exported. *None* of the embedded tax costs of American producers can be rebated to exporters or domestic companies that compete against imports. This increases the prices of American products, *giving foreign producers a significant tax advantage versus American producers.*

By unnecessarily imposing a heavy tax burden upon American companies which their foreign competitors do not have, we are "shooting ourselves in the foot" and hurting both American exporters and import-competing businesses as well. It has cost us millions of jobs, thousands of companies and factories and even many entire industries. In order to help level the playing field, *we need to remove those income and Social-Security taxes from American businesses.*

Debt and interest rates: Under our current tax code, interest payments are tax deductible for businesses. Dividends on stocks are not. This encourages companies to sell less stock and borrow more. Indeed, by making business interest payments tax deductible, our government actually *subsidizes* and thereby encourages businesses to borrow! Those companies thus burden themselves with more debt than they otherwise would, often much more than they should, much more than they can afford.

That extra debt increases the risk for many companies that, when their markets are weak or when credit becomes scarce such as during the global economic crisis of 2007-2010, they will be seriously hurt and perhaps even unable to survive. During that crisis, many debt-burdened companies failed and went out of business. Many others were taken over by other companies—or even by the U.S. Government in the case of General Motors, Chrysler, AIG, Fannie Mae and Citibank. That additional demand for loans by businesses also helps to *raise interest rates for the rest of us* when we purchase homes, cars and other credit purchases.

Federal Business Taxes under *Sensible Tax Reform*

Untaxing business: *STR* will totally revolutionize the business tax code. As was noted above, businesses do not actually pay taxes themselves but are effectively only passing to the IRS the taxes that they had charged to their customers or which had reduced the income of employees or dividends paid to shareholders. It would be much *simpler*, much more *just*, and much *more effective* if businesses did not pay those taxes. If an alternative tax system could be designed where the customers, the employees and the shareholders paid the taxes themselves, businesses could be effectively untaxed. ***Sensible Tax Reform*** does exactly that—*businesses will pay neither income taxes nor Social Security and Medicare taxes.*

The overall annual reduction under ***STR*** in federal corporate income, Social Security and Medicare taxes along with the associated tax-compliance costs (which are estimated by the Tax Foundation to be $160 billion annually) for American businesses will be more than $800 billion per year! That reduction of expenses *will allow American producers to compete much more successfully, both domestically and internationally*. Foreign businesses will still receive the rebate of their VATs, but American businesses will not be paying any federal taxes at all.

When we stop "shooting ourselves in the foot" taxwise, the international competitive playing field will be leveled significantly. That will greatly improve our horrible balance of trade deficit and reduce the need of American businesses and federal government to borrow so heavily abroad. And it will lead to a very significant increase in production and jobs in the US.

Business incentives under *STR*: Since corporations will pay no income taxes, the choice between borrowing and paying interest or selling stock and paying dividends will no longer be distorted by the current tax subsidy for interest payments. Relying more upon equity and less upon debt will *strengthen American companies and reduce their exposure to market downturns*. Also, a substantial decline in business borrowing, together with the elimination of taxes on interest earned by investors, will help to *reduce interest rates*. That will benefit not only businesses but households and the government as well.

And, if American companies will no longer be paying federal taxes in the US, *most of the incentives for amassing profits outside of this country will disappear.* Companies will bring home most of their worldwide profits to invest here. Both effects will be important for employment and for the value of the companies' stocks. [Chapter 9 will examine in detail the untaxing of businesses and what the results are likely to be.]

A Federal Consumption Tax

To replace all of the tax revenues that the above revolutionary changes will entail, the core of the ***Sensible Tax Reform*** proposal will be a *federal consumption tax* (FCT) on retail purchases.

- The FCT will be a *single flat-rate tax*
- Charged on the *retail* purchase
- Of both goods and services.
- *Everyone* will be subject to exactly *the same consumption taxes and tax rules* on what they purchase.

Unlike our existing tax system, the ***STR*** tax code will not have special rules for a few and other, less favorable and less just, rules for the many.

Tax Regressiveness

If the tax burden on the low and middle-income groups is higher than on the wealthy, the tax system is *regressive*. For example, our *Social Security and Medicare taxes* are *very* regressive, since they only apply fully to the income of the poor and middle classes. The Social Security tax only applies to income below $113,700 (2013). Individuals with very high salaries and bonuses, such as famous athletes, movie stars and top Wall Street managers, only pay the Social Security tax on that $113,700 maximum—a very small part of their income. Other very high-income individuals, who receive most of their income from sources that are *not* even subject to the Social Security and Medicare taxes (such as dividends and capital gains), pay very little if anything in payroll taxes.

Our existing federal *income taxes* are *progressive* (up to 39.6%) on wages, salaries, commissions, tips, bonuses, etc. but *very regressive* (20% maximum) on income from dividends, capital gains and the so-called "carried interest" income of hedge-fund managers. Warren Buffet, America's second-wealthiest man, has noted that with tens of millions of annual income he pays less than 17% in federal taxes—a lower rate than his secretary! Likewise, Mitt Romney, during his presidential campaign, admitted that he regularly pays less than 15% on millions of dollars of annual income.

Buffett was not bragging. He was holding his own personal situation up as an example of how unjust the American federal tax system is. Indeed, a report from the IRS (May 2013)[15] analyzing the 400 taxpayers with the highest incomes in the United States (minimum *annual* income of the 400: $109 million—a very exclusive club!) found that their average tax was only 18.1% of adjusted gross income. Millions of less-fortunate Americans paid much higher tax rates. This grave inequity will be eliminated under ***Sensible Tax Reform***: *all income will be treated alike, whatever the source.*

Flat Taxes

All *flat taxes*, whether a flat *income* tax such as advocated by Steve Forbes in his two runs for the presidency or a flat *sales* tax such as proposed by ***STR*** as well as the Schaeffer-Tauzin and the so-called "fair tax," are basically regressive. However, careful design of a tax system can incorporate provisions to not only reduce but also completely eliminate those regressive effects. Unfortunately, the Forbes and other flat-tax plans do very little to overcome the very regressiveness of their proposals. The fair-tax plan, although offering more buffers to the basic regressiveness of its proposal, still falls far short of eliminating regressiveness.

Under ***Sensible Tax Reform—Simple, Just and Effective***, several significant adjustments will effectively eliminate the regressiveness of the federal consumption tax and provide additional benefits to simplify the lives and raise the standards of living of poor and middle-income Americans. This will be accomplished primarily by (1) eliminating the very regressive Social Security and Medicare taxes, (2) providing a progressive *rebate* of the FCT on incomes up to the poverty level and (3) special rules that will soften the impact of the FCT upon several key categories of consumption. Another factor will be the very limited tax on very high incomes, which is discussed in the next section. [The federal consumption tax will be examined in detail in the next chapter.]

A Simple-and-Just Federal Tax on Very High Incomes

Those three provisions of ***STR*** will go a long way to mitigate the *regressiveness* of a single-rate sales tax. The elimination of income taxes will primarily benefit those with high incomes, since they pay the bulk of income taxes. If high incomes were to be totally untaxed, there would still be significant regressiveness due to huge differences in *income.* Since the poor and middle classes consume all or most of their income, they will pay the federal consumption tax (FCT) on most or all of their income as it is spent. The very wealthy, on the other hand, consume only a small share of their income and are able to save a high percentage of their income. Their FCT taxes will be a much smaller share of their income than that paid by the poor or middle classes. That would be very regressive. ***Sensible Tax Reform*** includes a provision that will moderate this extreme regressiveness: a *simple-and-just federal tax on very high incomes.*

American Taxpayers

STR *will totally remove the burden of income taxes from 99% of Americans.* All income (wages, salaries, bonuses, capital gains, dividends, interest, inheritance, Social Security, etc.) will be treated alike and subject to the same taxes and tax regulations. However, the first $1 million of total income each year will be completely exempted from federal income taxes. *No one with annual income of less than $1 million will pay any income tax.*

STR Income-Tax Rules

All taxpayers, whatever their income, will be *treated alike. All personal income, whatever its source,* will be *taxed alike.* There will be no deductions, no credits, only that single $1 million exclusion, no phase-ins or phase-outs, and no preferential tax rates that primarily benefit the privileged few. Even for those few who must pay income taxes, the process will be much simpler and much less expensive than today and the tax rates will be lower. It will no longer be necessary for the wealthy to hire expensive tax planners to "game" the system, since there will be no loopholes to game. And, there will be no alternative minimum tax and no tax withholding. For those with incomes of more than $1 million, there will be only three tax rates: 15%, 25% and 35%.

Political Appeal

The only way that there will ever be sufficient public and congressional support to get serious tax reform passed is if the proposal benefits the vast majority of Americans and attracts all parts of the economic and political spectrums—conservative, moderate and liberal. That will only be possible if the tax proposal eliminates most of the regressiveness of a flat tax and thereby helps the poor and middle classes as well as the very wealthy. That will be accomplished by incorporating this *simple-and-just federal tax on very high incomes.* Otherwise, moderates and liberals would not support it. This is especially true in our current political climate in Washington, where Congress seldom agrees on anything. [The tax on very high incomes will be discussed in detail in Chapter 7.]

A Return of Political Integrity and Public Confidence in Government

Our politicians are at the core of the tax-reform issue since they enacted the complex, unjust, and constantly-changing tax legislation that causes so much economic and personal distress now. However, they are also the mechanism that can eradicate that offensive system.

Politicians and Taxes

The public today perceives a tax system that is very unjust and a political system that is cynically manipulated for the wealthy, for large companies and for other powerful groups—to the detriment of the rest of America. However, *few taxpayers actually know how much they are paying in taxes.* Many politicians like it that way, since it grants them great power. Confidence and respect for Congress and members of Congress in general have fallen as low as 10%—below the level even of telemarketers. [President Reagan perceived a similar problem and once famously remarked that "*Diapers and politicians both need to be changed regularly—and for the same reason.*"]

Politicians like the current tax system because they have been able to riddle our federal tax code with loopholes that they can manipulate for the advantage of their rich contributors. With **STR**, our tax system will be open and transparent. A very beneficial side effect will be that it will be *very difficult for politicians to manipulate* our tax system with special provisions for a few companies or individuals, as they often do now. The entire tax code will be *open, easy to understand* and *everyone will be treated alike.*

The elimination, under ***Sensible Tax Reform—Simple, Just and Effective***, of most of today's *77,000 pages* of the Internal Revenue Code and its substitution with the federal consumption tax and the simple-and-just federal tax on very high incomes will help to reverse that negative image. Our politicians will no longer be accused of subverting our tax system. Under ***Sensible Tax Reform****, federal taxes will be simple to understand and easy to see.* We will all know how much we are paying in taxes.

Protecting against Manipulation

The current federal tax system has little integrity and little public respect. Cynics of revolutionary tax reform sometimes claim that lobbyists in cohort with politicians will quickly make the same mess out of any new tax system that they have made out of our current one. That must never be permitted to happen! In order for all Americans to be completely confident about the integrity of the new tax system, it must be protected from manipulation.

- *First*, the simplicity and transparency of ***Sensible Tax Reform*** will greatly reduce what can be manipulated in the tax system. *There will be few possible ways to distort the system*
- *Second*, any attempt to twist our federal taxes in a way that will benefit only a few to the detriment of the majority will be *discouraged by the transparency and simplicity of the new system*. Any such attempt would be visible, not hidden as are most such maneuvers today.
- *Third*, I believe that most congressmen wish to do what is good for their constituents and all of America. If the vast influence of tax lobbyists is removed, those congressmen will likely welcome the reduction of the pressure from the lobbyists.
- *Finally*, there will be a provision mandating *a super-majority of both houses of Congress to make any substantive changes* in the ***Sensible Tax Reform*** program (e.g., attempts to increase tax rates, inject exclusions or other special treatment). A 60% vote of *both* houses of Congress (i.e., 60 senators and 261 representatives, if all members vote) will be required.

If the tax code cannot be easily manipulated, then tax lobbyists will have to find something positive and productive to do with their time and money—rather than damaging our country.

Sensible Tax Reform: A Summary

It should be obvious that ***Sensible Tax Reform—Simple, Just and Effective*** is truly significant and truly revolutionary:

- *Total elimination of the Social-Security and Medicare taxes*—for businesses and individuals;
- *Total elimination of the corporate income tax*;
- *Elimination of the personal income tax* for 99% of Americans;
- *Elimination of all loopholes* (exclusions, deductions, credits and preferential tax rates), except for the annual income-tax exclusion;
- *Elimination of the estate tax* while treating inheritance income as part of ordinary income;
- *Elimination of most tax-compliance burdens* for both businesses and individuals; and
- Indexation of all appropriate measures to inflation.

To replace all of these taxes, ***STR*** will:

- Introduce a very broad-based federal consumption tax [Chapter 6] and
- A very simple-and-just federal tax on incomes above $1 million [Chapter 7].

Exhibit 5-4 illustrates the tax changes that ***Sensible Tax Reform*** will bring, together with the numerous benefits that will ensue. On the left is our current federal tax system, which is heavily reliant upon income and payroll taxes. In the middle of the diagram is ***STR*** that will rely primarily upon the federal consumption tax. On the right, can be seen many of the benefits accruing from the change from our current tax system to ***STR***—simplicity, justice and much greater economic effectiveness.

Conclusions

Businesses will be completely freed from most of their current federal tax burdens. The savings will be passed on to America in the form of lower prices, increased investments, more research and development, less business debt,

Exhibit 5-4

Sensible Tax Reform – Simple, Just & Effective

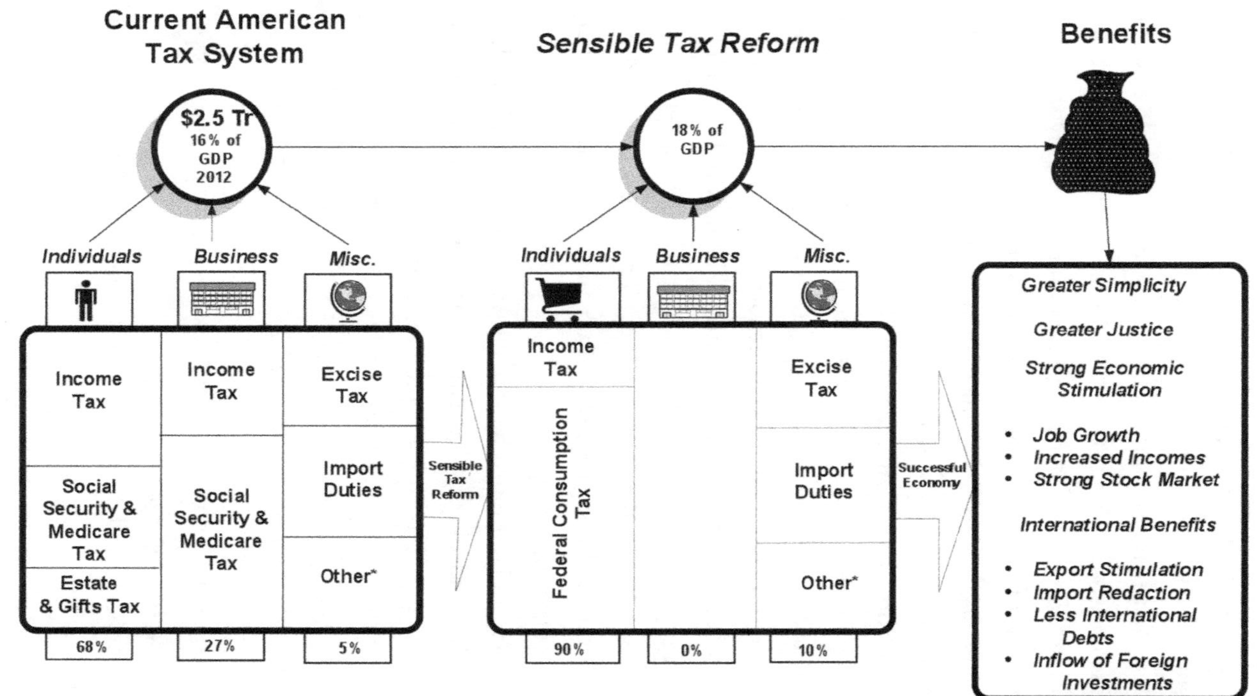

* Other sources of government revenue: primarily Federal Reserve profit

Korth©2014: *Sensible Tax Reform – Simple, Just and Effective!*

Designer: Andrew Targowski

lower interest rates, more jobs and increased income. It will greatly increase the ability of both American exporters and import-competing producers to compete against foreign companies.

Individuals and families will pay the taxes, even as they do now. However, instead of income, Social Security and Medicare taxes, tax collection will be primarily in the form of the federal consumption tax and only secondarily with the simple-and-just federal tax on very high incomes.

The federal tax base will be much broader. Everyone who makes retail purchases in the U.S. will pay the tax, including those with illegal income and also all visitors from abroad. All retailers will collect the tax, which will apply, to most retail purchases. There will be a minimum of limited exceptions (see Chapter 6). Few Americans will have any fear of the Internal Revenue Service; indeed, relatively few will even need to report annually to the IRS (Chapter 7). Our lives will be much simpler. Standards of living will be much higher for almost all who pay their taxes now. Those who currently evade taxes (e.g., drug dealers and those who use illegal tax scams) will pay more taxes under ***Sensible Tax Reform*** because, although we cannot tax their illegal income, they will be taxed when they spend.

Furthermore, unlike most other tax-reform proposals, ***STR*** is designed to appeal across diverse ideologies—economic, social and political. It is not a right-wing or left-wing issue. It is both a Republican and a Democratic issue. It should appeal to conservatives, independents and liberals. That is why it can overcome the natural cynicism of those who assert that serious tax reform is not feasible. That is why *this very practical tax-reform proposal can become law.*

- Chapter Six will examine in detail the *federal consumption tax* portion of ***Sensible Tax Reform***.
- Chapter Seven will do the same for the *simple-and-just federal tax on very high incomes.*

Endnotes

14 *The Budget for the Fiscal Year 2014*, Office of Management and Budget, February 2013; Tables 2.1 and 2.5

15 www.irs.gov/pub/irs-soi/09intop400.pdf

CHAPTER 6

FEDERAL CONSUMPTION TAX

The army of lobbyists in Washington (is) seeking to produce changes in the income tax, to introduce special privileges or exemptions for their clients, or to have what they regard as special burdens on their clients removed.
—Milton Friedman, Nobel laureate in economics

Chapter 5 summarized the changes that ***Sensible Tax Reform—Simple, Just and Effective*** will bring: complete elimination of the Social Security, Medicare, estate and corporate-income taxes, together with the elimination of the personal income tax for 99% of Americans. What makes all of this possible will be a new federal consumption tax (FCT) on *retail* expenditures.

By shifting to the ***STR*** federal consumption tax, Milton Friedman's concerns about "the army of lobbyists" introducing "special privileges or exemptions" will no longer be a threat. The income tax will be virtually eliminated. What remains of the income tax will be so simple and transparent that it will be difficult, if not impossible, for tax lobbyists to manipulate. A simple and just tax on consumption will be completely beyond their ability to distort.

The Nature of the Federal Consumption Tax

The FCT will satisfy all of the criteria that were set forth in the previous chapter for the design of a new consumption-tax system to replace the tax monstrosity that we have now:

- *It will be very simple*:
    - o *Single-level*
    - o *Retail only*, which
    - o *Everyone will pay*,
    - o Regardless of where they shop and which
    - o *Will apply to the purchases of most goods and services.*
- *It will be very just*:
    - o *All taxpayers will be treated the same.*
    - o There will be no specially favored groups.
- *It will be economically very effective*. The new tax climate will
    - o Provide a very strong boost to the economy,
    - o Stimulating businesses,
    - o Making US businesses much more competitive in world markets and
    - o Creating millions of jobs.
- *It will be free of manipulation*: The new, very simple federal tax code will be difficult to change and distort. And it will be indexed to inflation.
- *It will bring us much greater privacy*: We will no longer be reporting medical costs, charitable donations, *et cetera*, as we now do with our annual tax returns.
- And, the vast majority of taxpayers in this country will be much better off financially than they are under our current tax system.

The Federal Consumption Tax: Who? Where? What?

Who Will Be Subject to the FCT?

The "who" question of the federal consumption tax under ***Sensible Tax Reform*** is very simple and very just.

- *Every retail customer* will be subject to the federal consumption tax
- *Whenever and wherever they shop* and
- *Whatever the source of their income*—whether:
    - o Earned or unearned,
    - o Legal or illegal, and
    - o From this country or abroad.

STR is a system of ***universal inclusion of all retail customers***. If some groups of customers were to be exempt, that would not only be unjust but also the tax rate on the purchases by the rest of us would need to be higher.

We must be confident that everyone is being treated justly. The federal consumption tax will be very carefully structured to insure this. Everyone will be taxed in exactly the same way—a very different situation from our current tax system.

Where Will Purchases Be Taxed?

The "where" question of the FCT under ***Sensible Tax Reform*** will, as promised, also be simple, just and effective. One of the unfair aspects of our current state and local sales-tax systems is that different retailers can be subject to different sales-tax laws. The *local* retailer, whether locally owned or part of a national chain, is often at a competitive disadvantage relative to alternative retailers, such as Amazon or mail order. That is unjust and will be eliminated under ***STR***. All retailers will be treated the same.

Does that mean that Internet purchases will be taxed? Yes. Governments selling garbage collection? Yes. Goodwill Industries selling donated items? Yes. Flea markets selling both new and used goods? Yes. This will basically be no different than what is already done with state and local sales taxes in many states. All retail sales will be subject to the same tax rules.

It is obvious that, if we exempt some groups of sellers, it would not only be unfair to retailers who are not exempt, but it would also shrink the tax base, increase the tax rate on everything else, add complications, and open the door for manipulations. ***STR*** is a system of *universal inclusion of all retailers*.

What Expenditures Will Be Assessed the Federal Consumption Tax?

The "what" question of the federal consumption tax proposal under ***STR*** is also very simple and very just. The FCT will apply to the purchase of:

- Both goods and services,
- Used as well as new goods,
- Wherever they are bought, and
- However they are paid.

That is important not only for simplicity and justice of our tax system but also to broaden the tax base as much as possible in order to keep consumption tax rates as low as possible. It also removes loopholes through which tax lobbyists could squeeze special treatment for favored clients, which would be to the disadvantage of the rest of us.

Does that mean that groceries will be taxed? Yes. A visit to the barber? Yes. Football games? Yes. Used cars? Yes. A pedicure? Yes. Water and sewer services? Yes. There will be virtually *universal inclusion of consumer goods and services* under the FCT system.

What Expenditures by Individuals Will *Not* Be Taxed?

The FCT under ***Sensible Tax Reform*** will involve universal inclusion of all retail customers, all retailers and the purchase of most consumer goods and services. However, not all retail expenditures are purchases for consumption. Accordingly, several types of expenditures by individuals will not be subject to the federal consumption tax: financial investments, charitable donations, the payment of state and local taxes, and the premiums on insurance policies.

Financial investments: ***STR*** will exempt all financial savings from the burden of taxation. Deposits in savings accounts or the purchase of certificates of deposit, stocks, bonds or mutual funds are investments—not purchases for consumption. If income is not spent to buy goods and services, it will not be taxed.

In effect, under ***Sensible Tax Reform***, all financial savings will be tax-sheltered. This will substantially increase America's capacity for saving. That is extremely important since Americans collectively have a dismal record of savings. And, we will not need complicated retirement programs, such as 401(k)s and IRAs. We will have more income available for savings and investing those funds will be much easier.

Insurance: The purchase of insurance is a very special category of expenditure, somewhat akin to investment—planning for and protecting against the possibilities of the future. It is not for "consumption." Health, property and casualty and life insurance are all generally prudent and cautious efforts to plan for the future. The federal consumption tax under ***STR*** will not tax insurance premiums.

However, the expenditures resulting from health and P&C claims or proceeds from life insurance would be taxed. For example, the repairs to a car damaged in an accident will be subject to the FCT. Similarly, the income from life insurance policies would be subject to the simple-and-just federal tax on very high incomes.

Charitable donations: Financial donations to charitable organizations are not for personal consumption and will *not* be subject to the FCT tax. ***STR*** will encourage charitable giving since the real incomes of most people will be much greater. [Donations of tangible goods, such as clothing and food, are obviously not expenditures and will not be taxed either.]

State and local taxes: Municipal income, sales and property taxes, as well as excise taxes (for example, gasoline or tobacco taxes), are not voluntary expenditures. Nor are they for consumption. Therefore, they will *not* be subject to the FCT. No government should tax the payments of taxes to government agencies, at either the state or federal level. Under ***STR***, it will not occur.

Will Expenditures by Businesses and Governments Be Taxed?

Purchases by businesses: As was seen in Chapter 5, one of the key parts of ***Sensible Tax Reform*** will be the untaxing of business. The federal consumption tax will be a tax on *retail* purchases only. Purchases by businesses are costs of their operations. They will *not* be subject to the retail tax. [The impact of ***STR*** upon business will be examined in detail in Chapter 9.]

Purchases by government agencies: In a similar fashion, purchases by governments and their agencies occur for the purpose of providing public services.

Government agencies will *not* be subject to the tax for the same reason as with businesses. Only retail purchases will be subject to the FCT—*not wholesale.* [The impact of ***STR*** upon the government and its agencies will be examined in detail in Chapter 10.]

A Single FCT Tax Rate

Under ***Sensible Tax Reform—Simple, Just and Effective***, the U.S. Government will be receiving no corporate income taxes, no Social Security taxes, no Medicare taxes, no estate taxes and substantially lower personal income taxes. The new federal consumption tax will be the source of most of the replacement revenue for the federal government. Those will be sweeping, revolutionary innovations.

STR will involve major personal changes, but will bring significant financial rewards. The proposal in this chapter is for a radical change in our tax system. However, once it is considered relative to all of the reader's current taxes and other expenses and once the reader realizes how much better off he / she is, then the promises of the new tax system will be seen to be *very beneficial.* It will certainly be much more attractive than our current income-based tax system.

One Tax, One Rate

Sensible Tax Reform will introduce a single flat-rate federal consumption tax. In order to maintain *revenue neutrality* for the federal government, several economic studies have suggested 26-34% as a reasonable estimate for the FCT rate. Retail purchases of both goods and services, by all buyers and from all retailers will thus be taxed at the same rate: about 30%. This is necessarily a rough estimate. Once it has been tested by sophisticated economic models, we will be able to determine a more specific rate.

A tax of 30% sounds high—very high. At first glance, it is a shock. However, *all of us are now paying higher taxes than that—often much higher*!!! First, we pay visible taxes (i.e., the Social Security, Medicare and personal income taxes) directly to the federal government. We also pay invisible taxes that were paid by businesses and are then embedded in the prices that we pay, even though we do not see them. That can add 10%, 15% or even more to the price of what we buy. The FCT will replace most of the federal taxes that we now pay—with one consumption tax, one rate. Everyone will pay it. And that tax will be very visible.

The nominal rate of the FCT will indeed be high. However, when all of the savings and benefits are considered, the federal consumption tax will be seen to be not an increase in our individual taxes but rather a substitute for other taxes—a lower-tax substitute. As shown later in this chapter, the vast majority of Americans will be substantially better off under the 30% federal consumption tax of the ***STR*** than they are now. They will be paying lower taxes, enjoying a higher standard of living and be able to save much more. Also, the annual tax-compliance burden (i.e., April 15) will be virtually eliminated for more than 98% of Americans.

We need a federal consumption tax. Taxes will be simpler and more just. The economy will be stronger. We can't afford *not* to move forward and make the necessary changes. We need ***Sensible Tax Reform—Simple, Just and Effective***. We need it now!

The *Rebate* of the Federal Consumption Tax

A flat sales tax, including any federal consumption tax such as ***STR***, is basically *regressive*. Unless provisions are incorporated in the tax plan to protect the less fortunate and to insure that all are treated justly, the poor and middle-income groups will bear a heavier tax burden than will the wealthy. The poor will pay the new federal consumption tax on 100% of their income, since they will spend it all. Middle-income groups will pay it on the bulk of their income.

The wealthy, on the other hand, will legally avoid paying the federal consumption tax upon any income that is not spent on goods and services—money which is saved. If no other tax applies to very high incomes, that could leave the majority of their income completely untaxed, their average tax rates (FCT as a percentage of income) very low and America's income and wealth gaps would continue to broaden. That would be very regressive and clearly not just.

As can be seen in Exhibit 6-1a, total expenditures [Column 2] are comprised of the base price [Column 3] plus the 30% FCT [Columns 4]. A 30% federal consumption tax could well absorb 23% of the incomes of the poor and middle classes [Column 5]. [23% would be the maximum effective tax, because the table is measuring the tax as a percent of the total expenditure. Thus, the spending of the family with $20,000 would be $15,400 plus the 30% FCT ($4,600). The tax rate would be $4,600 / $20,000 = 23%.]

Exhibit 6-1a

Effective Tax Rates with a 30% FCT				
(1)	(2)	(3)	(4)	(5)
Income	Expenditures			Average
	Total	Base Price	FCT	Tax
$20,000	$20,000	$15,400	$4,600	23.0%
$50,000	$48,000	$36,900	$11,100	22.2%
$100,000	$93,000	$71,000	$22,000	22.0%
$250,000	$205,000	$153,800	$51,200	20.5%
$500,000	$385,000	$292,300	$92,700	18.5%
$1,000,000	$700,000	$538,000	$162,000	16.2%
$5,000,000	$3,000,000	$2,307,700	$692,300	13.8%
$10,000,000	$4,000,000	$3,076,900	$923,100	9.2%

As Column 5 and Exhibit 6-1b show, the flat consumption tax is *very regressive*. For high incomes the effective tax rate is much lower—and continues to fall rapidly as incomes reach very high levels (only 9.2% at an income of $10

Exhibit 6-1b

Effective Tax Rates with a 30% FCT

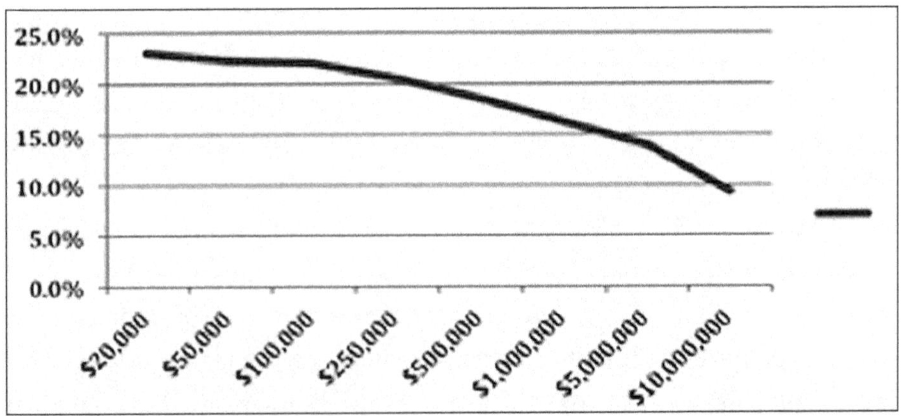

million in the example shown). Although *everyone pays the same rate of FCT for most of the goods and services that they buy*, the larger one's income, the smaller the share that is spent for consumption and the lower the percentage of income that is paid as consumption tax.

In order to offset the regressiveness of the FCT, there need to be compensations in the new tax law to protect lower-income groups. The elimination of Social Security and Medicare taxes (which are very regressive) from our current tax system will *indirectly* reduce the regressiveness of the new federal consumption tax. Also, as will be seen in the next chapter, those with very high personal incomes will still be subject to a revised and simplified income tax—the simple-and-just federal tax on very high incomes.

Rebate of the FCT on basic consumption: Since the poor need to spend most or all of their income, they would still be worse off with the FCT—unless they are protected from the tax. Therefore, ***Sensible Tax Reform*** will provide a direct offset to the FCT in the form of a *rebate*. The rebate would apply to the taxes paid on purchases up to the poverty level. [The US Department of Health and Human Services[16] (HHS) determined that the poverty level in 2013 was $11,490 for an individual and $23,550 for a family of four.]

As a very simplified example, assume that a poverty-level family has income of $20,000 and the federal consumption tax rate is 30%. When that poor family spent their $20,000 of income, the FCT would total $6,000 (30% * $20,000). The total cost would be $26,000—$6,000 more than their income. Therefore, the family would receive an annual rebate of that $6,000:

Cost of goods and services	$20,000
Federal consumption tax	+ $ 6,000
= Total expenditures	$26,000
(-) Rebate	- $ 6,000
= Net cost	$20,000

Since ***STR*** treats all legal taxpayers exactly the same, everyone would be eligible for the rebate. In effect, *purchases up to the poverty level will be completely* *free of the federal consumption tax*—for *all* Americans. HHS adjusts poverty levels annually for inflation. The annual rebate would adjust accordingly each year. Also, there will be a simple periodic re-application so that the rebate can be adjusted to changes in family size.

The rebate will thus pay for the FCT on purchases up to the poverty level. It would be remitted to each taxpayer on a monthly basis (e.g., $6000 ÷ 12 = $500 each month), paid at the beginning of each month. Thus, taxpayers would have the funds in advance to pay the tax on their purchases during that month.[17] Because of the elimination of Social Security and Medicare and the likely decline in prices, even low-income families will be much better off under ***Sensible Tax Reform***. [Chapter 8 will examine the impact upon individuals and households in detail.]

Costs versus Benefits of the FCT

"Okay, Korth!" you say. "Perhaps you are right in saying that we will all be much better off under your proposed ***Sensible Tax Reform—Simple, Just and Effective***. But is it absolutely necessary to tax necessities such as food, clothing, housing and used items?" The answer is "yes." Virtually everything needs to be taxed in order to keep the FCT as low as possible. 30% would be a high rate, but exclusions would force the rate even higher.

- There needs to be an *absolute minimum of exceptions.*
- *Everyone* must pay,
- Subject to the *same FCT rules,*
- *Whenever* they make their purchases,
- *Wherever* they make their purchases,
- *From whomever* the purchases are made,
- *However they finance those purchases* and
- For *any goods or services purchased.*

As the economic benefits of this improved tax system flow through, the economy will grow much faster.

Tax Advantages of _Sensible Tax Reform_

- You will no longer be paying Social Security taxes.
- You will no longer be paying Medicare taxes.
- You will likely no longer be paying federal personal-income taxes.
- You will no longer be paying estate taxes.
- You will receive a rebate of the FCT on basic consumption.
- The new tax system will be much more just with everyone paying their share—including crooks, illegal immigrants and foreign tourists. The US taxpayer's "playing field" will at long last be level.
- Your life will be much simpler. There will be much less financial record keeping, no need to file federal income taxes—and no need to fear IRS audits.

Non-Tax Advantages of _Sensible Tax Reform_

- With the elimination of embedded taxes and tax-compliance costs, the prices of goods and services will fall.
- Real net incomes and the standards of living for almost all Americans will increase.
- The planning of savings for your retirement, for your children's education, for your healthcare and for starting your own business will be much simpler and more affordable.
- The economy will boom, with millions of new jobs being created.
- Interest rates will fall.
- The stock market will likely soar and dividends rise sharply. And
- Our political leaders will be free from the disrupting influence of tax lobbyists. We will have more confidence in our federal government.

The reader is encouraged to remember what ***STR*** has changed in his/her favor. A summary of many of the principal benefits is summarized in the accompanying boxes. The first box highlights favorable *tax* implications.

The second box highlights *non-tax* improvements from the adoption of ***Sensible Tax Reform***.

FCT vs. Our Current Tax System

Exhibit 6-2 illustrates America's current situation for various levels of incomes. For simplicity, the table assumes that a family of four at the poverty level has approximately $20,000 of gross income. The family now pays $1,530 to Social Security and Medicare [7.65% of $20,000; Column 2], but pays no income taxes [Column 3]. Their net income is only $18,470 [Column 4].

A family with earned income of $100,000 would pay $7,650 in Social Security and Medicare taxes. The table assumes $10,000 of income taxes. That family would currently have $82,350 of income after taxes.

Exhibit 6-2

Income under the Current Tax System			
(1)	(2)	(3)	(4)
Gross Income	Payroll Tax	Income Tax	Disposable Income
$20,000	$1,530	$0	$18,470
$60,000	$4,590	$3,200	$52,210
$100,000	$7,650	$10,000	$82,350
$250,000	$10,000	$45,000	$195,000
$500,000	$14,000	$125,000	$361,000

Exhibit 6-3 illustrates how, under our current tax laws, families now might spend and save. Column 1 is total income (pre-tax). Column 2 is after-tax or disposable income [from Exhibit 6-2]. Column 3 illustrates possible levels of annual purchases.

Exhibit 6-3

Purchases and Savings under the *Current* Tax System				
(1)	(2)	(3)	(4)	(5)
Income		Purchases	Savings	
Gross	Disposable		$	%
$20,000	$18,470	$18,470	$0	0.0%
$60,000	$52,210	$51,000	$1,210	2.0%
$100,000	$82,350	$77,000	$5,350	5.4%
$250,000	$195,000	$170,000	$25,000	10.0%
$500,000	$361,000	$290,000	$71,000	14.2%

The savings [Columns 4 and 5] is the part of net income that is not spent on purchases. Not surprisingly, the poverty-level family since it is so poor, needs to spend all of its net income [Column 3] and is unable to save anything. For higher levels of income, the purchases shown are not precise, since different families will have very different spending and saving patterns. Nevertheless, savings by most of the middle class in the US remains very low.

Higher income groups do much better, even now. The family with $100,000 of earned income and disposable income of about $82,350 [Column 2] would spend perhaps $77,000 and save $5,350—a savings rate of about 5.4%. [With the pathetically low savings patterns of most American families in recent years, even this would be above the norm for most families.] Those with higher incomes obviously are capable of saving significantly more—both in dollar and percentage terms.

Sensible Tax Reform—Simple, Just and Effective

As has been noted repeatedly, our current tax system is a mess—complicated, unjust and hurting our economy. It needs to be completely overhauled. It needs to be replaced with ***Sensible Tax Reform—Simple, Just and Effective***. The American people need it. Our businesses and the economy need it. And our government needs it.

The *STR* Impact upon *Income*

Exhibit 6-4 shows what America can expect with the adoption of ***STR***. As was shown in Chapter 5, no one will pay Social Security or Medicare taxes [Column 2]. And no one with income of less than $1,000,000 will pay any income tax [Column 3] In addition, taxpayers will qualify for the annual rebate of $6,000 that was discussed above [Column 4]. [Note that the rebate will be the same for families of equal size, regardless of income—everyone will be treated alike.] With ***Sensible Tax Reform***, for more than 99% of Americans, disposable income will equal the gross income that they receive now plus the rebate [Column 5].

Exhibit 6-4

The *STR* Impact upon Income

(1)	(2)	(3)	(4)	(5)
Gross Income	Payroll Tax	Income Taxes	Rebate	Disposable Income
$20,000	$0	$0	$6,000	$26,000
$60,000	$0	$0	$6,000	$66,000
$100,000	$0	$0	$6,000	$106,000
$250,000	$0	$0	$6,000	$256,000
$500,000	$0	$0	$6,000	$506,000

The *STR* Impact upon *Purchases*

Other very favorable developments from the introduction of ***STR*** will be the demise of embedded *business* taxes and tax-related compliance and planning costs of businesses. As a result, both wholesale and retail prices will fall. Exhibit 6-5, Column 1 shows disposable income from Column 5 above, including the ***STR*** rebate. Column 2 shows the same level of purchases as was seen above in Exhibit 6-3. Column 3 below assumes a modest *decline* in prices of only 6%, although the actual decline will very likely be more.

Exhibit 6-5

The *STR* Impact upon Purchases				
(1)	(2)	(3)	(4)	(5)
Disposable Income	Current Purchases	Lower Prices (-6%)	Cost w/ 30% FCT	Total Savings
$26,000	$18,470	$17,362	$22,570	$3,430
$66,000	$51,000	$47,940	$62,322	$3,678
$106,000	$77,000	$72,380	$94,094	$11,906
$256,000	$170,000	$159,800	$207,740	$48,260
$506,000	$290,000	$272,600	$354,380	$151,620

The final variable will be the 30% federal consumption tax [Column 4]. Nominal costs will be higher than now [Column 2]. However, real income [i.e., total disposable income in Column 1] will be much higher for almost all Americans. As a result, the relative costs of what we buy will be substantially less than they are now. This can be observed at all income levels by the considerable increase in our capacity to save [Column 5 and Exhibit 6-6]—the result of having paid less for our purchases, despite the 30% FCT. Our standard of living will rise.

The *STR* Impact upon *Savings*

Exhibit 6-6 shows how substantial the increase in our *total savings* might be under ***Sensible Tax Reform***. Columns 2 and 3 are drawn from the above tables. Column 4 shows plausible *increases* in savings for various income levels (that is, the difference between Columns 2 and 3). Column 5 shows what the percentage increase might be (Column 4 divided by Column 3).

Middle-income groups will be the biggest winners. With an income of $66,000 [$60,000 plus the $6000 rebate], a family could experience an increase in savings of more than 200% [Column 5]! A middle-income family with $106,000 of income [Line 3] would also enjoy a huge increase in savings—122%.

Exhibit 6-6

The *STR* Impact upon *Total Savings*				
(1)	(2)	(3)	(4)	(5)
Income:	Savings			
Total	Total Savings		Savings	%
STR	*STR*	Pre-*STR*	*Increase*	Change
$26,000	$3,430	$0	$3,430	n.m.
$66,000	$3,678	$1,210	$2,468	204.0%
$106,000	$11,906	$5,350	$6,556	122.5%
$256,000	$48,260	$25,000	$23,260	93.0%
$506,000	$151,620	$71,000	$80,620	113.5%

The sharp increase in their standards of living opens many possibilities to the families. We cannot, of course, actually say how that "savings" will be used. As has been noted before, the poor are in fact likely to spend most or all of their increase in income rather than to actually save it. Whatever their decisions, they will enjoy a much higher standard of living. Many in higher income groups will indeed sharply increase their savings, pay off debt or send their children to a better college. Some may buy a larger home or a newer car. Others will save to start their own businesses.

Finally, Exhibit 6-7 shows the plausible impact of ***STR*** on *savings rates* (that is, savings as a share of total income in Column 1). The low-income family will experience $3430 more of real disposable income. If saved, that would correspond to more than 13% of their ***STR*** income. However, most of the poor will utilize their higher income to increase their purchases. At middle-income levels with pre-***STR*** savings rates of 2-14% [Column 4], many families are likely to actually increase their savings and investments substantially [Column 5].

Exhibit 6-7

The ***STR*** Impact upon the ***Savings Rate***				
(1)	(2)	(3)	(4)	(5)
Income	Savings			
	Total Savings		Savings Rate	
	STR	Pre-*STR*	Pre-*STR*	*STR*
$26,000	$3,430	$0	0.0%	13.2%
$66,000	$3,678	$1,410	2.0%	5.6%
$106,000	$11,906	$7,350	5.4%	11.2%
$256,000	$48,260	$30,100	10.0%	18.9%
$506,000	$151,620	$75,000	14.2%	30.0%

Advantages of a Federal Consumption Tax

This section will focus upon the implications of ***Sensible Tax Reform—Simple, Just and Effective*** for simplicity, justice, increased income, honesty of government and privacy.

Simplicity

One of the most attractive aspects of ***STR*** will be what we will no longer need to do. More than 98% of Americans will never again even need to file income taxes. Fewer than 1% will actually pay any federal income taxes at all [Chapter 7]. Further, an estimated $110 billion in monetary and time costs every year will be eliminated.

We also spend countless millions of hours and billions of dollars in *planning* for our retirement and our estates [e.g., 401(k)s, IRAs, Roth IRAs, etc.], for our children's education [e.g., 529 and Cloverdell plans] and for our health [e.g., health savings accounts]. Such special-purpose programs exist primarily because of our tax system. Under the ***STR***, such tax-avoidance schemes will no longer be necessary, since there will not be any income taxes to avoid. Each of us will have much more time to do what we would really like—spending time with our families, exercising, pursuing a hobby, starting a business, doing charitable work, or writing a book.

Justice

One of the key aspects of ***STR***'s federal consumption tax is that everyone will pay it when they spend, which will be quite just. One of the most discouraging aspects of our current system is the almost universal view that it is grossly unjust, that many avoid paying income taxes with sleazy scams or even evade taxes illegally. Our system hurts those most who can least afford it: the low and middle-income groups who comprise 75% - 85% of the population. They are the core working and administrative groups who rely almost completely upon earned income. At the same time, our existing system unfairly benefits groups that can avoid or evade income and Social Security taxes. Groups that legally avoid paying federal taxes now but that will pay the full federal consumption tax include:

- The very wealthy who live on trust funds, loans or non-taxed or preferentially-taxed investments, such as dividends and capital gains (especially the misleadingly named "carried interest"); and
- The 50,000,000 annual visitors from abroad who now pay only embedded taxes—a much lower effective tax than the FCT. However, when we travel to Canada, Europe, Japan, etc., we pay their federal consumption taxes (the VAT). With ***STR***, they will likewise pay similar explicit taxes (our FCT) when they visit here and spend on travel, hotels, restaurants, souvenirs, gifts, etc.

Groups that now *illegally evade* paying income, Social Security, Medicare or estate taxes but which will join the rest of us in paying the federal consumption tax include:

- *Crooks*: The mafia and other criminals do not pay income taxes or Social Security and Medicare taxes on their illegal earnings from drugs, money laundering, gambling, prostitution, etc. However, when ***STR*** is in effect, they will pay the FCT when they spend their ill-gotten gains on normal purchases.
- *Tax evaders*: Those who hide legally-received income or exaggerate deductions or who do not even file any income-tax returns (e.g., the

movie actor Wesley Snipes, the Grammy-winning singer Lauryn Hill and the billionairess Leona Helmsley, all of whom were jailed for tax evasion) would pay federal consumption taxes.

- The "*underground economy*": Often "casual" employees (e.g., day laborers, lawn services, nannies, flea markets, etc.), are hired by either families or businesses to work "off the books." These groups commonly escape income and Social Security taxes now, but they will join us in paying the federal consumption tax when they spend.
- *Illegal immigrants*: Foreigners who are in the US illegally are also frequently paid without being charged either income or Social-Security taxes. They will likewise be taxed when they spend.

In order for there to be general support for the tax system upon which our government relies, the people must have confidence that everyone pays their just share of taxes. That confidence is lacking now. It will be re-established with ***Sensible Tax Reform—Simple, Just and Effective***.

Increased Income

There will be a very real and very substantial increase in income for almost all Americans—no Social Security taxes (6.20% of earned income), no Medicare taxes (1.45%), no personal income taxes (10-39.6%), and no compliance costs (priceless). Most Americans will receive a monthly rebate. And, prices will fall when businesses pass their savings from the elimination of their taxes unto their customers. *Income for almost all of us will increase much more than will the new taxes.*

This is especially true of the poor, who spend all of their income. Under our current system, we have the absurd situation where those below the poverty level are paying 7.65% in Social Security and Medicare taxes and some even pay income taxes. There is something ethically wrong when people who qualify for welfare benefits, such as food stamps, lunch programs for their children and rental assistance are at the same time paying federal income taxes. How much better it would be if they received all of their income and had much less need for government assistance.

STR will encourage work and reduce the need for welfare. The poor will pay the federal consumption tax—as everyone else will as well. However, everyone will also qualify for the rebate of the FCT. That will help all consumers to the same extent. In the case of the poor, it will completely shield them from the actual burden of the FCT. For the rest of us, it will shield us from taxes on an equal amount of consumption.

Privacy

Americans are very concerned, and rightfully so, about the incursion of government and business into their private lives. How often do we hear about private financial information being inadvertently released on the Internet, improperly accessed from credit agencies or being stolen by crooks?

Since few Americans will be submitting the detailed information that is currently part of filing our federal income taxes every April 15, the ***STR*** will greatly reduce the amount of prying into our lives by the federal government and the accumulation of private information. Let us take back our privacy!

Conclusions

We have seen that the core of ***Sensible Tax Reform*** will be the elimination of many different business and personal taxes and their replacement primarily with a federal consumption tax—with its:

- *Universal inclusion of all retail customers,*
- *Universal inclusion of all retailers* and
- *Inclusion of most consumer goods and services purchased.*

That will provide the broadest and fairest possible tax base for our economy.

The ***STR*** will:

- Increase the justice of the federal tax system,
- Substantially simplify it,
- Strengthen our economy,
- Create millions of new jobs,
- Greatly increase our real incomes,

- Greatly increase our standards of living,
- Make manipulation of the tax system much more difficult,
- Greatly reduce the corrosive influence of tax lobbyists, and
- Protect us from prying by the government into our private finances.

The new federal consumption tax will seem very high initially, but will actually be much less of a tax burden for most individuals than the total of all of our existing taxes that it will replace. More importantly, at the same time that our current taxes paid will fall for most of us, there will be the increase in income that will result from the ***STR***. The bottom line is that we will be much better off. When you, the reader, fully understand the advantages of ***Sensible Tax Reform—Simple, Just and Effective***, *you will become a confirmed supporter!*

Chapter 7 will complete this second part of the book with a discussion of the other leg of the ***STR***: the simple-and-just federal tax on very high incomes.

Endnotes

16 aspe.hhs.gov/poverty13poverty.cfm

17 The concept of a rebate of FCTs is also included in other national sales-tax proposals, beginning with the *Schaeffer-Tauzin National Retail Sales Tax Act of 1997.*

CHAPTER 7

A SIMPLE-AND-JUST FEDERAL TAX ON VERY HIGH INCOMES

When a tax is not visible, it can be easily retained or raised with little, if any, awareness among taxpayers about how the tax affects them.
—Tax Division, American Institute of Certified Public Accountants

Chapter Five introduced the overall proposal for ***Sensible Tax Reform—Simple, Just and Effective***. Chapter Six examined the federal consumption tax (FCT) component of the proposal. This chapter will explore the other component—a *very simple-and-just federal tax on very high incomes*. Unlike our current federal income-tax system, the income-tax component will be very visible. Taxpayers will know very well how it affects them. Washington will no longer be able to manipulate our taxes in secret. The new tax system will be very easy to understand and very easy to implement:

- *All taxpayers* will be treated the same.
- *All income* will be treated the same.
- There will be *no exemptions, deductions, credits or preferential tax rates* for privileged groups.

- A *single large* ***exclusion*** *every year* will shield 99% of taxpayers from the income tax.
- There will be a simple *three-tier income tax* on income above the exclusion.
- The exclusion and the tax brackets will all be *indexed for inflation.*
- There will be *no alternative minimum tax.*

Why Do We Still Need an Income Tax?

The corporate income tax will be completely removed under *STR*. In addition, most of the personal income tax will be eliminated. However, there are a number of reasons why the *retention of a personal income tax on very high incomes is warranted*: economic necessity, ethical necessity, and political necessity.

Economic Necessity for an Income Tax

Tax neutrality: ***Sensible Tax Reform*** has been designed with *tax neutrality* for the federal government in mind. That is, the government will collect approximately the same amount of taxes that it is projected to attract under our current tax system. The 30% FCT alone may not fully compensate for such massive reductions in government revenue. Therefore, *economic necessity* requires a *simple-and-just federal tax on very high incomes* in order to supplement revenues from the federal consumption tax and to keep its rate as low as possible.

Exhibit 7-1 shows total revenues of the US Government for 2012. It can be seen that the federal government's lost revenues will be very high when the Social Security, Medicare, estate, corporate-income and most personal income taxes are eliminated—$2.3 *trillion* [Column 5, Lines 1 and 2] of the $2.4 trillion of federal government revenue in 2012—almost 96% of the total.

The personal income-tax burden on those high-income taxpayers who will still be subject to the tax will be much lower than it is now, but an *income tax* on incomes greater than $1 million will be included as part of ***Sensible Tax Reform.***

Income tax on high incomes: Despite the many personal income tax loopholes available today, many of the wealthy pay a lot of their income in taxes. However, few pay anywhere near the 39.6% maximum statutory rate [Exhibit

Exhibit 7-1

U.S. Government Revenues: 2012[18] (Billions)					
	(1)	(2)	(3)	(4)	(5)
	Individuals	Corporations	Other	Total	
				$	%
Income Taxes	$1,132	$242		$1,374	56.1%
Social Security					
& Medicare	$422	$422		$844	34.5%
Estate and Gift Taxes	$14			$14	0.6%
Excise taxes	$79			$79	3.2%
Import duties	$30			$30	1.2%
Miscellaneous	———	———	$107	$107	4.4%
Total Value ($)	$1,677	$664	$107	$2,448	
Share of taxes (%)	68.5%	27.1%	4.4%		100.0%

7-2, Column 5]. According to the IRS[19], the top 1% of taxpayers pay an average of only 23-24% of their income in federal taxes. Of course, some taxpayers

Exhibit 7-2

Income & Taxes under the Current Tax System				
(1)	(2)	(3)	(4)	(5)
Gross Income	Payroll Tax	Income Tax	Disposable Income	Tax as %
$500,000	$14,000	$125,000	$361,000	27.8%
$1,000,000	$22,000	$275,000	$703,000	29.7%
$10,000,000	$30,000	$2,350,000	$7,620,000	23.8%
$25,000,000	$45,000	$5,750,000	$19,205,000	23.2%

would pay more and some much less (for example, Warren Buffett's famous 17% and Mitt Romney's 13%).

An individual with $1 million of annual income might easily pay $275,000 or more in federal income taxes today [Column 3] in addition to a relatively small payroll tax [Column 2]. Someone with income of $25 million might pay $5 million or more.

Our federal budget cannot afford to lose such tax revenue. Therefore, *economic necessity* alone offers a very strong reason for retaining an income tax on very high incomes along with a federal consumption tax. However, there are also ethical and political arguments as well for taxing the income of those with very high incomes.

Ethical Necessity for an Income Tax

Switching to a consumption tax: High-income individuals will benefit very handsomely from the introduction of ***Sensible Tax Reform***. The simplification of income taxes together with the single large exclusion and the elimination of the estate tax will reduce their income taxes substantially. As seen in the above exhibit, if the federal personal income tax were to be completely eliminated, someone with $25 million of income would receive an income-tax cut of more than $5 million [Column 3].

With the switch to a federal consumption tax, *everyone will pay a tax on what they spend on consumption*—not on what income they receive. Most of those with low incomes will not get much benefit from the elimination of income taxes. They will also likely spend all of their income and will need to pay the new federal consumption tax on most of it. The very wealthy, of course, will pay the same FCT rate on what they buy. However much, if not the vast majority, of their very high incomes will *not* be spent and therefore *not* be subject to the consumption tax. They would therefore pay very low average consumption taxes. Without any tax on the unspent (i.e., "saved") portion of the income of those with very high incomes, the overall tax effect would be regressive—very regressive.

Income and Wealth Gaps: A related ethical issue involves the increasing awareness that our society is being divided by a growing *income gap* and *wealth gap* between the very rich and the vast majority of Americans—the middle class. In an article in Barron's[20], the conservative financial newspaper, Michael Santoli observed menacingly: "*Never in history have the haves had so much. Burgeoning wealth and incomes...are accruing disproportionately to the entrepreneur class and the already rich... The long-term pattern in which the rich get rapidly richer seems durable.*"

Those who would remove all federal income taxes from these very-high income groups sometimes assert that our current tax system is onerous, some even claim that the current rates (top rate: 39.6%) are confiscatory for those with high incomes. Such claims are unrealistic. Even now *Americans pay some of the lowest income taxes in the developed world.*

In Exhibit 7-2 above, despite fairly high taxes, after-tax disposable income [Column 4] is very high for the very wealthy under our current tax system. Exhibit 7-3 below illustrates how even now those with very high incomes can enjoy very high after-tax *savings rates* [Column 5]—more than 20% for someone with income of $1 million and almost 60% for someone with $25 million of gross income.

Exhibit 7-3

Spending and Savings under the Current Tax System

(1)	(2)	(3)	(4)	(5)
Income		Spending	Savings	
Gross	Disposable		$	%
$500,000	$361,000	$310,000	$51,000	10.2%
$1,000,000	$703,000	$500,000	$203,000	20.3%
$10,000,000	$7,620,000	$3,000,000	$4,620,000	46.2%
$25,000,000	$19,205,000	$5,000,000	$14,205,000	56.8%

Failing to tax very high incomes would continue to enlarge the very wide income and wealth gaps that are increasingly dividing America. Simple justice as well as political common sense should alert us to the need to end this gross inequity. The elimination of income taxes on very high incomes is clearly not necessary to make wealth accumulation possible.

Plutocracy: In his Barron's article, Michael Santoli described our current environment as a "*winner-take-most economy.*" We are creating a *plutocracy*—an *economic aristocracy*, a system where the political power does not result from merit or social rank or inherited titles but merely from wealth.

The danger of such income and wealth disparity has been recognized since the very founding of this nation. More than 200 years ago, Thomas Jefferson warned about this threat from an "*aristocracy of moneyed corporations.*" J. Pierpont Morgan, one of America's most successful and very-wealthy entrepreneurs, similarly warned 100 years ago against "the tyranny of mere wealth, the tyranny of plutocracy." Jefferson and Morgan knew intimately about what they were speaking, since they were warning about the economic class of which they were very prominent members.

Extreme wealth has been amassed in other corners of the world as well as here in America—from Germany to Mexico, from Russia to India and from Spain to China. However, nowhere else in the world is the opportunity to amass extreme wealth, or even "modest" wealth, so widespread and the unique entrepreneurial environment so supportive as in the United States. The American free-enterprise system is an unparalleled environment in which very high incomes and great wealth are available for hundreds of thousands, even millions, of Americans. More than 1 million American families have more than $5 million of wealth in addition to their home.

Every year we hear more and more of very high incomes for professional athletes, movie stars, corporate CEOs, financial wheeler-dealers, and ultra-wealthy heirs and heiresses. Hundreds of hedge fund, investment-bank and private-equity fund managers on Wall Street have received annual incomes of $25,000,000, $100,000,000 and even billions of dollars.

Wealth and Income Gaps: *The gaps in American income and wealth are the highest of all of the major industrialized countries in the world*[21] Indeed, the income gaps are little better than for such countries as Russia and China and on a par with India and Indonesia—hardly the norms by which Americans want to be judged. Our income gaps are much worse than Canada, Western Europe and Australia[22].

As was noted above, the income and wealth gaps between the ultra-rich and the other 99% of Americans have become the *highest in American history*. Unless our tax system changes, it appears likely that these gaps will continue to grow much wider in coming years. That is inexcusable! ***STR*** would help to counter that trend by eliminating these and all other loopholes that distort our tax system and treat different groups of taxpayers differently.

War on taxes: Despite their very high incomes, savings rates and enormous wealth, many of the ultra-rich pay large sums to lobbyists in order to try to eliminate ALL income and estate taxes. [They seem to share Leona Helmsley's famous quip that, "*Only the little people pay taxes!*"] That is something that our federal government with its huge budget and debt imbalances cannot afford. It would not be good for our economy and would be dangerous for our society! Therefore, on the basis of justice, a *simple-and-just federal tax on very high incomes* will be *ethically necessary* along with the federal consumption tax.

Political Necessity for an Income Tax

In addition to the economic and justice arguments, if very-high incomes and large bequests are not taxed, there will be no possibility of mobilizing the broad-based political support necessary to get the ***Sensible Tax Reform***, or any other true tax reform, passed by Congress! This proposal would then go the way of other ambitious tax proposals—and *not* be approved by Congress. The Armey and Forbes flat income-tax proposals as well as the flat sales-tax proposals of Schaeffer-Tauzin and the "fair tax" have floundered in Congress. Without exception, every one of them has been viewed by moderates, both Republicans and Democrats, as too skewed economically, politically and socially for the benefit of the wealthy at the expense of the middle class. *None* of them have come close to being passed by Congress.

In order to bridge the political and social gulf and make passage of ***STR*** possible, *a realistic tax-reform plan must be more balanced* than those proposals. For passage by Congress and signing by the president, a tax proposal must appeal to a broad political spectrum. If we are serious about real tax reform, a tax on very high incomes will be necessary. If *you*, the reader, are really serious about eliminating all of your business taxes and compliance costs, are truly serious regarding the elimination of the personal tax burdens of more than 99% of Americans and are very serious about actually seeing such a simple, just and effective income-tax system passed, then political necessity also requires a tax on very high incomes in conjunction with the FCT.

In summary, a *simple-and-just federal tax on very high incomes* is needed as part of ***STR*** for reasons of (1) government revenue, (2) taxpayer justice and (3) political feasibility.

A Simple-and-Just Federal Tax on Very High Incomes

All Taxpayers and Income Will Be Treated the Same

Under our current income-tax system, the *earned* income of the farmer, the factory worker, the store clerk, the teacher, the waitress, the entrepreneur who starts his own business, and the manager who runs a corporation is now charged significantly higher income-tax rates (up to 39.5%) than is the income of those who live off of *unearned* income in the form of dividends, capital gains and "carried interest" (all currently taxed at a maximum rate of 20%). That imbalance is contrary to all principles of meritocracy and justice. *Our current tax system rewards wealth and power—not merit*! Under ***Sensible Tax Reform—Simple, Just and Effective***, *all taxpayers and all income will be treated alike and subject to the same tax rates*. Earned income and merit will no longer be treated less favorably than "unearned income."

A Simple and Just Tax System

Since its founding 100 years ago, our federal tax system has become extremely complicated via countless changes to it in Washington—more than 700 changes per year on average.

Justice and transparency: Our federal tax system should be simple, open, just, effective and protected from behind-the-scenes special political deals for the favored few. We need fair rules that everyone understands and that apply the same to everyone.

Under our current federal tax system, some of the loopholes favor the poor (for example, the earned-income tax credit). However, most income-tax deductions and credits primarily favor those with high incomes and with a lot of political influence: mortgage-interest deductions on million-dollar mortgages, tax-free capital gains of $500,000 on the sale of houses and the obscene favoritism accorded to "carried interest."

Taxation—not social engineering: The government needs to stop pursuing non-tax goals and calling it tax reform. If there are special social goals that the government wishes to promote, then it should openly and clearly create programs to support those goals directly— not bury them in our federal taxes.

Our current income-tax system is riddled with complicated, inconsistent, conflicting and often-unjust loopholes. Regardless of how meritorious some of the loopholes might be (for example, the deduction for interest on home mortgages and credits for energy efficiency), there are better ways to attain those goals than manipulating tax exclusions, exemptions, deductions, credits, tax rates, phase ins, phase outs and numerous other loopholes to accomplish these goals. And, those programs should be very visible, subject to periodic critical review and perhaps even include *sunset provisions*, which would automatically terminate the programs if Congress chose not to renew them.

Tax lobbyists: The group that most clearly wants to retain the current corrupt tax system is the *tax lobbyists*. They have created an atmosphere in Washington where they have obtained a disproportionate amount of influence. They even sometimes actually write parts of changes in the tax laws—always to their own advantage, of course. It is time to return the Internal Revenue Code to what it was intended to be—a tax system that is simple, just and effective! It is time that the American people reclaim control over our tax system.

Preparing Tax Returns under *STR*

Calculating Total Income

The process of calculating an individual's income will be very simple. *All income, from whatever source, will be treated the same and be included as part of total income.* Exhibit 7-4 shows the new simplified IRS Tax Form 1040 HI (high income) that might result from the adoption of the ***STR***.

One Exclusion but No Deductions, Credits or Exemptions

Under the simple-and-just federal tax on very high incomes, there will be no deductions, credits, exemptions, preferential tax rates or any other type of special

Exhibit 7-4

Form 1040 HI: Income

Sum all sources of income:

Salaries and wages
Bonuses and commissions
Tips
Interest and dividends
Capital gains
Health premiums paid by employer
Employer contributions to retirement
Social Security benefits
Pensions and annuities
Profit (self-employed)
Rents
Royalties and licensing fees
Option premiums
Alimony
Gifts and inheritances
Gambling winnings

= ***Total income***

tax treatment. However, there will be one exclusion: The first $1 million of income will be totally excluded from the federal income tax. That will *exclude 99% of taxpayers from having to pay any federal income taxes.* When the federal income tax was first introduced in 1913, it only applied to ½ of 1% of Americans. Now it applies to virtually all of us. ***Sensible Tax Reform*** will return our federal income taxes to about that 1913 ideal again.

Taxable Income

About 140 million personal income tax returns are filed each year under our current federal tax system. Once ***STR*** is implemented:

- 98% of those tax returns (more than 137 million) will no longer need to be filed—ever again.

- Most of us will no longer need to keep the extensive financial records that are necessary now.
- Life will be a lot simpler and less stressful—especially near April 15.

For those who must file taxes, the process will be very simple:

1. Record and sum all income [Exhibit 7-4 above]
2. Subtract the $1 million exclusion:
   Total income - $1 million = ***Taxable income***
3. Calculate the taxes due

Tax Rates

Calculating the taxes due will also be very simple. There will be only three income-tax rates:

- 15% for annual *taxable income* between $0-10 million
- 25% for annual taxable income between $10-25 million
- 35% for annual taxable income in excess of $25 million

Exhibit 7-5 shows the *current* federal tax brackets for a married couple filing jointly. In contrast to the ***Sensible Tax Reform*** with a 15% tax rate beginning only at $1 million of income, today a mere $17,851 is enough income to be taxed at that rate. Likewise, in comparison to the maximum 35% tax rate, which only falls upon taxable incomes greater than $25 million, under our present system the highest income-tax rate of 39.6% begins at $450,001 (in 2013).

This proposed system will clearly save high-income households hundreds of thousands or even millions of dollars annually when compared with our current income taxes. A simple-and-just federal tax on very high income would not only be justified but would still leave most high-income households better off than today. The difference would be that those gains would have been realized under the same tax rules as for everyone else—not via special tax breaks designed only for the very wealthy.

Exhibit 7-5

Tax Brackets for Married Taxpayers Filing Jointly		
Taxable Income	Marginal Tax Rate	
	2013	*STR*
$0-$17,850	10.00%	0%
$17,851-$72,500	15.00%	0%
$72,501-$146,400	25.00%	0%
$146,401-$223,050	28.00%	0%
$223,051-$398,350	33.00%	0%
$398,351-$450,000	35.00%	0%
$450,001+	39.60%	0%
$1,000,000+	39.60%	15%
$10,000,000+	39.60%	25%
$25,000,000+	39.60%	35%

Income Taxes Due

Exhibit 7-6 gives illustrations of ***STR*** income taxes due for income levels up to $40 million. As can be seen, on the first $1 million of income, there is no *taxable* income [Column 2], so no income taxes will be due [Column 6] and the tax rate will thus be 0%. Even at $10 million of total income, the average tax rate will only be 13.5%, 20.0% with $25 million of income and only 26.3% with $40 million of income. However, some ultra-high income taxpayers (for example, those receiving "carried interest") may pay more under the simple-and-just federal tax on very high incomes than they do currently.

Whether to Tax Estates or Inheritance?

America is the land of opportunity. Nowhere else in the world, indeed nowhere else in history, has there ever been such a confluence of economic opportunity, political stability, economic infrastructure, and a just and efficient legal system. Centimillionaires and billionaires are being created at an unprecedented rate.

Exhibit 7-6

Income Taxes Due under *STR*					
(1)	(2)	(3)	(4)	(5)	(6)
Income		Marginal Tax Rate			Total
Total	Taxable[a]	15%	25%	35%	Taxes
$500,000	$0	$0	$0	$0	$0
$1,000,000	$0	$0	$0	$0	$0
$2,000,000	$1,000,000	$150,000	$0	$0	$150,000
$5,000,000	$4,000,000	$600,000	$0	$0	$600,000
$10,000,000	$9,000,000	$1,350,000	$0	$0	$1,350,000
$25,000,000	$24,000,000	$1,500,000	$3,500,000	$0	$5,000,000
$40,000,000	$39,000,000	$1,500,000	$3,750,000	$5,250,000	$10,500,000
a. (Column 1) - $1 Million Exclusion					

Many of these people have contributed greatly to this country. We should all be proud that our free-enterprise system allows the likes of Sam Walton, Steve Jobs, Jeff Bezos, Larry Ellison, Oprah Winfrey and Steven Spielberg to use their ideas, their genius and their hard work to amass great fortunes. They have all contributed greatly to our economy and quality of life.

Every year, Forbes Magazine publishes a list of the 400 wealthiest individuals in the country—all billionaires. [There are other billionaires who did not even make the list.] A concentration in family dynasties is evident on the Forbes list. On the 2013 list[23], of the top twenty richest Americans, three of the Mars candy dynasty heirs were worth $17 billion each ($51 billion in total). Two of the Koch oil and commodity heirs are each worth $34 billion ($68 billion together). And four of the ten wealthiest Americans all have the same last name—Walton, with $26-27 billion each (a combined fortune of over $107 billion within the Walton family). That is an enormous concentration of wealth: nine of Forbes' richest twenty fortunes are concentrated in just those three families—almost a quarter of a trillion dollars.

The opportunity to generate high incomes and to amass great wealth is the right of everyone in this country. Each and every one of us, including the poor and middle class, have benefited greatly from *this* unique American environment. *Each of us also has an obligation to give back to our country.* Those who have been fortunate enough to receive great income and accumulate great wealth have a special obligation to pay back and to share with the nation that has made their success possible.

Taxation of Wealth

A special form of income tax is the taxation of the transfer of wealth—in the form of estate and gift taxes. Like the rest of the Internal Revenue Code, the taxation of estates and gifts is very complicated, often contradictory and widely perceived to be unfair. Nevertheless, today's estate tax is not oppressive. The vast majority of large estates are totally shielded from taxes—due to a large estate-tax exclusion ($5.25 million in 2013) and additional provisions favoring spouses and capital gains, along with special help for the estates of farmers and small businesses.

In recent years with more than 2,300,000 deaths annually in the United States, fewer than 4,590 estates (about one out of every five hundred) even needed to *file* estate taxes in 2011[24]. Only one third of those, 1480 estates, had to pay *any* federal taxes at all. *99.9% of estates pay no estate taxes*!!! And, the average estate tax of those few that did actually have to pay was only 15.5%—not at all onerous for wealth that may have been growing untaxed for many years.

Dishonest and Misleading Criticism of the Estate-Tax System

While complicated, the estate tax is clearly not the horrible "death tax" that radical attacks claim it to be. Despite these facts, a well-financed and aggressively-marketed campaign to abolish the estate tax has been mounted by a small group of the ultra-wealthy.

Typically, opponents of the estate tax argue that the wealth has already been taxed, which is patently dishonest. In reality, much or even all of the wealth in the largest taxable estates is in the form of capital gains, *which has never been taxed*! The aforementioned special estate-tax provisions protect most of that wealth accumulation from paying any income taxes at all.

Misleading information: There is much mis-information and deliberate dis-information regarding America's estate tax that is constantly spewed by extremist media in the United States. These groups sometimes try to minimize the importance of the estate tax as a revenue source for the American government. However, a tax that might yield "only" $13-18 billion annually in tax revenue would produce an additional $130-180 billion over a ten-year period. If that tax revenue were eliminated, our federal debt would be that much higher.

Those critics do not seem to think that the very wealthy have any tax obligation to the U.S. Government and the American people. They appear to believe that rules designed to benefit the very wealthy, rules that disproportionately benefit themselves, are good for the entire country. That is certainly not true. What would truly be good for individuals, businesses and America as a whole would be tax laws that are just, simple, consistent and which apply the same way for everyone.

True Flaws in our Estate Tax

If we can get beyond all of the anti-estate-tax hyperbole and dishonesty, we can clearly see that there are actually very real and serious flaws with our current estate tax:

- As with other federal income taxes, the laws involving estates and inheritances in the United States are incredibly complicated, confusing and contradictory.
- Estate planning is very difficult and often extremely expensive.
- The effective *marginal* rate on most taxable estates is 40%—the highest income-tax rate.
- All estates are *not* treated alike. The *ultra-wealthy* receive advantages via loopholes that the majority of *merely wealthy* individuals with taxable estates cannot receive. As a result, the effective estate-tax rate is often much higher for mid-sized estates than for the very largest.
- Taxation of an entire estate is generally much heavier than if each heir were to be taxed upon his/her own share of the inheritance.

Patents for avoiding taxes: Our existing estate-tax laws are so ridiculous that some law firms have even been able to obtain more than 100 *patents* for their clever schemes to avoid estate taxes to which only the firm's wealthy clients would have access. What could be more damning evidence of the absurdity of our existing federal estate-tax system than that such egregious loopholes exist that a proposal for scamming our tax system might be patentable! Our tax system needs to be simple, just, transparent and equally available to everyone! Our existing estate-tax system fails that test completely.

Taxation of estates today: Consider a $20 million estate with four heirs (Exhibit 7-7]. Under the current estate-tax system (2013), the estate will have a $5.25 million exclusion [Line 2]. The net taxable estate of $14.75 million [Line 3] might then be subject to a flat 40% estate tax, $5.9 million [Line 4]. The total after-tax estate would be $14,100,000 [Line 7], comprised of the after-tax estate [Line 5] plus the untaxed exclusion [Line 6]. Assuming that each heir would receive the same amount, his or her individual bequests would then be about $3,525,000 [Line 8].

Exhibit 7-7

Estate Tax under our *Current* Tax System

1. Total estate	$20,000,000
2. (-) Exclusion	($5,250,000)
3. = Net taxable estate	$14,750,000
4. (-) Tax (40%)	($5,900,000)
5. = After-tax estate	$8,850,000
6. (+) Exclusion (from Line 2)	$5,250,000
7. = Total after-tax estate	$14,100,000
8. (÷ 4) = Individual after-tax bequest	$3,525,000

Wealth Taxation under *STR*

Another part of the simple-and-just federal tax on very high incomes will be the taxation of wealth transfer. As noted above, most accumulated wealth in large estates is in the form of *capital gains that has never been taxed.* Under ***Sensible Tax Reform—Simple, Just and Effective***, that estate will not be taxed. Instead, the bequests and donations will be distributed tax-free. Bequests will be subject to taxation as part of the income of heirs—not as a separate inheritance tax. The new system:

- Will *tax at moderate levels,*
- With *no loopholes* and
- With *everyone treated the same.*

A simple-and-just federal tax on wealth transfer: With ***STR***, wealth and its transfer will be protected from today's convoluted estate-tax rules, which are difficult to understand and expensive to follow. It will also provide protection from complicated estate-tax scams that now distort the system. And, the process of transferring businesses and farms as bequests will be simple and will protect those who wish to continue to operate the enterprise.

Lower wealth-transfer taxes: All sources of personal income (including inheritance) will be treated exactly the same. All income will be summed up and then benefit from the same simple-and-just federal tax on very high incomes that was discussed earlier in this chapter.

Using the above example, since there would not be an estate tax [Exhibit 7-8, Line 2], each of the four heirs might receive equal bequests of $5 million [Line 4]. The combined income taxes due on the *inheritance* of each of the four bequests would be much less under ***STR***. Heirs who had the full unused $1 million income-tax exclusion [Line 5] could pay as little as $600,000 in taxes [Line 7] on their $5 million of inherited income—an effective tax rate of only 12%. That compares with the 40% rate that could apply to the net taxable estate under our current tax system.

If each of the four heirs were in the same situation, the total tax bill would be $2.4 million ($600,000 * 4)—a reduction of $3.5 million versus today's estate tax of $5.9 million [Exhibit 7-7, Line 4]. That would yield to each individual an after-tax income of $3.4 million [Line 8] *plus* the $1 million that had been excluded from their individual taxes [Line 9] for a total of $4.4 million each [Line 10]—an increase of $875,000 in the inheritance of each in comparison to our current tax law. The total after-tax inheritance, if all four heirs receive equal shares, will be $17.6 million [Line 11] versus $14.1 million now.

Exhibit 7-8
Estate Tax under *Sensible Tax Reform*

1. Total estate	$20,000,000
2. (-) Estate tax	($ 0)
3. = Remaining estate	$20,000,000
4. Individual inheritance	$5,000,000
5. (-) Individual annual exclusion	($1,000,000)
6. = Individual taxable income	$4,000,000
7. (-) Income tax (15%)	($600,000)
8. = Individual total after-tax	$3,400,000
9. (+) Individual annual exclusion	$1,000,000
10. = Individual after-tax bequest	$4,400,000
11. (* 4) = Total after-tax inheritance	$17,600,000

Benefit to heirs: Clearly, the heirs can generally expect to receive a much larger after-tax bequest with the *simple-and-just federal tax on very high incomes* under ***STR*** than they do currently:

- First, the estate will have been divided up among the heirs *before* being subject to the income tax. That will greatly increase the amount of the total inheritance.
- Second, for most heirs, the bequest will benefit from the annual $1 million income-tax exclusion.
- Third, tax rates will be at a much lower level (15%) than the current rates (40%).

The *Simple-and-Just Federal Tax on Very High Incomes*—Summary

The federal income tax under ***Sensible Tax Reform—Simple, Just and Effective*** will not be merely an evolutionary, but a true revolutionary, change in the income-tax system of the United States:

- All income will be treated equally.
- There will be no exemptions, deductions, or credits.
- Estate taxes will be eliminated.
- Inheritance will be combined with all other income for income-tax calculations.
- The first $1 million of income each year, from whatever source, will be excluded from the tax. That will exclude 99% of all potential taxpayers from paying *any* income taxes.
- The only income-tax brackets for those with very high incomes will be: 15%, 25% and 35%, with the top bracket only applying to net taxable incomes greater than $25 million.
- There will be no alternative minimum tax (AMT).
- The brackets, along with the exclusion, will be indexed for inflation.

A Need for Change—Now!

A simple-and-just federal tax on very high incomes is mandatory if we really:

- Hope to *maintain tax neutrality* for our federal government and to finance the enormous reduction in income, estate, Social Security and Medicare taxes that the ***Sensible Tax Reform*** will entail.
- Hope to *maintain fairness, the perception of justice and avoid accelerating the social and economic divisions* in America via the rapidly growing wealth and income gaps.
- *Want federal tax reform* to be passed by our politicians in Washington.

These three chapters, Chapters 5-7, comprise the core of ***Sensible Tax Reform—Simple, Just and Effective***. The next three chapters will examine in detail the impact that the two components, the federal consumption tax and the simple-and-just federal tax on very high incomes, will have on families [Chapter 8], businesses and the overall economy [Chapter 9] and the government [Chapter 10].

Endnotes

18 *The Budget for the Fiscal Year 2014*, Office of Management and Budget, February 2013; Tables 2.1 and 2.5

19 http://www.irs.gov/uac/SOI-Tax-Stats-Individual-Statistical-Tables-by-Tax-Rate-and-Income-Percentile

20 "Rich America, Poor America," *Barron's*, Michael Santoli, January 23, 2007

21 OECD Factbook: 2013, p. 67

22 oecd-library.org/sites/factbook-2013-en

23 "*The World's Billionaires*," Forbes, March 4, 2013 (www.forbes.com/billionaires)

24 "Estate Tax Returns Filed in 2011," *Internal Revenue Service*, Statistics of Income Division, Table 1, August 2012.

PART C

THE IMPACT OF THE *SENSIBLE TAX REFORM* TAX PLAN

Chapter 8: ***Sensible Tax Reform* for American Families**
Chapter 9: ***Sensible Tax Reform* for American Businesses**
Chapter 10: ***Sensible Tax Reform* for the American Government**

CHAPTER 8

SENSIBLE TAX REFORM AND AMERICAN FAMILIES

People want just taxes more than they want lower taxes.
—Will Rogers, American humorist

Chapters 5-7 detailed the basic elements of ***Sensible Tax Reform—Simple, Just and Effective***. This chapter will address the impact of the new tax program upon families and individuals. *We are the taxpayers who pay most of the federal taxes now*—not businesses,. We pay whether directly in the form of Social Security, Medicare, income and estate taxes or indirectly through the embedded taxes that are included in the cost of what we buy. The new tax system will eliminate all of those existing federal taxes and replace them with the federal consumption tax [Chapter 6], coupled with the simple-and-just federal tax on very-high incomes [Chapter 7].

This chapter has two major parts. The first will explore the important impacts that this new tax program will bring at various income levels as well as for investors and retirees. The second part will examine those expenditures which will either *not* be taxed or be taxed under special provisions.

Impact of *STR* upon all Americans

The previous three chapters have stressed again and again how, in contrast to our current unjust tax system that treats and taxes different taxpayers differently and often very inequitably, ***Sensible Tax Reform*** will treat everyone the same:

- The new tax system will be much simpler, easier to understand and free of complicated loopholes.
- The system will be much more just. Everyone will be treated alike and everyone will share the tax burden, which will be very difficult to evade.
- Taxes will be reduced for the vast majority of Americans, with the total elimination of Social Security, Medicare and estate taxes and of most income taxes.
- Incomes, standards of living and family savings will rise.
- There will be no alternative minimum tax.
- And, the new tax system will be much healthier for the overall economy, with millions of new jobs created.

All of us will benefit greatly from ***Sensible Tax Reform***. The following three sections will explore the specific impacts upon the three major income groups.

Impact of *Sensible Tax Reform* upon *Low-Income* Groups

STR will bring substantial benefits to low-income groups:

- Social Security and Medicare taxes replaced by funding from the federal general budget,
- More real income—even with the new FCT,
- Lower prices,
- A rebate of the FCT payments received monthly—in advance, and
- A healthy economy with strong job growth.

Current Taxes on the Poor

The treatment of the poor under our current tax system is irrational. For a poverty-level family of four earning $20,000, both parents are likely to need to work. They must pay Social Security and Medicare taxes and often income taxes as well, from the very first dollar that they earn. They spend everything they receive, saving nothing.

Payroll taxes are the heaviest federal taxes paid by most Americans. The poor, and even most of the middle class, do not benefit from the cap on Social Security taxes, which tops out in 2013 at income of $113,700—above which no more of the taxes are paid. [For instance, if Donald Trump had $30 million of annual income, he would only pay Social Security on the first $113,700.] Furthermore, though millionaires can currently deduct the interest on mortgages of up to $1 million and tens of thousands of dollars of property taxes from their taxable income, those benefits are of little help to the poor. Yet, payroll taxes are *not* tax deductible.

No Federal Taxes on the Poor

STR will effectively "untax" the poor from the federal tax burden. They will:

- Pay no income tax,
- Pay no Social Security tax,
- Pay no Medicare tax and,
- Although they will pay the federal consumption tax, the FCT *rebate* will totally offset the tax for them.

The poor will never again even need to file federal income taxes. ***STR*** will eliminate the current irrationality whereby the federal government taxes the poor and then creates special tax programs and subsidies (such programs as food stamps, free school lunches, child care and rent assistance as well as the earned-income tax credit) to give money back to many of the poor—*if* the poor apply for them. These programs are constantly under attack from groups opposing low-income assistance to the poor. With the elimination of all taxes on low-income groups and with the receipt of the monthly rebate, there will be much less need for such programs.

Consumption: Consider the income and consumption of a family of four with a poverty-level income of $20,000 in Exhibit 8-1. Even though the family is below the poverty level, it must now pay payroll taxes of $1530. They thus only have $18,470 to spend [Column 2], although many also pay income taxes. The poor are likely to spend all of their income, mostly on basic necessities: Their total consumption will equal their net income of $18,470.

Exhibit 8-1

The *STR* Impact upon the Consumption of Low-Income Groups					
(1)	(2)	(3)	(4)	(5)	(6)
Current	Pre-STR	Consumption under STR			Total STR
Income	Consumption	Price	w/ FCT	w/ Rebate	Savings
		(-6%)	(+30%)	(-$6,000)	
$20,000	$18,470	$17,362	$22,570	$16,570	$3,430

Under ***Sensible Tax Reform***, what they earn ($20,000) is what they will actually have to spend (less any deductions for healthcare and retirement programs by their employers). Since producers' costs will decline with the elimination of federal taxes, retail prices are also likely to decline, as was discussed in Chapter 6. Column 3 assumes a 6% decline, but it may well be more.

The 30% federal consumption tax will be added [Column 4] to yield a final purchase cost of $22,570. However, the FCT of $6000 (30% of $20,000) will be rebated. Thus, the net cost will be only $16,570 [Column 5]. With their income of $20,000, the real incomes of a typical poor family will increase by $3,430 [Column 6 and Exhibit 8-1b]. Even if the additional purchases bear the entire 30% FCT, that will represent $2,638 of additional consumption for the poor—a real 15.2% increase in income ($2,638 / $20,000), as well as in consumption and standards of living. Although most of the poor will be unable to save much, they will clearly benefit greatly from the new tax system.

Impact of *Sensible Tax Reform* upon *Middle-Income* Groups

70-80% of Americans fall into the very broad category of "middle income." They pay most of the Social Security, Medicare and income taxes. They have *not* been well served by recent tax "reforms." Many of the tax benefits that have been designed for the advantage of the very wealthy and big companies during the past decade have done little to help the middle class. While real incomes of those with very high incomes have risen sharply over the past twenty years and even since the economic collapse in 2008-10, for lower and middle-income groups *real incomes have fallen.* In addition, reduced government support for social programs have served to deepen the pain.

Sensible Tax Reform—Simple, Just and Effective will offer very real and very substantial improvement to the standards of living of virtually all middle-income families. Important benefits (in addition to those for the poor) include:

- Much greater ability to actually save;
- Much more flexibility in planning and saving for retirement, healthcare and education;
- Much greater ability for their employers to adequately fund retirement and healthcare;
- No tax withholding;
- No alternative minimum tax (AMT); and
- An end to the constantly-changing tax rules.

More than $1.5 trillion of Social Security, Medicare and income taxes will be eliminated for middle-income individuals and families. Tens of billions of dollars in tax preparation costs will also be saved. The marriage tax penalty will be gone. Everyone will be eligible to receive the sales-tax rebate (the same dollar amount as for the poverty-level family of the same family size)

Greatly Increased Income

The financial welfare of middle-income Americans will improve greatly under ***STR***, as Exhibit 8-2a illustrates.

Consumption: Consider a family of four with $100,000 of income and purchases of $77,000 (as was discussed in Chapter 6). As with the poor, middle-income groups will experience declining prices [Column 3]. Nominal prices including the 30% FCT will increase to more than $94,000 [Column 4], but the *ability to pay* those higher prices with their much higher spendable income will increase even more. The rebate [Column 5] will help, but the elimination of most existing federal taxes on income will have the greatest impact.

Exhibit 8-2a

The *STR* Impact upon the Consumption of *Middle-Income* Groups					
(1)	(2)	(3)	(4)	(5)	(6)
Current Income	Pre-STR Consumption	Consumption Under STR			Total STR Savings
		Price	w/ FCT	w/ Rebate	
		(-6%)	(+30%)	(-$6,000)	
$60,000	$51,000	$47,940	$62,322	$56,322	$3,678
$100,000	$77,000	$72,380	$94,094	$88,094	$11,906
$250,000	$170,000	$159,800	$207,740	$201,740	$48,260

The 30% FCT portion of the price will equal $21,714 [Column 4 minus Column 3]. That will be reduced by the $6,000 tax rebate, so that the net tax will be $15,714, which represents an effective tax rate of 15.7%. Thus, the actual tax bite will only be around half of the full 30% FCT nominal rate.

Savings: Another way to evaluate the overall effect of this increased real income is to observe the impact upon savings [Column 6 above and Exhibit 8-2b]. Despite the 30% FCT, the family's total savings will have more than doubled from before [Columns 2, 3 and 4 below]. The potential savings rate will jump to about 12% [Column 5] up from only 5.4%.

At all income levels shown, there is a very substantial increase in *potential* savings [Column 5 versus Column 6]. Middle-income households may choose to spend some of the increase in disposable income rather than save it. However, the greatly increased opportunity to save will be there. The majority of the middle class will likely increase their saving, many by very significant amounts—for retirement, to buy a home, education of their children or opening their own business. In any event, the household's standard of living will have increased

Exhibit 8-2b

The *STR* Impact upon the Savings of *Middle-Income* Groups					
(1)	(2)	(3)	(4)	(5)	(6)
Current Income	Total *STR*	Pre-*STR* Savings	*STR* Savings	*STR* Savings	Pre-*STR* Savings
	Savings		Increase	Rate	Rate
$60,000	$3,678	$1,210	$2,468	6.10%	2.00%
$100,000	$11,906	$5,350	$6,556	11.90%	5.40%
$250,000	$48,260	$25,000	$23,260	19.30%	10.00%

greatly. The total advantage will actually be even greater since some expenditures (for example, insurance premiums, charitable donations and part of the cost of buying basic medical care, a home and a car) will not be taxed. [See the last section of this chapter.]

Impact of *Sensible Tax Reform* upon *High-Income* Groups

Most taxpayers with high incomes will also benefit from ***Sensible Tax Reform.*** Advantages will include most of those listed above for middle-income taxpayers. In addition, there will be:

- The first $1 million of income will be excluded from the income tax.
- Much lower effective tax rates than now on income above $1 million,
- Replacement of the 40% estate tax with much lower effective tax rates on inheritance,
- Much simpler retirement and estate planning, and
- Much greater capacity to donate to charity.

Also, high profits and freedom from paying taxes will allow companies to pay much higher dividends. And, stock markets will likely be very strong. The wealthy will be the principal beneficiaries of those trends since they make the vast majority of investments by individuals and therefore receive most of the dividends and capital gains.

Federal Consumption Tax

Most wealthy households consume a much smaller share of their income than the rest of us (Paris Hilton perhaps being an exception). They will avoid the 30% FCT on what they do *not* spend, which is often most of their income, as was seen in Chapter 7. Exhibit 8-3a illustrates a family with $1,000,000 of annual income and paying no income taxes that might spend $500,000 [Column 2]. The ***STR***-related impacts will be the same as with low and middle-income groups. The price decline is assumed to be about 6% and the 30% FCT will be added before deducting the $6000 rebate for a family of four [Column 5]. They would still realize savings of almost $400,000 [Column 6]. The nominal cost of their consumption will have risen sharply (from $500,000 to $605,000). However, their ability to pay (that is, their income) will have grown much more—as will their savings.

Exhibit 8-3a

The STR Impact upon the Consumption of High-Income Groups

(1)	(2)	(3)	(4)	(5)	(6)
Current Income	Consumption				Total STR
	Pre-STR	Price	w/ FCT	w/ Rebate	
		(_6%)	(+30%)	(-$6000)	Savings
$500,000	$300,000	$282,000	$366,600	$360,600	$139,400
$1,000,000	$500,000	$470,000	$611,000	$605,000	$395,000
$10,000,000	$3,000,000	$2,820,000	$3,666,000	$3,660,000	$6,340,000
$25,000,000	$5,000,000	$4,700,000	$6,110,000	$6,104,000	$18,896,000

Tax on High Incomes

Taxes paid: Exhibit 8-3a also shows how the household with $10 million of income would pay only $840,000 of federal *consumption* taxes [(Column 3) * 0.3 - $6,000]. If that were the only tax to which they were subject, the family would owe 8.4% in taxes ($840,000 ÷ $10 million), which is much lower than what will be paid by middle-income families—and very regressive. Therefore as was explained in Chapter 7, on the basis of justice ***Sensible Tax Reform*** includes a provision for simple-and-just federal taxation of very high incomes. That family would pay combined total of $2,190,000 in consumption plus income taxes, an effective tax rate of 21.9% for the two taxes together, which is likely less than they are now paying:

Consumption tax [($2,820,000 * 0.3) - $6,000]	$840,000
+ Tax on very high incomes [($10,000,000 -$1,000,000) * 0.15]	$1,350,000
Total taxes	$2,190,000
Tax rate [$2,190,000 / $10,000,000]	21.9%

Those with very high incomes will no longer be able to utilize tax loopholes. However, they will no longer be threatened by the alternative minimum tax and their financial planning will be much simpler and less expensive. For higher levels of income, the personal income tax rates will also be at much lower rates. Between $10-$25 million of total taxable income per year, the rate will be 25%. The top rate of 35% will only apply to that share of annual taxable income that is above $25 million. [Under our current system, taxable income as low as $450,000 is taxed at the top rate of 39.6% rate.] The income-tax savings for most people with very high incomes will be quite substantial.

Savings: As shown in Exhibit 8-3b, Column 5, at $500,000 and $1 million of income, savings rates (adjusted for both income and sales taxes) [Column 5]

Exhibit 8-3b

The STR Impact upon the Savings of High-Income Groups

(1)	(2)	(3)	(4)	(5)	(6)
Current Income	Total STR Savings	Pre-STR Savings	STR Savings Increase	STR Savings Rate	Pre-STR Savings Rate
$500,000	$139,400	$61,000	$78,400	27.9%	10.2%
$1,000,000	$395,000	$203,000	$192,000	39.5%	20.3%
$10,000,000	$4,990,000	$4,620,000	$370,000	49.9%	46.2%
$25,000,000	$13,896,000	$14,955,000	($1,059,000)	55.6%	59.8%

will rise sharply from current levels [Column 6]. Those with high incomes will clearly do very well under the new tax program. Furthermore, those savings rates will have been realized without deductions, credits or any of the other existing tax loopholes. Even at $10 million of income, savings rates will increase—to almost 50% [Column 5]. At income of $25 million, it can be seen that savings may decline but still be at a very high level.

Sensible Tax Reform is clearly *not* an assault upon the wealthy or high-income individuals. Most of them will benefit in comparison to our current income tax and estate tax systems. It will also reduce most of the temptation for wealthy taxpayers to illegally hide income abroad.

Impact of *Sensible Tax Reform* upon Investors

Simplicity

The ability to save will be greatly abetted by the much greater simplicity that the new tax system will bring to the saving process. Middle-income investors will no longer need sophisticated tax-sheltered investment vehicles such as 401(k)s, 403(b)s, Keoghs, IRAs or Roths, all of which gained their popularity because of their tax-deferring or tax-saving characteristics. Since only the very high-income individuals among us will pay any income tax at all, the rest of us (98-99% of all Americans) will generally not even need to consider the tax angles when we buy and sell stocks, bonds, derivatives, etc. We will have much more money to invest and our tax-planning endeavors will be much simpler. The investment process will be easier. The rate of return on our investments will be much greater. Compliance and planning costs will be much lower.

The Economy and the Stock Market

Businesses will be "untaxed" under ***Sensible Tax Reform—Simple, Just and Effective***. Also, the economy will be very strong.

- Companies will be much more profitable and competitive.
- They will be much stronger financially.
- Their ability to pay dividends will be much greater.
- The stock market will likely be very strong.

Individual investors will, at the same time, have an increased incentive to demand higher dividends. The taxes on dividends and capital gains will decline from a current maximum of 20% down to 0% for the majority of investors, while even those with income up to $11 million will only be paying 15%. Also, the need by individuals to borrow will likely be much less. When they do choose to borrow, the interest rate will decline after the introduction of ***STR***.

Foreign investors: The dynamics of the American financial system along with the increased strength of our economy will appeal not only to American investors but foreign investors as well. That appeal will be enhanced by the end to tax withholding on dividends and interest paid to foreigners, since very few of them will owe any income taxes on earnings here in the US. American financial markets will become even more attractive to foreigners than they already are.

The Market for Real Assets

Wealth creation under ***STR*** will be dramatic. Many assets that owners might like to sell (e.g., land, vacation homes, works of art, even small businesses and farms) may now remain off the market because of the desire to postpone today's capital-gains taxes. The elimination of capital gains taxes for most Americans will free many to sell those appreciated assets. ***STR*** will likely lead to a surge of such property unto the markets. That would benefit the economy (e.g., the real estate) and also collectors and museums.

Impact of *Sensible Tax Reform* upon Retirees

Higher Real Income

Retirees (and those planning for retirement) will benefit from many aspects of the ***Sensible Tax Reform***. Retirees live primarily upon Social Security, pensions and their retirement funds. With the $1 million annual income-tax exclusion, *few retirees will ever pay any income tax*. Most will never even need to file with the IRS. Life will be simpler and financially more secure. Also, it must be remembered that all of us are paying for hefty embedded taxes now. When those taxes are removed from our producers, prices will decline. That will provide further benefits for retirees.

Tax-Sheltered Accounts

Savings that have accumulated in *tax-sheltered accounts* (for example, 401(k)s and IRAs) have completely avoided income taxes. For millions of Americans, such investment programs are some of the most positive features of our much-maligned Internal Revenue Code. Tax sheltering will no longer be necessary. Such programs will be phased out.

Social Security and Medicare

Payroll *taxes* will be completely eliminated under the *Sensible Tax Reform*. However, the *benefits* of the programs will not be affected. They will remain based upon earnings, just as they are now. Employers will continue to report employees' annual earnings to the Social Security Administration, just as they do now. The only change will be that the source of the funds in those two programs will be from the federal government's general tax revenues. That will provide a much stronger and more stable funding base for the entire Social Security and Medicare systems. It will provide retirees and those nearing retirement much more confidence in the long-term viability of both programs.

The existing tax-sheltered investments will be added to all other income and be subject to the same tax rules as all other income. Since the first $1 million will be completely excluded from income taxes, *the vast majority of taxpayers will owe no taxes on their tax-sheltered savings*. Even for those with more than $1 million of tax-sheltered investments, few people would pay more than 15% since very few have more than $11 million in tax-sheltered accounts. In almost all cases, this will mean much lower taxes on their withdrawals from those accounts than they would have had under today's Internal Revenue Code.

Non-Sheltered Accounts

Past savings that were not tax-sheltered were made *after* income taxes had been paid. Such investments will not be taxed again. *Future* dividends, interest or capital gains on those accounts will be taxable but will also benefit fully from the new tax rules and be completely tax-free for anyone with income of less than $1 million. Thus, few people with investments will need to pay any income taxes on investment income.

Expenditures with Special *STR* Taxation Rules

STR stresses the importance of applying the FCT to *all* retail purchases of goods and services. However, a small number of *non-consumption expenditures*, because of the special nature of each, enjoy special rules. Each is discussed below.

Investments

Investments are provisions for the future, not for current consumption. Therefore, as was mentioned above, investments will not be taxed. Only when they are sold in the future and the money is spent will the savings be taxed—with the federal consumption tax.

The purchase of any assets that have only investment value (for example, bank accounts, stocks and bonds, mutual funds and even gold bars) will not be taxed. However, if the purchase has value as a collectible or has other utility (for example, gold coins or jewelry, artwork or rare postage stamps), it will be taxable.

Students and Education

Higher education is an *investment*—in our children's futures, our own futures, and the nation's future. The entire economy and society will benefit from a better-educated workforce. This has never been more important than in our current high tech, rapidly changing and globalized world. Therefore, there will be special provisions for higher education.

Students: In order to focus this special educational benefit directly where it will have the desired effect, *career-related* education at *post-secondary* institutions (colleges, universities, community colleges and tech schools, whether public or private) will be eligible for special tax rules. *Tuition* up to $15,000 per year per student plus *educational fees* and *mandatory materials*, including textbooks, will be excluded from the FCT. [That $15,000 exclusion will be indexed annually to the cost of higher education at the best public universities.]

The special educational provision will apply equally whether a student attends a community college or Harvard University. In the former case, of course, all educational expenses are likely to be tax free since the tuition is unlikely to approach $15,000, while at a very expensive private school, such as Harvard, only the first $15,000 of tuition will be tax free. [At a University of Notre Dame reunion where I presented my ***Sensible Tax Reform*** proposal to a large audience, an agitated alumnus came up to me after the presentation and said: "I have two children attending Notre Dame, where tuition is over $40,000 per year per kid. Do you mean to tell me that your tax plan would require me to pay a hefty consumption tax on all tuition above $15,000 for each child"? My response: "Yes, but you won't be paying any income tax on income up to $1 million!" When he heard that, he smiled and thanked me. As he had realized, it is critically important for everyone.

Insurance

Insurance is another expenditure that provides for the future. It is not for current consumption or utility. Generally, neither health, property and casualty nor life insurance premiums will be taxable. When you collect on insurance to repair your house or car or to get medical care, those expenditures will be taxable, but the up-front premiums will not be.

Life-insurance proceeds will be added to all other sources of income and will be subject to income taxation. Since most life-insurance beneficiaries will not have income greater than the $1 million annual tax-free allowance, they will avoid taxation. However, if the recipient's total annual income including the insurance exceeds $1 million, it will be subject to the same tax rules discussed in Chapter 7. Most taxation would be at the 15% tax rate.

Taxes

The payment of taxes is obviously not for consumption. Therefore, tax payments will not be taxed. Neither excise taxes (such as those on gasoline, alcohol or tobacco) nor municipal income, sales and property taxes will be subject to the FCT. One level of government should not tax the payment of taxes to another level of government.

Interest Payments

Like all services, interest payments by individuals will be subject to the FCT. *Interest is the cost for borrowing* (that is, renting) money. Like any rental service (whether a car from Hertz, a hotel room from Marriott or power tools from a rental store), renting money will be taxed.

Our existing Internal Revenue Code perversely allows a tax deduction on the interest payments when we borrow money to buy a house (up to a $1 million mortgage). That is a subsidy from the government, which encourages us to borrow—often more than we should, as was seen with the millions of home foreclosures in recent years! That is crazy! Rather than subsidize and encourage excessive borrowing, the FCT will apply to all payment of interest on personal loans, just as with any other form of rental. That will encourage more responsible financial habits by Americans.

Charity

If individuals choose to donate money to charities, the donors are not consuming. Indeed, they are giving others the right to consume with the money. Therefore, the gift will not be taxed. ***Sensible Tax Reform*** will greatly benefit charities. Since most people's income will not have been taxed at all, they will have much greater income and much more capacity for donating. In addition, their charitable donations will still not be subject to federal taxes or require federal reporting.

Housing

If only new but not used homes were to be taxed, as the "fair tax" does[25], it could cripple new-home construction. It would also cause very severe inflation in used-home prices. Under ***STR***, all purchases of homes will be taxed, whether new or used.

However, the full 30% FCT would cause serious trauma to buyers of homes, especially low and middle-income groups, as well as to the home-construction industry. And needing to pay the entire FCT at the time of purchase (even if lenders would finance it) would deter large numbers of potential buyers. Therefore, as shown in Exhibit 8-4, ***Sensible Tax Reform*** will provide a special program for determining the taxes due on the purchase of a home.

First, there will be a *$100,000 tax-free allowance* [Column 2]. Purchases up to $100,000 of any homes for personal use would be completely free from all

Exhibit 8-4

FCT on the Purchase of Homes (New or Used)					
(1)	(2)	(3)	(4)	(5)	(6)
Purchase Price	Tax-Free Allowance	Adjusted Price[a]	50% Exclusion	Tax Due 30%	Average Tax
$50,000	$100,000	$0	$0	$0	0.0%
$100,000	$100,000	$0	$0	$0	0.0%
$150,000	$100,000	$50,000	$25,000	$7,500	5.0%
$200,000	$100,000	$100,000	$50,000	$15,000	7.5%
$300,000	$100,000	$200,000	$100,000	$30,000	10.0%
$500,000	$100,000	$400,000	$200,000	$60,000	12.0%
$1,000,000	$100,000	$900,000	$450,000	$135,000	13.5%
a: (Column 1) - (Column 2)					

FCT. Since everyone will be treated the same under all parts of the tax system, the $100,000 tax-free allowance will apply to the purchase of any house, regardless of price.

The tax-free allowance will protect those with lower incomes and also purchasers of lower-cost vacation homes. That will cushion the impact upon all homebuyers as well as to protect the housing and home-construction industries. Consider the purchases of a $150,000 home and a $300,000 home:

Purchase price	$150,000	$300,000
(-) Tax-free allowance	($100,000)	($100,000)
= Adjusted price	$ 50,000	$200,000

Second, half of the remaining price would also be excluded from the FCT [Column 3]. Thus, the purchasers of a $150,000 house would receive an initial $100,000 exclusion [Column 2] as well as an additional 50% exclusion of $25,000 [Column 4]. Continuing with the example above:

Adjusted price	$50,000	$200,000
(-) 50% exclusion	($25,000)	($100,000)
= *Net taxable price*	$25,000	$100,000

Third, the purchaser would only be assessed the FCT on the remaining balance [Column 5]— $7,500 for the $150,000 house, an effective tax rate of 5.0% [Column 6]. For the $300,000 house, the tax would be $30,000 and the effective tax rate of 10.0%.

Net taxable price	$25,000	$100,000
Tax due	($ 7,500)	($ 30,000)
Average tax	5.0%	10.0%

Fourth, even the reduced tax could discourage home buying by those who intend to own for only a few years. For example, if you bought a $300,000 house, paid $30,000 in FCT taxes and then decided to move two or three years later, the tax that you had paid could cause a significant loss. In order to avoid this, only 10% of the entire tax will be due at the time of the closing, with the other 90% to be financed over the next ten years, along with the mortgage.

The purchaser of the $150,000 home, instead of paying the entire $7,500 tax, would only pay 10% ($750) at the time of sale. The financing of the rest ($6750) over a ten-year period at 6% would add about $75 per month to the mortgage package. [That would be similar to the inclusion of property taxes and home insurance as part of the monthly payments—though the FCT component would cease after ten years.] Likewise, the buyer of a $300,000 home, instead of paying a $30,000 tax at the time of the purchase, would pay 10% of that ($3000) at closing and the balance in monthly payments.

The final part of the housing-tax program will provide for *paying the tax only in the years that you own the house*. A purchaser who only owned the home for two years would only pay the tax at the time of purchase and for those two additional years, but not for the remaining eight years. Short-term buyers will thereby not be severely penalized.

To summarize the five parts of the ***STR*** program for taxing the purchase of homes:

1. A $100,000 tax-free allowance on the purchase price of any new or used home [Column 2];

2. Half of the balance excluded from the FCT [Column 4];
3. Only the net taxable price subject to the 30% FCT [Column 5];
4. 10% of the tax due and payable at the time of the purchase with the balance financed over ten years; and,
5. The tax only due for the years that the buyer owned the home.

Automobiles

The United States has poor public transportation in most cities. For most Americans, owning an automobile is a necessity—to get to the store, to a job, to the doctor, to visit friends, etc. However, cars are very expensive, one of the largest lifetime expenditures. The full federal consumption tax could be a traumatic shock to both the American consumer and the automobile industry.

All automobile purchases, whether new or used, will be subject to the tax. However, as with houses, ***STR*** provides special provisions that will bring the effective FCT down significantly. First, the initial $10,000 of the purchase price of any car will be excluded from the tax [Exhibit 8-5, Column 2]. Thus, students,

Exhibit 8-5

FCTs on the Purchase of Vehicles (New or Used)					
(1)	(2)	(3)	(4)	(5)	(6)
Price	Tax-Free Allowance	Taxable Base	50% Exclusion	Taxes Due	Average Tax
$10,000	$10,000	$0	$0	$0	0.00%
$15,000	$10,000	$5,000	$2,500	$750	5.00%
$20,000	$10,000	$10,000	$5,000	$1,500	7.50%
$25,000	$10,000	$15,000	$7,500	$2,250	9.00%
$30,000	$10,000	$20,000	$10,000	$3,000	10.00%
$40,000	$10,000	$30,000	$15,000	$4,500	11.30%
$50,000	$10,000	$40,000	$20,000	$6,000	12.00%
$75,000	$10,000	$65,000	$32,500	$9,750	13.00%
$100,000	$10,000	$90,000	$45,000	$13,500	13.50%

young families and retired couples could buy a $10,000 car and pay no FCT. Second, as with the purchase of homes, 50% of the balance will be excluded from the tax [Column 4].

No FCT would be due on a $10,000 car [Column 5]. A $20,000 car would bear a $1,500 tax, an average tax rate of only 7.5%. If the car was financed, the tax could be included. That would add $29 per month for a five-year loan at a financing cost of 6%. The tax on a $30,000 car would be $3,000, an effective rate of 10.0%, at a cost of about $58 per month.

To summarize the three parts of the ***STR*** program for taxing the purchase of automobiles:

1. The first $10,000 of the purchase price of any car, new or used, will be tax-free for all buyers [Column 2].
2. There will be an additional 50% exclusion from the taxable base [Column 4].
3. The tax due on the car will equal 30% of that amount [Column 5].

Healthcare

The final special expenditure category of ***STR*** is healthcare, one of the biggest financial burdens for millions of families and also one of our most rapidly rising costs. *Basic healthcare* will not be taxed.

Healthcare costs that will *not* be taxed: The cost of basic preventive, emergency and remedial medical procedures will be exempt from the FCT. *Basic preventive medical* costs will include such items as biannual teeth cleaning, annual physicals, blood and urine tests and mammograms, as well as prescription drugs and equipment. *Emergency medical* costs are fairly self-explanatory: ambulance, doctors, hospitals, etc. *Remedial medical* costs would include rehabilitation, physical therapy, kidney dialysis, etc. Non-taxed hospital care would be limited to the "normal" facilities and procedures, such as a semi-private room (unless there was an over-riding condition, such as the danger of infection) and one physical per year. None of these expenses would be subject to the FCT.

Healthcare costs that will be taxed: Many other health-related costs would be taxable. Elective surgeries and procedures (e.g., face lift, lens implant, boob job, hair implant, teeth straightening, etc.) would be taxable. Also, extraordinary care in hospitals, such as a full-time nurse or family suites in luxury facilities, as do exist in many major hospitals, would have deductions for the cost of normal care but be taxed on the balance of the cost. Consider a case where the "normal" cost for a semi-private room with the "normal" services as determined by standards of the health-insurance industry was $1,000 per day. On the other hand, a patient in a "Cadillac plan" for a private room with private nurse and other special services cost $4,000. In that case, the first $1,000 of the bill would be excluded from taxation, but the balance ($3,000) would be subject to the FCT.

Conclusions

We have seen how the ***Sensible Tax Reform—Simple, Just and Effective*** will bring a myriad of advantages to all income classes. Income, living standards and savings will all increase. Our lives will be much simpler and filled with fewer worries. The economy will be very healthy and job growth will also be very strong. Stock markets will be strong. ***STR*** should be heartily welcomed by most Americans!

The next chapter will examine how simple, just and extremely beneficial this new tax system will be for businesses and the overall American economy. Chapter 10 will do the same thing for governments and their agencies.

Endnotes

25 The "fair-tax" proposal would only tax new homes—very stimulating and inflationary to the *used-home* market (which accounts for 85% of home sales) but devastating to new-home construction.

CHAPTER 9

SENSIBLE TAX REFORM FOR AMERICAN BUSINESSES

Killing the corporate income tax would improve the efficiency & competitiveness of U.S. business; eliminate incentives to relocate overseas or to engage in mind-boggling shelter transactions, .. eliminate disincentives to pay dividends & foster more efficient corporations, sensibly valued. Who can argue with that?
—Edward J. McCaffery

Chapters 5-7 introduced ***Sensible Tax Reform—Simple, Just and Effective***, the revolutionary tax system that will replace most of our current federal tax mess. Chapter 8 examined in detail its impact upon individuals and families. This chapter will explore its impact upon American businesses.

Perhaps the strongest argument for passage of this revolutionary new tax system is the immediate and dynamic impact that it will have upon American businesses:

- Federal business taxes and tax-related regulations will largely disappear.
- Costs will decline dramatically as suppliers pass on some of their own cost savings.

- The ability of our exports to compete internationally and of domestic businesses to compete against imports will improve greatly.
- Profits will soar.
- Millions of jobs will be created.

STR will change the economic "rules of the game." Collectively these effects will revitalize our economy. American business is over-taxed. This seriously handicaps its competitiveness and our prosperity. The tax burdens are serious, shortsighted and avoidable. ***Sensible Tax Reform*** will help "level the playing field" for American businesses versus foreign competition. That will provide substantial benefits for American workers, consumers, investors and the government as well.

Why Shouldn't Businesses Pay the Federal Consumption Tax?

Before examining how the introduction of ***Sensible Tax Reform*** will help American businesses, it is worth responding to an inevitable question: Why does the new proposal totally remove taxes from businesses?

Existing Federal Taxes on Businesses

Total federal income taxes on businesses have fallen significantly over the years as tax rates have decreased, as tax rules have become more accommodating and as companies find ways to game the system domestically or hide their profits abroad. In FY 2012, federal *corporate* income taxes were down about 35% to $243 billion compared to $370 billion in 2007, while *personal* income taxes declined only 3%. The burden has been increasingly shifting to individuals. Would the proposed tax system not make that apparent injustice even worse? If we, the consumers, must pay the tax, then shouldn't businesses pay as well?

The answer is "no." When tax reforms cut the taxes on wealthy *individual* taxpayers, then the burden *does shift* to others—especially to the middle class. However, that is not what occurs with business taxes.

Where do businesses get the profits and funds to cover all of their expenses? From sales. To whom do final sales go? To individuals and families who are the final consumers. From whom do businesses obtain the money to pay all of those costs, including tax payments. From these same retail customers. Therefore, *WE* even now pay for all of their costs. Businesses are just an expensive extra layer of tax compliance and planning. By eliminating the tax burdens on businesses (which total more than $825 billion annually in federal income, payroll and Social Security and Medicare taxes, plus compliance costs), we are *not* adding additional burdens upon ourselves. We are eliminating the middleman and in the process reducing the cost to the American economy and to ourselves as well.

Therefore, a key part of ***Sensible Tax Reform*** will be the untaxing of business—no income tax, no Social Security tax and no Medicare tax.

No Tax on Business Purchases

A related question involves taxes on purchases between businesses. The new tax code will be introducing a purchase tax on individuals in the form of the federal consumption tax. Since businesses will not be paying the federal income and payroll taxes, should they pay a similar tax on business purchases? Again, the answer is "no."

Business-to-business taxes: As was argued in preceding chapters, a critical part of ***STR*** will be removing taxes from businesses as completely as possible so that they can eliminate those costs from their pricing and be free to compete more aggressively and successfully. If business had to pay a federal business-to-business purchase tax, that would undo many of the advantages of removing our current income taxes from business.

The imposition of such taxes would also provide a very strong incentive for companies to integrate vertically. The retail store might buy the distributor, the baker, the miller and perhaps even the farmer, which would eliminate all of the business-to-business taxes. That would give those companies a major competitive advantage, since sales and transfers within the company would not be subject to business-to-business taxes. This would obviously be a significant economic distortion caused solely by taxes. It would lead to substantial consolidation within all industries. It would be the death knell of tens of thousands of small, independent businesses.

Therefore, for many reasons, it will be important that business be untaxed. It will be important for business, important for the overall economy and important for individuals.

Value-added tax: Some economists, such as Bruce Bartlett[26], favor a variation on a purchase tax for businesses in the form of the value-added tax (VAT). However, although each business pays the tax on the value that they have added (that is, the increase in price above their costs), in reality the final customer actually pays the entire tax—just as with the federal consumption tax that STR will introduce. Each of the businesses gets reimbursed for the taxes they had paid. Thus, the VAT is not actually a tax on business purchases but on *retail* purchases.

What Changes Does *STR* Bring for American Businesses?

The replacement of our existing tax systems with ***Sensible Tax Reform*** will immediately change many things for businesses in this country. Most industries, indeed most businesses, will benefit greatly:

- Increased justice—*equal treatment of all businesses,* large and small;
- Simplicity—*sharp reduction in tax-compliance and tax-planning requirements and costs*;
- *Complete elimination of almost all federal taxes* on businesses;
- *Much more time* for management to focus on making business better, not just trying to minimize taxes; and
- Equity financing will become much more attractive relative to debt financing.

These will each be discussed in the following sections.

Justice

The most important characteristic of the ***STR*** is its justice. As it does with individuals, our current tax system treats some businesses much less justly than other *similar* businesses. Small businesses especially pay a disproportionately heavy burden in comparison to large companies. Even among large businesses, government favoritism has granted extraordinary tax benefits to select industries (such as forestry, farming, oil, ethanol, sugar and pharmaceuticals) while denying the same benefits to other businesses. However, to manipulate our federal tax system, favoring some businesses to the disadvantage of others, is bad economics and bad public policy as well.

The oil industry is an especially egregious example of governmental misfeasance in this area. In recent years, American oil companies, by exploiting soaring oil prices, brought in *hundreds of billions of dollars in profits*. Exxon-Mobil alone had $45 billion of net income in 2012. Shamelessly, it and many of its peers still turned to the federal government for free handouts in the form of tax credits and subsidies. *Shamefully*, our federal government granted tens of billions of dollars in special tax benefits to those companies—which they can prosper very well without and which our government cannot afford.

Credits are hidden *subsidies*, which reduce taxes dollar for dollar. Hiding subsidies in the tax code and calling them "credits" must be ended. If the federal government wants to subsidize oil, pharmaceutical companies and the sugar industry, let it be done openly. If the government deems tax credits to be desirable, they should be replaced with subsidies—that are not part of the tax code and that are visible to the public and subject to periodic review.

No "free lunch": Of course, as with any of the special tax treatments for favored groups, "there is no free lunch" for the rest of us. If those companies that receive such preferential treatment save tens of billions of dollars via tax credits or subsidies, then the rest of us must pay for it. It might be through higher taxes, lower services (e.g., national security, highway repairs or education) or a higher national debt, upon which the government must pay interest and which must be repaid by us or by our children.

Are those tax credits for wealthy industries like oil and pharmaceuticals worth it? No! Let us return to a simple and just tax system that does only what it was intended to do—collect taxes. Social and economic policy should be handled separately from taxes.

Simplicity

The current federal-tax system is far too complicated and difficult for businesses to readily understand—and getting more complicated by the year. Mention was made in an earlier chapter of how Citicorp's annual tax filing has more than 20,000 pages and GE's more than 57,000! [GE is reported to employ more than 1000 tax accountants. It also pays very little in US federal income taxes.] It is absurd that companies must spend so much time and money solely preparing their tax returns. It is also absurd to believe that the Internal Revenue Service can actually understand those returns—if indeed anyone at the agency even reads them in detail.

Sensible Tax Reform will lift a very heavy burden from businesses in this country with the elimination of income and payroll taxes. That will greatly simplify the financing and managing of American businesses.

Elimination of Taxes

Companies will effectively be "untaxed" under ***STR***. They will pay no federal taxes on profits, employees or purchases. None! Nada!

- No corporate income taxes
- No Social Security taxes
- No Medicare taxes
- No embedded taxes
- No tax on their own purchases
- Elimination of most tax compliance costs
- Elimination of tax planning and simplification of investment planning

The greater the *current* tax burden is on a company then the greater the tax benefits are going to be. Companies will be enjoying an unparalleled opportunity to improve, grow and become more profitable. The impact upon economic growth and the creation of new jobs will be very impressive.

Management Time and Focus

Under ***Sensible Tax Reform***, most of today's wasted time, paperwork and money from tax compliance will no longer be necessary. All businesses will still report employees' earnings to the Social Security Administration, but will neither pay nor collect Social Security and Medicare taxes. And retailers, but not manufacturers or wholesalers, will collect the FCT and submit it to the government, but will not be paying income and payroll taxes. Managers will be able to focus upon running their businesses, making a profit and making a productive contribution to the country—not just trying to minimize taxes.

Studies have estimated[27] that businesses spend as much as $165 billion each and every year just complying with the federal income-tax obligations—recordkeeping, collecting and remitting the taxes, and complying with the annual reporting requirements. The total direct cost savings from the elimination of all federal business taxes and tax-related expenses for companies, large and small, is more than $825 billion dollars ($242 billion of business taxes, $422 billion of Social Security and Medicare and the $165 billion of tax-compliance costs)—and that will be repeated every year!

Those compliance and tax-planning costs are nothing but "empty calories." They do not add to our economy or improve our living standards. But those costs add to the prices for customers and lose business for American companies—both domestically versus imports and abroad when they export.

Making Equity Financing More Attractive

Reducing funding costs: Interest rates, which are the primary cost of borrowing, are another type of embedded expense that ***STR*** will eliminate. Lending is a very competitive business. If the lenders did not have to pay profit taxes on their earnings or Social Security taxes on their workers, they could afford to charge a lower interest rate. That will lower the cost of financing cars, houses, credit card purchases, educational loans and many other consumer expenditures and increase demand for them.

Financing with debt: The potential impact of eliminating taxes on lenders can be seen somewhat even today in the difference between the interest rates paid on municipal bonds that are tax exempt and U.S. Treasury bonds that are not. Even though Treasury bonds are much safer than municipals, they pay a higher interest rate than do good-quality "munis," because the interest paid on treasuries is not tax-free for investors.

Interest must be paid, whether the business is profitable or not—but is now tax deductible. Dividends on stock, on the other hand, need only be paid if the board of directors chooses to pay them—and, if paid, are *not* tax deductible. As a result of the tax deductibility of interest payments, *our tax system encourages companies to borrow more than they otherwise would*, just as it does with families [Chapter 8]. The more debt a company has, the greater its risk of being forced into bankruptcy if it runs losses, as occurred so often during the Great Recession of 2007-2010 and its aftermath.

Financing with equity: In contrast to debt, a company's equity (that is, its common stock) provides an important safety net for the company, its workers and for the overall economy. With the elimination of interest-payment deductibility under ***STR***, companies will likely rely more upon equity financing—both via retained earnings and the sale of new stock. Business profits will also likely rise significantly which will make the issuance of new issues of stock much easier. This will increase the financial strength of companies and decrease the likelihood of bankruptcy.

How Will Businesses Respond to the *STR* Changes?

Sensible Tax Reform will quickly and permanently change how businesses operate. Managers will need to think differently about how they manage their businesses, how they finance their operations and how they invest for the company's future.

Making American companies more effective, competitive and profitable is one of the most important results of this tax proposal, which will present business with unique opportunities. There are obviously many different ways in which businesses can productively employ that $825 billion windfall. This section will explore how businesses might use the opportunity:

- Lower prices,
- Increase profits,
- Pay higher dividends,
- Pay off debt,
- Buy new equipment,
- Increase R&D,
- Hire more employees, and / or
- Fund employee healthcare and retirement programs.

STR will usher in an era of exciting opportunities and innovation. All businesses in America will experience major changes. Each of these alternative results is examined below.

Lower Prices?

Industries differ greatly in the degree of price competition. Some industries, such as the big national retailers like Costco, traditionally operate on thin profit margins and may indeed pass the tax and tax-related savings on quickly to customers. Some highly-competitive industrial and commodity businesses, such as steel and wheat, might do likewise. However, in industries such as pharmaceuticals and cable television, price competition is much lower. Prices are unlikely to fall as far or as rapidly in more competitive industries. Collectively we can expect price declines of perhaps 5-10% over several years. [However, prices certainly will not fall the 20%+ that is forecasted by very optimistic proponents of the "fair-tax" plan.[28]

Increase Profits?

In the highly-competitive global markets of today's economy, many American companies are under intense price pressure, often operating with unhealthy profit margins. Dissatisfied stockholders clamor for higher profits and dividend distributions. The ***STR***-induced drop in taxes and costs will provide an opportunity for many businesses to increase their profit margins, their return on assets, their return on equity and their retained earnings.

Higher Dividends?

The payment of dividends by American companies has been seriously lagging economic growth for many years. Dividend yields are much lower than they were in the 1960-1980s. The increase in profits will allow companies to increase dividends, which will likely lead to higher prices of those companies' stocks.

Pay Off Debt?

The tax deductibility of interest payments under our current federal income-tax system encourages companies to increase their debt burden. That excessive debt hurts companies' financial ratios and credit ratings. The stock value of many companies languishes as a result. The appeal of selling new issues of stock versus more debt will increase dramatically. Businesses will become less reliant upon debt to finance their operations and expansion. At the same time, reduced interest rates will further reduce the risk for American companies, especially when the economy slows down.

New Investments in Capital Equipment and R&D?

Some businesses will use their greater prosperity to modernize their plant and equipment. Others will expand their operations, either in existing businesses or new ones. Companies may also increase investments in research and development or new marketing or employee-training programs.

Increased Hiring and Improved Employee Benefits?

The incentive that will be provided by the elimination of US federal taxation under ***Sensible Tax Reform*** will induce domestic businesses to expand and also attract many expatriate American companies to return to the US. These trends will create hundreds of thousands or even more of new jobs. Also, intense cost pressures have forced many companies to limit wages and salaries or retirement and health programs. ***STR*** will provide the opportunity to improve such employee benefits.

Lower prices. Higher profits. Higher dividends. Fewer debts. New investments. Better employee benefits. All of these are plausible, and indeed desirable, responses to the unparalleled opportunities that ***STR*** is likely to bring. And, all of these will be very beneficial to America's economy, families and even government as well.

Increased Honesty

The avoidance and evasion of federal and state taxes in this country has become a serious problem with businesses, large and small. Many are notorious because of the widespread financial and legal gimmicks that they have designed to (legally) avoid or (illegally) evade their federal and state tax obligations in the US. For example, the very profitable General Electric[29], while apparently using legal maneuvers, has paid federal income taxes of less than 2% on the average since 2002. On the other hand, Merck, the giant pharmaceutical firm, illegally funneled American profits abroad to evade American taxes, but was caught and paid $2.3 billion in unpaid taxes and penalties[30].

When ***STR*** is operational, these practices will no longer be an issue—indeed, they will have lost most of their appeal. Businesses will not owe federal taxes. The incentive for skirting or violating the law will be eliminated. Businesses will be able to operate freely without fear that their activities will draw IRS scrutiny. Profits will return from abroad. Foreign tax havens will lose their appeal for American companies. Indeed, the US will become a tax haven for foreign companies.

Contractors who now illegally fail to pay and collect Social Security or withhold income taxes will no longer have that obligation. Small businesses, which the IRS now identifies as major evaders of profit taxes, will no longer have any incentive for hiding income or exaggerating expenses. The new tax system will increase the honesty of businesses and ease the consciences of their managers.

Our current tax system may be unjust and opaque—but it is the law. When the rest of us obey the laws and scofflaws evade them, then their share of financing our federal government shifts to us. We will all benefit when greater honesty returns to the tax system.

American Businesses in the Global Economy

International competition is very intense. While there are many very successful American companies worldwide (for example, Apple, Coca-Cola, International Harvester and Boeing), overall our companies' international performance is inadequate and has produced many serious and damaging effects on our economy.

- Our *exports* are significantly reduced.
- Our *imports* are greatly increased.
- American *companies move abroad.*
- Millions of *American jobs have been lost to foreign producers.*
- *American companies keep trillions of dollars abroad to avoid U.S. income taxes.*
- *Foreign companies* are less likely to invest here.

While there is no a single simple cause for this very poor international performance, one of the most significant factors is certainly our existing tax system. Fortunately, the tax burden is also the one cause of these damaging effects that intelligent change in governmental policy could quickly and dramatically improve. The introduction of ***STR*** will bring dramatic improvement.

STR will sharply reduce taxes and tax-related costs for American exporters and import-competing businesses, just as it will for the rest of the economy. Since foreign competitors will not be realizing similar cost savings, American exporters should be able to win back many export markets that they have lost in recent years—and win some new ones as well. Domestic businesses will likewise be able to win back much of the business that had been lost to imports.

Since there is an alternative tax system that would greatly increase the international competitiveness of American businesses, it would be tragic if we do not take advantage of it. ***STR*** is designed to help redress the disadvantages for American producers of both goods and services. When companies here no longer need to pay profit and Social Security taxes as well as high compliance costs:

- They will regain much of their international competitive ability.
- American production of goods and services will grow.
- Millions of jobs can be saved or recaptured.
- Our balance-of-trade deficit will fall sharply.
- The American government and companies will not need to borrow nearly as much abroad.
- The US dollar will likely strengthen.

Exports

Foreign exporters: Taxes can be an important factor in a country's international-trade success or failure. Most of the rest of the world has a very different primary tax system than the U.S. has—the value-added tax (VAT). It is a form of *sales tax* which is paid by businesses at each level of production on the "value added" at that stage of production.

All of the taxes get rolled forward and ultimately charged to the final retail customer, unless the government chooses to exempt a particular customer or group of customers from paying the tax. Governments *always* exempt their country's exports. Accordingly, when foreign companies export, all of the VATs that have been paid up to that stage of production are rebated by their governments. Corporate *income* taxes, which cannot be rebated by the governments, are generally a much smaller source of government tax revenues in those countries and correspondingly a much smaller tax burden on their companies.

American exporters: US federal business taxes are primarily in the form of taxes that fall *directly* upon our businesses (Social Security and Medicare taxes plus corporate income taxes), rather than *indirectly* upon their customers in the form of a VAT. US taxes cannot be rebated to exporters. American exporters therefore embed all of their costs and desired pre-tax profit margins, including income and payroll taxes, into their pricing. Then, when the goods reach foreign countries, the products will be assessed the VAT. The foreign-produced products, which compete with our exports, do have to pay that tax also, but not the additional tax-related costs that are embedded in *our* exports. American products are more expensive because of tax and tax-related costs here in this country. We export much less as a result.

Imports

America imports more than $6.5 billion of goods per day, $195 billion per month and around $2.3 *trillion* per year[31]. Products from foreign countries arrive on our shores with a cost advantage due to the rebate of the VAT taxes that is similar to their advantage in foreign markets against our exports. That allows them to reduce their export prices to this country. Thus again, just as with our exports, American products are at a tax disadvantage versus imports. Our companies lose sales to foreign competitors, which translates into lost profits and millions of lost American jobs.

Another devastating import loss to the American economy and American workers is the massive "off-shoring" of American *service*-industry jobs, such as customer-service centers, legal and accounting services and credit-card operations. This is a massive import of services into this country, which causes the loss of hundreds of thousands of American service jobs. To the extent that foreign competitive edges are the result primarily of inexpensive labor, this is understandable. However, to the extent that US government tax policy has shifted the cost advantages against our companies, that is discouraging—and foolish and unnecessary.

Balance of Trade

A large negative balance of trade deficit is the excess of merchandise imports over exports. Many industrialized countries, such as Germany and Switzerland, export more than they import. Others, like Canada, run small deficits. America's trade deficits are huge. Most *developing* countries run trade deficits. America is more like a developing country in terms of our international competitiveness. The U.S. annual balance of trade deficit has *exceeded* $400 billion every year since 2000 and has *averaged* over $700 billion annually since 2004[32]. That is very bad for the U.S. economy. It is also bad for the rest of the world that must finance those obscene US trade deficits.

Profits Held Abroad

The United States is one of very few countries that tax the *foreign* income of their businesses. American companies can defer such taxation as long as they keep the earnings of foreign subsidiaries abroad rather than bringing them home. This is capital that companies do not have readily available to them to expand and modernize here in America. The amount kept abroad by American companies is more than two trillion dollars!

Repatriation scandal: We have seen earlier how in 2005 that tax lobbyists wrangled an especially sweet loophole that benefited only a relatively small number of companies, primarily in pharmaceuticals, like Merck, and electronics, such as Apple. Companies were allowed to bring profits back from abroad and pay only 5.2% in taxes the lowest federal corporate tax rate in the country! Pfizer, the giant pharmaceutical firm, alone brought back $37,000,000,000 (billions of dollars!!!) of profits that it had accumulated abroad. The program, which was poorly conceived, badly designed and horribly administered, attracted 840 companies to bring more than $360 billion of profits back to the US and pay only 5.2%.

"A Wall Street Journal analysis of 60 big US companies (each with at least $5 billion held offshore) found that, together, they parked a total of $166 billion offshore" (in 2012 alone)[33]. Exhibit 9-1 lists the largest of the users of this tax maneuver to avoid US taxes by shifting and/or keeping net income abroad. Some of the firms legitimately utilized the offshore funds in productive investments abroad. However, much of the tax avoidance is a scam and the funds are kept abroad only to defer taxes. Those companies give a bad name to the entire program.

Exhibit 9-1

Assets "Permanently Reinvested" Overseas (2012)

General Electric	$108,000,000,000
Pfizer Inc.	$73,000,000,000
Microsoft Corporation	$60,800,000,000
Merck & Company	$53,400,000,000
Johnson & Johnson	$49,000,000,000
IBM	$44,400,000,000
Exxon Mobil Corporation	$43,000,000,000
Citigroup Incorporated	$42,600,000,000
Cisco Systems, Incorporated	$41,300,000,000
Apple, Incorporated	$40,400,000,000
Abbott Laboratories	$40,000,000,000
Proctor & Gamble	$39,000,000,000

The 2005 profit-repatriation program promised that firms would use the profits for the benefit of our economy in the form of tens of thousands of new jobs, substantial capital investment, more research and development—very attractive promises. However, the program was a colossal failure in attaining the goals. Instead, with clear distain for the intent of the law, many companies simply increased executive salaries, dividends and stock buybacks—and *cut* employment. Such flagrant favoritism for the clients of high-paying lobbyists is a scandal. When a repeat of the income repatriation was proposed a few years ago, it was promptly rejected by both liberal and conservative economists[34].

Bringing profits home: ***Sensible Tax Reform*** will eliminate all profit and Social Security taxes from American businesses—all American businesses, small as well as large, not just a favored few. Those companies will no longer be taxed in the United States for profits earned abroad. Companies will be free to bring home any or all of their *future* foreign profits without fear of tax consequences.

American companies will no longer be tempted to manipulate export prices in order to shift profits abroad or to create foreign subsidiaries whose sole function is to avoid American taxes. They will no longer shift valuable patents and copyrights on goods and services that had been developed here in the US to foreign tax havens and then pay high fees to use their own patents and copyrights! American businesses will be free to plan their investments for efficiency and true profitability, and not distort those plans in order to game the tax system. The attractiveness of business in this country will be so appealing that many companies will be able to bring back home a lot of the operations that they have moved abroad.

Foreign investment in America

The proposed ***STR*** changes in tax laws will have an interesting collateral effect—our corporate tax-free environment, lower operating costs and competitive environment here in the United States will attract many foreign companies to invest here and create even more jobs. For some companies in high-tax countries (such as in many western European countries), the United States will be a *virtual tax haven.* [See Chapter 10.]

Impact of *STR* upon American *Retailers*

All American businesses, including retailers, will enjoy the elimination of income and Social Security taxes and the reduction of tax-related expenses resulting from ***Sensible Tax Reform***. However, most retailers will need to collect the new FCT.

Tax collection: Forty-five out of the fifty states now charge sales taxes. Most retailers of goods and some retailers of services already have the experience and equipment for collecting sales taxes. The collection of the FCT will not be very different. However, there are many retailers, especially providers of services (for example, plumbers, dentists, hospitals, yard services, etc.), which may not now be required to collect sales taxes but will be required to do so for the federal consumption tax.

Retailers will bear much of the cost of collecting and remitting the FCT taxes. However, their tax savings from the elimination of income, Social Security and Medicare taxes will be much greater than the costs of their federal consumption tax obligations.

Internet sales: Internet shopping grows rapidly every year. Many "brick and mortar" retailers are encountering strong online competition. Amazon has become one of the largest retailers in the world, with more than $50 billion of annual online sales. Most of the Internet sales escape the state sales taxes that local retailers must collect. That is an unjust advantage for online sellers versus local retailers, a problem that some state legislatures are already addressing. Under ***STR***, the playing field will be leveled, since all retail sales, whether purchased in stores, by mail or online will be subject to the FCT rules. State and local governments will find it easier to collect their own taxes as well. Local retailers will benefit.

Impact of *STR* upon American *Small Businesses*

Tax Compliance

The compliance burden of our *current* federal tax system can be very difficult for small businesses. Small businesses generally have neither the skills nor the time to handle all of the tax planning, bookkeeping and complying with the tax requirements. Even the Internal Revenue Service reports that it commonly costs small and medium-sized companies more to comply with the tax requirements than they actually pay in taxes. That is ridiculous! The elimination of these burdens will provide extra advantages for small businesses—whether corporations, proprietorships or partnerships.

A Double Payroll Tax

Small proprietors and partnerships must now pay not only their own personal payroll taxes (Social Security and Medicare), but must also pay the business' obligation. This "self-employment tax" totals 15.30% —7.65% for the entrepreneur himself plus 7.65% for the business' share. That is truly a heavy tax, especially for start-up companies. Most new businesses fail within four or five years. The single major cause is inadequate financing. The self-employment tax, as well as the cost of those payroll taxes for employees, is a major hurdle for aspiring entrepreneurs.

We can remove that hurdle with ***Sensible Tax Reform—Simple, Just and Effective***. The greater freedom that the elimination of tax regulations and costs will bring will allow small-business managers to focus upon competing and succeeding in their markets. The reduction of labor and income tax costs will make it less expensive for small businesses to be started and make it easier for them to survive. Fewer funds will be needed. Their very high attrition rate will decline.

Impact of *STR* upon the Housing and Automobile Industries

Two critical industries could be devastated by the federal consumption tax: housing and automobiles. They are *necessities* for families and they are expensive, generally the most expensive purchases for most households. Those industries also employ millions of workers. Because of the high price of cars and houses, a 30% tax (even net of whatever price decline is realized from the elimination of embedded taxes) would greatly increase their costs—and hurt their sales, perhaps critically.

Because of the importance and economic sensitivity of these two "big-ticket" industries to both households and the overall economy, our new tax system treats the housing and automobile industries differently from all other industries. As with all sales under ***STR***, both new and used houses and cars will be subject to the FCT. However, the FCT rules for these two industries will have special provisions [Refer back to Chapter 8].

Conclusions

The previous chapter stressed the advantages of ***Sensible Tax Reform*** for individuals and households. However, another very important benefit from its passage will be the impact upon the American economy in general and upon American businesses in particular.

Sensible Tax Reform will allow American businesses to operate much more effectively:

- Elimination of most federal income taxes on businesses:
  - No Social Security taxes
  - No Medicare taxes
  - No income taxes
  - No business-to-business purchase tax
- Lower operating costs:
  - Lower interest rates
  - Lower costs of purchases
- Minimum of tax-compliance costs
- Less debt and more equity financing, which will provide more financial stability for the businesses
- Much greater ability to compete against foreign companies
- Future foreign profits can be freely brought home and invested here productively and
- Foreign producers, which export here to the US, will need to confront the same federal consumption tax as American companies.

We must level the economic playing field with foreign competitors. We must improve the business climate. We must end the ridiculous, inefficient and even dangerous arena of tax manipulation that has become the "field of dreams" of Wall Street.

If businesses no longer need to pay taxes, no longer have a heavy tax compliance obligation and can plan their futures without worrying about distorting their financing in order to minimize future taxes, managers will be able to focus upon what is good for their company, their employees, their customers, their shareholders and the national economy—managing a successful business. We must free American entrepreneurial skills. ***STR*** will do that. Chapter 10 will explore its overall impact upon the government and its agencies.

Endnotes

26 Bruce Bartlett, *The Benefit and the Burden*, Simon & Schuster, 2012

27 Tax Foundation estimate

28 For example, the "fair-tax" proposal assumes that intense competitive pressures will force companies to quickly pass *all* of their savings to customers in the form of significantly lower prices, averaging 22-23%. Those assumptions are very naïve.

29 "The US Has a Low Corporate Tax," *Center for Tax Justice,* April 5, 2012

30 "How Merck Lost $2.3 Billion in the Bermuda Triangle," *CBSNews*, November 17, 2009

31 www.census.gov/foreign-trade/statistics/historical/goods

32 www.census.gov/foreign-trade/statistics/historical/goods

33 Scott Thurm and Kate Linebaugh, "More U.S. Profits Parked Abroad, Saving on Taxes," *Wall Street Journal*, March 10, 2013

34 Kevin Drawbaugh, "Twin Rebukes Jolt Business Tax Holiday Campaign," *Reuters*, October 4, 2011

CHAPTER 10

SENSIBLE TAX REFORM FOR THE AMERICAN GOVERNMENT

Taxes...are dues that we pay for the privileges of membership in an organized society.
—Franklin Roosevelt

In the previous two chapters, the impact of ***Sensible Tax Reform—Simple, Just and Effective*** upon individuals, businesses and the overall economy was discussed. In this chapter, the impact of the proposed tax reform upon the government will be examined.

Tax neutrality (keeping government revenues approximately the same as with our current tax system) was one of the goals in the design of ***STR***. The entire existing tax structure will be over-turned and replaced with a very different system, which will bring many benefits to the government while *maintaining its current projected revenue*:

- The new system will be much simpler and much more just, resulting in fewer complaints about our federal tax system.

- Both tax collection and enforcement will be much easier for the IRS, since there will be fewer than 20 million taxpayers (primarily retailers) instead of more than 170 million as there is now.
- The government's tax revenues will not be as volatile as under our current systems, since the tax base will be much larger and consumption (and therefore consumption taxes) is much more stable than income.
- The ***STR***-generated acceleration in economic growth will also enhance future government revenues that will reduce the budget deficits.
- America's international trade performance will greatly improve, with great improvement in our government's international debt and a substantial reduction of our government's need to borrow abroad.

Federal Income

Different Tax Sources

The U.S. Government collects a wide variety of taxes, including personal and corporate income taxes, Social Security and Medicare taxes, as well as estate and gift taxes. Under ***STR,*** the principal source of federal revenue would be the federal consumption tax. Personal income taxes would only be paid at income levels above $1,000,000, with inheritance income being included with all other sources of income and taxed accordingly. Corporate income taxes, Social Security and Medicare taxes (for both individuals and businesses) and estate taxes would be totally eliminated—a thing of the past.

Broadening the Tax Base

The federal consumption tax under ***Sensible Tax Reform*** will greatly increase the tax base by increasing the number and variety of taxpayers and the income that they will spend:

- The Mafia and other *crooks*, who do not now pay income and Social-Security taxes on their illegal earnings (from drugs, money laundering, gambling, etc.), will pay the federal consumption tax.
- Those living on the "*underground economy*" will join us in paying the FCT.

- Very wealthy people, who are now able to avoid income taxes by *living on loans or non-taxed investments*, will pay their share of consumption taxes.
- *Visitors from abroad*, who now only contribute to federal tax revenues via embedded taxes on their purchases, will pay the federal consumption tax just as we will.
- The *much stronger economy*, which will follow from the introduction of ***STR***, will increase both employment and incomes. This will increase consumer spending and the federal consumption tax that will be received by the federal government.

Tax Neutrality

Irresponsible government: Our current tax system allows far too much manipulation by lawmakers. Tax neutrality is virtually never a part of the process. President Bush proposed and Congress passed a large tax cut in 2002—*after* the tragic events of 9/11, *after* large tax cuts in 2001 and *after* a presidential declaration of war on terrorism, which everyone knew would lead to huge increases in the government's budget. As a result of the predictable increase in federal spending and the tax cut, the large budget *surpluses* that a fiscally-responsible Republican Congress and Democratic president had fashioned during the late 1990s were quickly transformed into massive and unending budget *deficits*.

Responsible government: Most major tax bills combine efforts for some minimal degree of fundamental reform with efforts to reallocate the tax burden and tax advantages. This invariably leads to the typical "Christmas-tree" tax bill that becomes laden with tax or special-treatment "ornaments" to please diverse groups and to garner votes as well as tax increases or decreases. This process has added greatly to the tax monstrosity in Washington that we are now combating. ***Sensible Tax Reform*** will replace that system completely and usher in an era of responsible government.

We must stop using the same insane tax-writing process that has given us today's tax mess [Chapter 4] while expecting sane results. *We must focus* upon *fundamental reform of the taxation process alone*, while eliminating ALL of the ornaments. We want a simple, just and effective tax system. Under the ***STR***, the bells and whistles that complicate and undermine our current system will be largely eliminated.

Do I expect that the ***Sensible Tax Reform—Simple, Just and Effective*** will truly maintain tax neutrality for the American Government when it is introduced? Yes. Can I guarantee it? No, of course not. [Although it may be true, as the great American statesman Benjamin Franklin said, that "the only sure things are death and taxes," neither the time or manner of death nor the amount or type of tax revenues is a sure thing.] The intention when introducing ***STR*** is to provide tax neutrality in the first year of the new tax regime. International *crises* and many other factors can shift the economic climate and reduce anticipated tax revenues. Anyone who claims anything else is naïve about the volatile nature of the economy. However, that uncertainty is just as true under our current tax system. Also, *favorable* international developments (for example, a strong European economy) could well improve the American economy and produce more federal tax revenue than expected.

Domestic Impacts of *STR* upon our Government

Sensible Tax Reform—Simple, Just and Effective will have many *dynamic impacts* upon the government other than merely changing the source and amount of federal income:

- The structure of Social Security and Medicare will change.
- Most of the social engineering that has so badly complicated and distorted our current tax system will be gone.
- The Internal Revenue Service will find its functions greatly simplified.
- Tax lobbyists will lose most of their influence in Washington.
- And, state and other municipal governments will need to make major adjustments to the new federal tax systems—especially if they currently collect income taxes.

Social Security and Medicare

As has been noted repeatedly, Social Security and Medicare taxes are the most regressive of the federal *income taxes* that Americans pay. All wage and salary earners must pay them—teenagers earning money for college and even families below the poverty line need to pay. When the share of payroll taxes that employers must pay on the earnings of their employees is added to those same taxes paid by the employees directly, most Americans pay more in Social Security and Medicare taxes than they do in *income* taxes. Indeed, for a very large share of the poor and lower middle-income Americans, Social Security and Medicare are the *only* income taxes that they pay.

However, "unearned income" (especially interest, dividends and capital gains), which is the principal source of income for most of the very wealthy, is not charged those payroll taxes at all. Also, those with incomes of more than $113,700 of salaries and wages do not pay the 6.2% Social Security tax (2013) for any income above that level. ***Sensible Tax Reform*** will eliminate not only personal income taxes for most Americans, but totally eliminate Social Security and Medicare taxes for both individuals and businesses. That will greatly reduce the regressiveness of our tax system.

Social Security and Medicare *benefits*, however, will not *be* affected by these tax reforms. The funding for these benefits will be paid out of the general tax revenues of the federal government. That provides a much stronger funding base for the entire system. Benefits will be determined by what an individual has earned—not by the payroll taxes they have paid.

Social Engineering

One of the most complicated aspects of the current federal tax code is its effort to design special tax-related benefits for different social and economic groups: The earned-income tax credit and the child-care credit only benefit the poor. The mortgage, property tax and charitable-donation deductions primarily benefit the wealthy. Generous estate-tax deductions and exemptions only benefit the wealthy. These and many of the dozens of other deductions, credits, exemptions, exclusions, special tax rates, etc. can be shown to provide real benefits to some groups, but not to others.

A strong case can be made that *some* of these provisions are good for the country. In some, but not all, cases that may be true. However, *these loopholes should not be part of the tax system.* If the government wishes to promote such social engineering by creating special provisions for some groups but not for others, then let it provide open, equitable and simple programs as part of its budget. It is very inefficient, complicating and often devious to hide them in the tax code.

Sensible Tax Reform—Simple, Just and Effective almost totally eliminates these "ornaments" on the tax tree. The proposed tax reform attempts to honestly and openly focus on cleaning up the tax system alone. In order to do that, *we need to get rid of as much as possible of what is not truly part of the tax system.* Will it be possible to entirely get rid of all the "ornaments"? No, a few special provisions will be part of the proposed legislation but each will apply to all taxpayers equally. Indeed, ***STR***'s major social impact is to entirely remove most social elements from the tax system. It will bring fundamental tax reform—just, effective and very simple.

The Internal Revenue Service

Some tax-reform proposals (e.g., the "fair" tax) make emotional claims that they would abolish the Internal Revenue Service and "free all IRS employees to pursue productive careers." Not surprisingly, this notion appeals to people who either have had bad experiences with the agency in the past, or who simply hate the nightmare that it imposes upon us every April. However, planning to totally eliminate the IRS is rather naïve. The agency's name might change (e.g., maybe the "Treasury Revenue Agency"). But, as long as we have a government, as long as the government spends money, as long as the U.S. Treasury collects taxes (whether based on income or sales), there will be an agency like the IRS to collect the taxes and prevent violations of the tax laws.

There will be a big difference in the IRS though under ***Sensible Tax Reform***. Since the number of individual and business tax returns will decline from more than 170,000,000 annually to less than twenty million (primarily the retailers who collect and process the sales taxes), the Internal Revenue Service will be much smaller than it is today (saving the federal government billions of dollars annually). For the same reason, the agency's enforcement mechanism will be much smaller—and, perhaps most importantly, will not be a threat to most individual Americans. There will be many fewer people who need to worry about running afoul of the IRS. Our lives will definitely be simpler and less worrisome. Most of us will never again deal with the agency. Any audits of retailers that do take place will be much simpler than now because tax reporting will be so simple, free of numerous deductions, credits, exclusions, exemptions, etc.

Tax Lobbyists

One of the most unsavory aspects of the present income tax and estate tax systems is the way in which tax lobbyists are able to buy special treatment from lawmakers for their clients. Our system is riddled with loopholes and unfairness. It is virtually designed for such abuse!

We must have no delusions about the fact that when these shady deals are made and these individuals and companies rip off the American government, *we* pay the bill. It is *our* government. Those are *our* tax receipts. The government is spending *our* money. If special-interest groups (such as the oil and pharmaceutical industries) can save their billions each year because of special tax loopholes, then what they save comes out of *our* pockets!

America will be much better off if the influence of tax lobbyists is marginalized. The federal consumption tax will accomplish that. Ending the influence of the unsavory gang of K-Street tax lobbyists in Washington will vastly improve the nation's tax climate. Under ***STR***, they will be marginalized. [It is worth noting that the term "lobbyists" has become so unsavory that they are trying to find a new name for what they do—a name that camouflages an occupation that has brought so much contempt upon itself.]

State Governments

There will be a lot of "soul searching" at the state level with the introduction of ***Sensible Tax Reform***. The federal consumption tax will rewrite the tax environment at all levels of government. States that now impose *income* taxes will be under great taxpayer pressure to eliminate them when the national income taxes are eliminated. At the current time, complying with state income taxes is not a huge burden for most taxpayers. After we first go through the nightmare of calculating our federal income taxes, it is generally a relatively simple process to adapt the federal totals in order to make the state and local income-tax calculations.

If the federal government eliminates income taxes, then things will be very different. If a taxpayer no longer needs to keep extensive financial records for federal purposes and does not need to calculate federal income taxes, he or she is not likely to be happy to still have to go through the process of calculating state income taxes. Either the states will need to greatly simplify the income-tax process (e.g., "Add your total W-2 income, plus dividends, interest and capital gains. Your tax due is 2% of the total.") or replace their income-tax systems with a sales tax designed like the *federal* consumption tax.

International **Impacts of *STR* upon our Government**

This book has argued strongly that our current federal tax system seriously harms both American exporters and import-competing companies—an unlevel playing field of our own creation! The form of business taxes that we now impose cannot be rebated to American companies while the consumption-based VAT that most other industrialized companies charge can be rebated to theirs. The result has been a huge increase in our trade deficit, the off-shoring of American factories and hundreds of thousands of jobs, and a horrendous and dangerous international debt that has led to our federal government borrowing trillions of dollars from other governments.

In addition, many Americans and U.S. companies as well hide trillions of dollars of income and profits in foreign tax havens as a way of avoiding or evading American taxes. How will the ***Sensible Tax Reform*** impact upon these and other issues that can affect our relations with other governments?

International Approval

Our system of direct taxation of our businesses has aggravated a number of serious international economic problems, which continue to fester and threaten our well being, as well as that of other countries. This is especially true of our very huge and unsustainable trade deficits and massive international debt. *The longer it takes us to acknowledge the nature and source of those problems and recognize the need to seek remedies, the greater the ultimate pain will become.*

More and more leaders around the world recognize that, while America's import folly has been the economic engine that has provided much of the zip to the world's economy for many years, our excesses are simultaneously distorting that economy:

- Our trade deficits are excessive.
- Our international debt is frightening.
- Our massive international borrowing increases interest rates worldwide and can freeze less creditworthy countries out of the financial markets because of our borrowing.

There will be much international approval of the changes to our economy that ***Sensible Tax Reform*** will introduce since they will also benefit the rest of the world. Its introduction will ease or totally eliminate many economic irritations that strain America's economic relations with other countries and threaten their future well-being as well as our own.

Leveling the International Playing Field

While many foreign governments will view some of the changes and the implications of the ***STR*** favorably, they will simultaneously dislike the economic ramifications of some of the changes. The rest of the world relies heavily upon the U.S. to serve as the economic engine for world prosperity. Even our staunchest allies, such as Canada, Mexico, the United Kingdom, Germany and Japan, have benefited from our system of taxation, which hurts our companies to the advantage of theirs.

Many foreign governments have exercised their diplomatic rights to object via international economic forums, such as the World Trade Organization, when the American government has attempted in the past to institute creative but improper export-promoting entities. This has often strained international relations.

What is proposed in ***Sensible Tax Reform—Simple, Just and Effective*** is completely legitimate and above reproach. We will be playing completely by the international rules. We will actually be doing what many of them have been advising us to do for many years—fundamentally revising our tax system to a consumption-tax-based system. They just never expected that we would actually do it.

What will be even more aggravating to them will be the way in which we have done it. Instead of instituting a VAT while maintaining corporate profit and payroll taxes, ***STR** will completely re-write the rules of the tax game.* Indeed, foreign firms will suddenly be placed upon the defensive:

- American *exporters* will become much more competitive internationally.
- American *import-competing companies* will become much stronger against foreign competitors.
- The *drop in U.S. interest rates* will provide a competitive advantage for American companies.
- The *dynamic stock market* here will make the sale of new issues of stock more attractive and allow our companies to strengthen their equity base.
- The *tax-free business environment* here in the United States will attract foreign companies to expand, or even move, here—with the U.S., in effect, becoming a tax haven.
- Americans and American companies will bring home hundreds of billions of dollars that have been accumulated abroad.

The changes that ***Sensible Tax*** Reform will bring will be very noticeable abroad, both to businesses and to governments. The international playing field may still be unlevel, but it will have become *unleveled in our favor*!

Massive trade deficit: America's balance of trade is huge, unsustainable and dangerous. We do not export enough and we import way too much. The US exported $1.6 trillion in 2012, which appears impressive. However, a much smaller economy, China, exports much more than we do—$2.1 trillion. Germany, an even smaller country with higher production costs than ours, exports almost as much we do—$1.5 trillion.

Our weak export performance would be bad enough if we showed any restraint on our *imports*. However, America is totally profligate and irresponsible—importing $565 billion more ($2.3 trillion) than the next largest importer, China.

The combination of weak exports and massive imports yields our very high balance-of-trade deficits: $785 billion in 2011 and $741 billion in 2012—more than $2 billion *per day*. Exhibit 10-1 illustrates how countries of very different size, from large Germany and China down to little Switzerland, run healthy *trade surpluses.* In contrast, countries such as Canada and Japan run modest deficits, while India and the UK run large deficits. The US, on the other hand, is in a class by itself—running trade deficits that are five times as large as any other country.

Exhibit 10-1

Balance of Trade[35]
($ Billions; 2011)

Germany	$220
Russia	$199
China	$155
Saudi Arabia	$132
Switzerland	$27
Canada	($10)
Japan	($32)
India	($154)
United Kingdom	($163)
United States	($785)

Our massive trade deficit has a very high cost. It means the loss of millions of jobs, thousands of factories, even the loss of entire industries. And, when we spend more overseas than foreigners spend here, most of the imbalance must be financed by our borrowing abroad.

Reducing the deficit: The world simply cannot continue to finance deficits of such magnitude. Yet, expressions of concern now generally fall upon deaf ears in Washington, where Congress and the White House seem incapable of confronting any of America's strategic economic problems and taking appropriate action. ***Sensible Tax Reform—Simple, Just and Effective*** will simultaneously greatly increase exports while greatly reducing imports. That significantly-reduced trade deficit will strengthen the American economy and, at the same time, remove a dangerous tension in the world's economy. Those prospects should find widespread bipartisan support in Washington.

Foreign countries cannot dictate our tax decisions. When our exports go to Europe, they are subject to value-added taxes that can exceed 20%. The European Union is fully within its rights to impose whatever taxes they choose. So are we.

International Indebtedness

In order to finance our horrendous deficit, the American government and businesses borrow very heavily from foreign lenders. The US Government alone owes more than $5 trillion to foreign lenders, including almost $1.4 trillion to the Chinese government and $1.1 trillion to Japan's. Exhibit 10-2 shows the foreign countries that have purchased the most US Treasury bills. When we owe such huge amounts, we are placing ourselves at the mercy of the willingness of foreign lenders, especially foreign governments, to continue to finance our profligacy.

Exhibit 10-2
Major Foreign Holders of Treasury Securities[36]
($ Billions, June 2013)

China	$1,376
Japan	$1,083
Caribbean banking centers	$291
Oil exporters	$257
Brazil	$254
Taiwan	$186
Switzerland	$180
Belgium	$176
United Kingdom	$163

America's international borrowing pushes up interest rates worldwide. Many foreign lenders are approaching, or have already reached, the limit to their willingness to hold American debt in their portfolios—regardless of how attractive that debt, especially U.S. Government debt, may be. The overall magnitude of the debt is an uncomfortable overhang for the entire international debt market.

Sensible Tax Reform will not reduce our *existing* international indebtedness. However, it will significantly slow down its *increase* and will accelerate the growth of the American economy, which supports that debt. Foreign officials and business leaders will find that desirable.

International Reserves

Many countries with trade surpluses have recently amassed unprecedented amounts of international reserves in recent years. The highest level of international reserves *in world history* is the $3.3 trillion of China—three times the second largest amount, the $1.2 trillion of Japan. Exhibit 10-3 shows those countries with $250 billion or more of international reserves. [US international reserves are about 140 billion.] Most of those foreign countries invest the bulk of their reserves in US Treasury debt. Indeed, they provide the financing for about one third of the US Government's debt.

Exhibit 10-3
International Reserves[37]
(Billions; 2012)

China	$3,331
Japan	$1,227
Saudi Arabia	$656
Russia	$487
Switzerland	$477
Brazil	$370
Korea	$323
Hong Kong	$317
India	$270
Singapore	$260

Our government's fiscal irresponsibility legitimately worries not only credit-rating agencies but foreign governments as well: huge, unending budget deficits;

$16 trillion federal debt; $5 trillion international debt of our government; drastic under-funding of Medicare; no energy policy; a shaky national health policy—the list of our government's economic flaws is very long! The abject failure by the US Congress and president to take decisive action to remedy these critical issues is all too obvious.

Sovereign wealth funds: As their international reserves have mounted to levels far above any point they had ever imagined, governments have been searching for alternatives to the traditional practice of simply investing in US Treasury debt. Increasingly, they are investing in the private sector—including buying stock in foreign companies. These special sub-funds of those countries' international reserves are called *sovereign wealth funds.* China has become the most aggressive and imaginative country in how it invests those sovereign funds. For example, in 2007, it invested $3 billion in the Blackstone private-equity fund here in the US.

This entire issue of foreign governments acquiring U.S. *private* assets will likely become an increasing irritant in coming years. Several years ago, the American Government refused to allow a sovereign wealth fund from Dubai to buy a company that managed several major American ports, because of concerns regarding national security. If we reduce our foreign indebtedness relative to the size of our economy by the fundamental tax reform that ***STR*** will bring, it will help reduce this growing diplomatic tension.

Bringing Profits Home

At the same time that the US Government is borrowing heavily overseas, American businesses and individuals are estimated to be holding more than $3.5 trillion abroad. That is money that generally is not used to help the US economy.

Business profits abroad: Chapter 9 illustrated how American companies are subject to taxes on what they earn abroad. However, they are allowed to legally defer taxation on those profits almost indefinitely. $2 trillion of profits of American firms is currently residing abroad.

The law was passed in order to help companies that earn foreign profits to remain competitive with their foreign competitors. However, US businesses have distorted this loophole out of all recognition. By careful manipulation of export prices (called transfer pricing), many companies can shift the profits from their domestic operations to low-tax or no-tax jurisdictions overseas. Other companies shift patents and copyrights that were developed in the United States, often at high cost, to foreign affiliates at a low price. The parent company here then pays high, inflated royalties to themselves overseas, where they are largely or completely shielded from US taxes—indefinitely.

Under ***Sensible Tax Reform***, businesses could continue to amass profits abroad. However, since they will not be required to pay income taxes here in the United States, there will be little incentive to accumulate excess profits abroad—even in a tax haven where they owe no taxes. There will be strong incentive to keep their profits here at home.

The issue will still remain regarding the taxes owed on the $2 trillion of profits that they have deferred under the current tax code. The taxes were deferred. Those companies have enjoyed the benefits of using tax-free money, often for many years. However, the taxes will need to be paid when ***STR*** goes into effect, as will be described in Chapter 11.

Individual savings abroad: In the United States, taxpayers are subject to earnings both at home and abroad. Foreign earnings do not need to be brought back to the US, but taxes are payable each year.

Unfortunately, thousands of people in this country *illegally* hide not only foreign earnings but also move large amounts of income that had been earned here. That is a criminal offense. The IRS has estimated that more than $1.5 trillion is being *illegally hidden* abroad. That does not include the hundreds of billions of dollars that have been *legally* invested abroad by individuals. The Justice Department and the IRS have been aggressively pursuing them in recent years. Between 2009 and 2013, over 39,000 tax cheats came forward under a leniency program that said they would not go to jail. The IRS has collected $5.5 billion from them[38].

Under ***Sensible Tax Reform***, the temptation to evade taxes will be very much reduced since the first $1 million of income, from whatever source or country, will be excluded from taxes. The next $10 million will only be taxed at 15%. Those who have hidden taxes overseas in the past will still be subject to punishment according to the rules of our tax code now. That also will be explored in Chapter 11.

Since America's tax regime will be so attractive with ***STR***, the appeal of moving money overseas will be significantly reduced. Individual investors will still diversify their investments by investing some of their savings abroad. However, it will be open and legal—which is what most American investors with funds abroad are already doing now.

America, the Tax Haven?

A tax haven is a foreign jurisdiction that treats income or wealth much more generously than does the individual or company's home country. Although some tax havens are used illegally under American law, many of them are very legal. As we have just seen, American companies establish foreign tax-haven entities in which to accumulate their foreign profits rather than remit them to the U.S. and pay income taxes here. American insurance and other companies set up insurance tax havens in the Caribbean. And individuals establish sophisticated tax shelters abroad to hide their income and estates from American taxes. Most of these are complicated and expensive. They are primarily attractive because the cost of current American taxes is perceived to be very high. Because of the difficulties and costs involved, only the rich are generally able to take advantage of *legitimate* foreign opportunities. However, many businesses and thousands of individuals also legally invest money abroad.

The adoption of the ***Sensible Tax Reform*** will eliminate much of the appeal of these foreign tax havens. In fact, the elimination of income taxes here, including those on interest, dividends and capital gains, would *make the United States a tax haven for many foreigners.*

It would also greatly enhance the appeal of the U.S. for foreign companies to expand here, and even to establish their international headquarters here. If the United States, the largest economy in the world, was simultaneously one of the world's most attractive tax environments, it could revolutionize the flow of global investments. That would help keep borrowing costs low, help finance economic growth and help to finance our foreign expenditures.

Conclusion

As was seen with individuals [Chapter 8] and with businesses [Chapter 9], both the federal and municipal governments will be significantly affected for the better by the introduction of ***Sensible Tax Reform—Simple, Just and Effective***:

- The overall federal tax system will be much simpler, easier to administer and less subject to "gaming."
- Tax revenues will be less volatile, since consumption is much less volatile than income.
- The economy will be strong, increasing future tax revenues.
- The need for the US Government to borrow overseas will be much lower.

The next chapter will explore problems of transitioning from our current income-based federal tax system to the new consumption-based tax system.

Endnotes

35 docs.wto.org

36 "Major Foreign Holders of Treasury Securities," June 2013; www.treasury.gov/resource-center/data-chart-center/tic/documents/mfh

37 wdi.worldbank.org/table/4.17

38 Stephen Ohlemacher, "Tax Cheats Pony Up $5.5 billion in Amnesty Program," *Huffington Post*, April 26, 2013

PART D

MAKING *SENSIBLE TAX REFORM* WORK

Chapter 11: **Transitional Impacts of Implementing *Sensible Tax Reform***
Chapter 12: **Is *Sensible Tax Reform* Right for America?**

CHAPTER 11

TRANSITION TO *SENSIBLE TAX REFORM*

We can't solve problems by using the same kind of thinking we used when we created them!
—Albert Einstein, Nobel laureate

America needs and most Americans want change in our federal tax system—major and fundamental change. ***Sensible Tax Reform—Simple, Just and Effective*** will bring very significant and very beneficial permanent benefits. However, there will be major adjustments for families, businesses and our government as we shift from our current income-tax-based fiscal system to one based primarily upon a federal consumption tax.

In order to ease the change to ***STR***, the new tax system will be phased in over a five-year transitional period: Our existing income, Social Security and Medicare taxes will be phased out and the new federal consumption tax phased in over that period. This chapter examines the major transitional impacts.

Transitional Impacts of *STR* for American Households

The new tax system will bring very substantial advantages for most Americans—the poor, the middle class and even most of the wealthy, both in income and in spending.

Personal Income

With the introduction of ***Sensible Tax Reform***, almost all Americans will experience *significantly higher disposable incomes*. With our increased take-home pay that will result from the elimination of our income and Social Security/Medicare taxes plus the rebate, we will be able to buy everything that we had bought previously plus pay the new tax and *still have more money than before*—to spend or save or donate to charity. As noted above, the changes will be phased in over five years.

Eliminated taxes: The Social Security and Medicare taxes will decline from their current level of 7.65% down to 6.00% in the first year [Exhibit 11-1, Column 4] and then 1.50% each year thereafter until reaching 0% in the fifth year. At the same time, personal income taxes will immediately be simplified from our current seven rates (ranging from 10-39.6%) to the new simple three rates of 15%/25%/35% [Column 1]. During the first year, the first $100,000 of total income will be tax free [Column 2] and the top rate of 35% will only apply to income of $1 million or more [Column 3]. Each year both the tax-exclusion level and the level at which the top rate will apply will rise until the full $1 million exclusion will be introduced in the fifth year.

The take-home income from our very first paycheck will generally increase by the amount of the decline in our Social Security, Medicare and income taxes. Even with the introduction of the FCT, almost everyone's ability to pay it will increase even more.

FCT rebate: Like the other parts of ***Sensible Tax Reform***, the federal consumption tax rebate will be phased in over five years. Everyone will begin receiving the rebate at the beginning of each month. Since the tax will be introduced in five equal increments [Column 5], the rebate will also increase proportionately each year by the same increments [Column 6]. The total effect will be that the poor, the middle class and even most of the rich will enjoy higher total and disposable income—with less hassle and greater privacy. We will enjoy more income immediately, but it may not be obvious for a few months since prices will also have increased.

Exhibit 11-1

Sensible Tax Reform: Personal Taxes—5-Year Transition						
	(1)	(2)	(3)	(4)	(5)	(6)
	Personal Income Taxes			SS/M	Consumption Tax	
Year	Tax Rate	Exclusion	35% Income		Tax Rate	Rebate
Now	10-39.6%	_	$388,350	7.65%	0%	0%
1	15%/25%/35%	$100,000	$1,000,000	6.00%	6%	6%
2	15%/25%/35%	$250,000	$2,500,000	4.50%	12%	12%
3	15%/25%/35%	$500,000	$5,000,000	3.00%	18%	18%
4	15%/25%/35%	$750,000	$10,000,000	1.50%	24%	24%
5	15%/25%/35%	$1,000,000	$25,000,000	0.00%	30%	30%

Shopping

Anticipation: Shopping will be affected even *before* the FCT tax comes into effect. Anticipation of the new tax may well initiate strong retail sales for some goods or services in the months leading up to the beginning of the new tax system. Many purchases may be accelerated, especially consumer durables (for example, cars and appliances) and semi-durables such as clothing. That year's Christmas shopping season will be strong for retailers.

Federal consumption tax: In the first year, the tax will be introduced at about 6%. It will increase annually by the same amount until fully implemented in the fifth year.

Sticker shock: We will all experience some degree of "sticker shock." The *base prices* of most of what we buy will likely fall on average. But, when the federal consumption tax is factored in, the total cost will increase. The tax will generally be included in the price of what we purchase, just as excise taxes on gasoline or tobacco are included in prices now. The shelf prices may not always break out the base prices from the taxes, but at the checkout counter the receipt will show the total prices and the total FCT separately. We should always know what taxes we are paying.

Spending: Although the poor will benefit greatly from ***STR,*** they will likely spend all they receive; they need it and few people would begrudge them the opportunity. The wealthy will also enjoy greater disposable income. However, most of them already have the income they need to maintain their lifestyles. Their expenditures will not likely change dramatically.

The real question involves the middle 80% or so of Americans. Undoubtedly, many will spend much or most of their increased incomes. For some, the choice will be understandable—a better college for their children, better insurance protection, a nicer home, etc. During the early transition, many people may not realize how much more real income they have and may spend carelessly, at least until the novelty of the increased income wears off. Whether or not they save, that is their choice. ***STR*** will provide the opportunity but it cannot dictate how different individuals will use that opportunity. The first year of the phase-in will be a learning experience for us all.

Investors

In the months immediately before ***STR***, investors whose investments have been strongly influenced by tax considerations may be busy repositioning those investments. Since income-tax rates will decline, investors may logically sell their losing investments if it will reduce their taxes (a tax strategy known as "tax-loss harvesting"). On the other hand, the sale of their winning stocks may be deferred until the new tax comes into effect when the profits will be taxed at lower rates. Other investors will find it attractive to invest in the stock of businesses that they expect to benefit most immediately from the new tax system (for example, retailers such as Wal-Mart that both are very price aggressive and also pay high income taxes).

Once ***Sensible Tax Reform*** goes into effect, there will be many important impacts upon investors. Middle-income Americans will experience a healthy increase in investable funds. At the same time, stock markets are likely to do very well. Companies will also be paying more dividends, which will make investments in stocks even more attractive. These projections may encourage existing investors to keep their winning investments until the market has fully adjusted to the new tax system.

Tax-sheltered Accounts

One provision of our current Internal Revenue Code that is praiseworthy is the series of tax-sheltered accounts that have been provided to encourage saving for retirement: Individual retirement accounts (IRAs), 401(k)s, 403(b) s, 457(b)s, Roth accounts, et cetera. All of these offer some degree of partial or complete tax deferral. Roth accounts have been funded by after-tax funds with the promise that the earnings on those accounts will not be taxed. That will remain true.

The other accounts have been funded by pre-tax income—and have never been taxed. Both the invested funds and the earnings on those accounts are scheduled to be taxed in the future at the tax rates that the individual would be subject to at the time of the withdrawals. Those accounts will no longer be necessary with ***Sensible Tax Reform***. During the transition to the new tax program, those accounts will become taxable. However, with the phase-in of the annual income-tax exclusion, most investors will be able to totally avoid taxes on those investments.

Interest Payments

Federal consumption taxes will be new to everyone. So also will the breadth of the purchases that will be taxed, since most existing state and local sales tax systems exempt most services and many forms of merchandise (for example, groceries) as well. One totally unique aspect of the new tax is that it will apply to interest payments by individuals. Rather than being tax deductible as is now true on home mortgages, ***STR*** will apply the FCT to interest payments by individuals.

Why should interest payments be taxed? The answer is simple: Interest is the price that we pay for *renting money*. It will be treated the same way as any other rental. Hotels rent us rooms. Airlines rent us seats on their planes. Rental companies rent us cars, trucks, party equipment, tuxedos, tents, etc. For all of those services we pay rent. Those rents will be taxable under the FCT. Similarly, banks and other credit companies *rent* us money in the form of loans. Interest is the rental price for borrowing. That rental cost will be subject to the consumption tax.

Currently existing tax law encourages borrowing excessively for home mortgages. [The excess was extremely apparent when millions of homeowners were foreclosed upon during the Great Recession of 2007-2010.] The new tax will make borrowing more expensive. It will encourage less borrowing. It will also encourage using some of our extra income to pay debt off more rapidly. Both effects will be beneficial for both families and the overall economy.

Currently-existing mortgage contracts will be protected by a "grandfather" clause: They will not be subject to the tax. However, the interest payments on all *new* loans, whether mortgages or credit cards or any other type of loans, will be taxed once the new tax is implemented. However, as with all other purchases, the new FCT on interest payments will be introduced gradually over five years. Any new loan will be taxed for the life of the loan at the rate in effect when the loan is disbursed.

Past Tax Evasion

One of the most unfortunate legacies of our current tax system is the amount of tax evasion that occurs. Our income tax system now is so complicated and the ways by which income can be hidden or expenses exaggerated are so common that tax evasion is distressingly easy. We are not talking about tax evasion on illegal income of the mafia and drug dealers. We are talking here about *legal income* that is *illegally hidden* from the Internal Revenue Service.

The most egregious form of tax evasion is the hiding of income in tax-haven countries, such as Switzerland. Several years ago, the US Department of Justice released a report that "as many as 52,000 tax law violating US citizens .. had secret Swiss accounts at banking giant UBS"[39] alone—a single Swiss bank, but many other banks there have also been charged.

It has been estimated that wealthy Americans have hidden more than $1.5 trillion in illegal overseas accounts. That tax evasion swindled the American government of hundreds of billions of dollars in income taxes. It also penalizes all of the rest of us, those who do honestly pay our taxes.

Those tax scams occurred under our currently existing tax system. Those tax cheats have broken the law. They will still owe all of the taxes that they have evaded, along with any appropriate penalties. The passage of ***Sensible Tax Reform*** will not allow them to escape their punishment.

Transitional Impacts of *STR* for American Businesses and Economy

Just as with individuals, businesses will experience dramatic changes from the introduction of ***Sensible Tax Reform—Simple, Just and Effective***. Completely removing federal taxes from American businesses will have dynamic effects upon companies, sole proprietorships and partnerships. Millions of businesses will have unprecedented new opportunities to compete and prosper. The impacts will be most dramatic with regard to international trade and investment where American companies will be much stronger players. However, excellent domestic business opportunities will abound as well. One of the most important impacts will be the creation of millions of new jobs for Americans.

Sales and Profits

Most retail businesses are likely to have a very successful fourth calendar quarter just before the introduction of the new tax. In addition to the normal Christmas season, there will be the added incentive for buyers to stock up before the new tax goes into effect. Sales will be strong. Profits will be excellent.

Until the new tax plan is introduced, businesses will remain subject to both normal income taxes as well as alternative minimum taxes. With the new tax, they will be free of such threats. Businesses will thus, to the extent possible, have a strong incentive to incur expenses *before* the new tax arrives and defer profits until *after* it takes effect.

Elimination of taxes: As with the ***STR*** impacts upon individuals and households, the transitional effects upon businesses will be phased in over five years [Exhibit 11-2]. The current eight tax brackets ranging from 15-39% will be immediately reduced to three: 15%, 25% and 35% [Column 1].

In a similar fashion, the business share of the Social Security and Medicare taxes, which generally are exactly equal to those paid by their employees, which will also be phased out [Column 20. That is exactly the same phase-out schedule as for their employees [Exhibit 11-1].

As was discussed in Chapter 9, our new tax system will eliminate more than $825 billion annually of taxes and tax-compliance costs from American

Exhibit 11-2
Sensible Tax Reform:
Corporate Taxes—5-Year Transition

Year	Corporate Income Taxes	SS/M
Now	15-39%	7.65%
1	15%/25%/35%	6.00%
2	12%/20%/28%	4.50%
3	8%/14%/20%	3.00%
4	4%/7%/10%	1.50%
5	0%	0.00%

businesses. In addition, interest rates will decline and the costs for much of what companies purchase will decline with the elimination of embedded taxes. The total gain from all of those savings (that is, the ***STR*** "bonus") will far exceed $1 trillion by the time the entire new tax program has been phased in—an enormous amount of new usable funds for American businesses. Businesses will have many choices for employing such gains whether reducing prices or spending the funds—investing in new plant and equipment, paying down debt, improving employee benefits, increasing dividends, etc. The opportunity for making these choices will arrive very quickly during the transitional period.

Business Inventories: Existing inventories will create a transition problem for companies that will be selling those goods to retail customers after the new tax system goes into effect. Those pre-***STR*** inventories will have embedded tax costs while their retail sales will be subject to the 6% FCT. There will thus be a problem of some double taxation. Businesses may well reduce inventories in anticipation of the new tax program, but there will still remain significant inventory carryover. To avoid the double taxation, there will be special inventory provisions: The carryover inventories will be exempt from the new sales tax for a limited period of time. After the disposal of "old" inventories, of course, the exemption will no longer apply.

This transitional treatment of retail inventories will be especially important for "big-ticket" durable items such as cars, major appliances and new houses. These products are inventoried individually and have long "shelf life." Retailers will need to keep careful end-of-year record by individual item. They will be exempt from the federal consumption tax if sold within the first year of the new tax system.

Retailers

No businesses will be *paying* the federal consumption tax, since it will only be a tax on retail sales. However, *retail* businesses will be required to *collect* the tax. In 45 states, retailers already collect sales taxes, so with the introduction of the tax they will generally only need to modify what they are already doing. In states that do not now collect sales taxes or in industries that do not collect it, the impact will be greater. For them, there will be transitional expenses for equipment, software, training, etc. However, those expenses will be much smaller than the savings from the elimination of income and payroll taxes. The tax responsibilities of retailers will actually be much less than currently: They will only need to report total sales together with the taxes collected on those sales and then remit the latter directly to the US Treasury.

Retailer angst: Retailers may fear that customers will be slow to spend in the first weeks or even months with the FCT. To the extent that the shopping surge in the old year borrows sales from the new year, there will be some slowdown—although many of those same retailers will have done very well in the previous quarter. The first quarter under the new tax system will be transitional for retailers and may be somewhat soft until the tax benefits for producers, wholesalers and retailers filter through the system and help to reduce prices for consumers, and until the anticipatory inventories have been consumed. However, many retail industries customarily schedule special sales in January. That will help to cushion the cost. As a result, the "sticker shock" will be deferred somewhat until the end of those sales.

Financing

The elimination of income taxes will open many opportunities for companies to realign their finances in a more economically-rational way than is done now.

At present, interest payments are tax deductible for businesses, while dividends are not. As a result, our current tax system subsidizes corporate debts. That encourages companies to borrow more and use less equity, since the latter costs more than debt financing.

While that may make sense from a tax point of view, it may be very irrational from an economic perspective. The more debt a company has, then the more fixed expenses it has (i.e., its interest payments). And also the greater will be the risk to which it exposes itself in the event of a weak economy or credit crunch when re-financing is difficult (for example, the Great Recession of 2007-10).

Equity is permanent financing, while debt is temporary. Equity financing is safer. ***Sensible Tax Reform*** will encourage less reliance upon debt. Since businesses will not be paying any income taxes, there will not be any taxable income from which to deduct interest payments (or wages and supplies either). Debt financing will become less important and equity more so.

Interest rates: ***Sensible Tax Reform*** will have very significant indirect effects on interest rates. The interest rate that lenders (for example, those who invest in debt) require in order to induce them to lend depends significantly upon the after-tax rate of return that they will realize. With the elimination of all federal business taxes and a very substantial reduction in personal income taxes, lenders will realize their target after-tax rate of return at much lower interest rates. As a result, interest rates will fall. [For comparison, remember that even now investments in debt that are exempt from federal taxes (for example, municipal bonds) pay a lower nominal interest rate than does taxable debt, often even less than US Treasury interest rates.] The decline in interest rates will have very important implications for both investors in debt and the borrowers to whom they lend.

Loans, bonds and mortgages: The decline of interest rates will be very attractive to borrowers. At the same time, the lower cost of debt coupled with greater income will tend to make both corporate and household borrowers safer and more attractive customers for the lenders, since those payments will be a smaller part of corporate earnings or personal income. Many businesses and households will utilize the new opportunities to pay down debt. Therefore, at the same time that other borrowers are anxious to refinance, lenders will have abundant funds and likely be very accommodating to borrowers.

For businesses, short-term debt and callable debt will be refinanced quickly. In the months leading up to the introduction of ***STR***, companies with maturing debt may well shorten maturities on the refinancing. Since interest payments will no longer be deductible, it will be very important for companies to refinance to take advantage of the new lower rates. Floating-interest loans will automatically enjoy benefits from any decline in interest rates. It may take years before non-callable, long-term fixed-rate debt will be able to be re-financed.

Households will also have an opportunity to refinance at lower interest rates. There will be an excellent opportunity to refinance floating debt with fixed-income debt—especially long-term debt, such as mortgages. It will be especially attractive to household borrowers to be able to reduce interest payments as much as possible, since the interest that individuals pay will be subject to taxes as well.

Dividends: At the present time, dividends on stocks are now at a tax disadvantage for the companies that pay them since they are made *after* each has paid its income taxes. Unlike interest payments, they are not deductible for tax purposes. Dividends are thus far more costly now than interest payments for companies.

Once the new tax rules come into effect, companies will be paying dividends with non-taxed profits. The effective cost of equity financing will be lowered. Companies will be much better positioned to afford the payments and are likely to greatly increase dividend payouts. At the same time, their shareholders will be imposing much more pressure on the companies to increase the dividend payouts, since the dividends will be taxed at lower and lower tax rates each year and totally free of taxation to most investors in the fifth year. With the decline of the cost of equity, companies will finance more with equity and less with debt. As a result, debt ratios will decline. That will strengthen companies during recessions and credit crunches.

Tax Avoidance

Our current federal tax system allows American companies with foreign operations to defer American taxes that are due on their profits abroad to be deferred until a future time, if the funds are used abroad in production or commerce. Many companies do use this tax provision appropriately. Unfortunately, the terms of the provision are somewhat vague. Even more unfortunately, hundreds of

American firms do not use the tax provision for the reasons for which it was created but instead have created their scams to transfer money abroad. That is money, which should *not* be subject to the tax-deferral provision. But because the IRS has allowed such action to occur without penalties, its use has spread rapidly. The total of both the legitimate and scamming uses of this "tax arbitrage," as it is euphemistically called, now exceeds more than $2 trillion being held abroad and deferring U.S. taxes indefinitely.

International tax scams: Two of the primary scams involve the improper use of transfer pricing and the sale or transfer of very valuable intangible assets to foreign affiliates[40].

Transfer pricing is the manipulation of the prices for international transactions between the parent and the foreign affiliate (for example, the pricing of exports) so that most of the cost is incurred in the United States (thereby reducing taxes due here) while most of the profits are shifted abroad to tax-haven countries with very low or even zero tax rates.

The second scam involves companies that have developed very expensive intellectual properties here (such as patents, copyrights and data bases) and then selling or otherwise transferring them at very low prices to foreign affiliates in foreign countries with low or nonexistent taxes. The parent companies (for example, pharmaceutical companies which are especially egregious users of this technique) then lease the assets back for use here in the United States where the asset had originally been developed. The parent companies here pay high prices (and therefore provide high profits) to the foreign affiliate. Again, as with transfer pricing, the primary goal is to use the scam to greatly reduce or even eliminate taxes due in this country and to greatly increase profits abroad where little or no taxes will be due. Those untaxed profits being amassed abroad will continue to grow rapidly year after year.

Under ***Sensible Tax Reform***, businesses will no longer be subject to corporate income taxes in the United States at all. The tax deferral abroad will no longer be necessary. The tax books from our existing taxes will need to be closed. The tax bill on those untaxed profits will come due. Those profits held abroad will be taxed when the new program comes into effect. Much of those funds will be brought home—just as $300 billion was brought home in 2005 when a 5.2% tax holiday was offered. Along with the other phase-in provisions of the STR transition schedule (discussed below), those companies will be able to spread the taxes over several years.

Inflation

With this tax reform, the base prices of retail goods will fall. However, the FCT will cause total *costs* to rise. What the net impact will be on inflation depends upon how inflation is defined. Most inflation indexes calculate the overall change in prices for a large "basket" of goods and services. It is very important that the costs of all major categories of consumption be well represented in that basket: food, clothing, energy, housing, healthcare, education, etc. If any important consumer category is omitted, then there would be a serious flaw in the inflation index.

Existing inflation indexes: None of the principal inflation indexes (e.g., the consumer price index or the cost-of-living index) now includes the inflationary effects of changes in sales taxes, which is quite appropriate since those tax effects are regional rather than national. However, a changeover from our current complicated federal tax system, with its numerous elements of federal taxes, to a very simple national retail sales tax is a very different situation. Price indexes would indicate falling prices under ***STR***. That would suggest a *cost* reduction, which will obviously not reflect the entire cost effect of the new consumption tax.

Any inflation index that failed to include the imposition of a significant federal consumption tax, one that will grow from 6% in the first year to around 30% in the fifth year, would be very flawed. On the other hand, an inflation index that included the imposition of the sales tax but failed to take into account the reduction of the other taxes that the FCT is replacing would be just as erroneous, suggesting much higher inflation than actually exists.

A new inflation index: A new more representative and more realistic inflation index will need to be devised to include all of the relevant changes in prices and taxes. It will need to include the effects of the new consumption tax as well as the effect of the personal taxes that have been removed:

Price index
+ FCT
- eliminated income taxes
= ***STR*** inflation index

If separate inflation indexes are constructed for different income groups (such as the poor, middle income and high income), then the rebate would also need to be factored in. Such special consideration of taxes will likely only be significant factors in the first five years of the new tax system while the changes are being introduced.

The Speed of Price Adjustment: Business costs will decline significantly over the five-year transition to full implementation of the new tax. It will take awhile for the cost-cutting effects to fully filter through the economy. Even when managers want to take advantage of the cost-saving opportunities to lower prices, they may delay until they recognize that the savings are truly permanent. In some industries, intense competition will force prices to quickly reflect the falling costs. In other industries where there remains a large carry-over inventory (e.g., department and hardware stores), consumer costs will increase more slowly in the first months, since the sales tax will not be imposed on old inventory.

Sticky Prices: Many prices bear little relationship to the cost of production. For example, the prices of many commodities (e.g., oil, wheat, and gold) are determined by supply and demand in world markets, which will be little affected by ***STR***. Also, some industries, such as pharmaceuticals, computer software and diamonds, commonly charge whatever the market will bear. And the prices of some products are heavily influenced by trade barriers (e.g., sugar and coffee). Price adjustments in those industries may be quite muted.

In the absence of intense price competition, lowering prices is not the only option available to producers. As mentioned earlier, some companies will use the increased profits to fatten their profit margins, to pay off debt, to increase dividends or to fund stock buybacks. Other uses for the increased profits will be for companies to modernize or expand their operations, to increase their research and development expenditures, or to increase employee benefits. All of these alternatives for utilizing the cost savings of businesses from the elimination of federal taxes can be very beneficial to our economy. However, they are all alternatives to lowering prices. Therefore, there will be some underlying inflationary pressure from the conversion to the new tax system. Eventually, most industries will pass much of the tax savings to their customers via lower prices, but it will take the entire five-year transition period for all of the effects to be fully felt.

Transitional Impacts of *STR* for the American Government

The impact of ***Sensible Tax Reform*** upon the government will be profound. It will substantially change the entire foundation of our current federal tax system. Four key areas that will experience significant changes during the transitional period will be federal tax revenues, the Internal Revenue Service, the Social Security and Medicare programs and tax evasion.

Tax Revenues

The elimination of income, Social Security, Medicare, estate and alternative minimum taxes will revolutionize the revenue system of the federal government. The change to a system that is based upon a consumption tax along with an income tax only on very high incomes will greatly simplify tax collection for the government. Instead of the more than 160 million personal, business and non-profit tax returns that are submitted to the IRS now, there will be fewer than 20 million—mostly retailers. Also, since consumer spending is much more stable than income (i.e., although our income may vary from month to month or year to year, our consumption varies much less), the revenues from a federal consumption tax will be much more stable than are income and profit taxes.

Internal Revenue Service

The IRS is perhaps the most reviled agency of the federal government. Nobody likes to pay taxes. Most of us feel that our taxes are too high and unjust. Our tax compliance burden is oppressive, expensive and resented—especially in the weeks and months leading up to April 15. The IRS is commonly viewed as the tax enemy. Though some naive people would like to get rid of it altogether, the true enemy is not the agency but the tax laws that our government has imposed upon us and which the IRS must enforce. As much as we might dislike the IRS, it is a necessary evil. That will be true under the ***Sensible Tax Reform*** as well as under *any* alternative tax system.

The IRS will be a smaller, more specialized agency. However, it will survive and there will not be the destruction of the IRS coupled with the mass layoffs of many thousands of employees as proposed by the "fair-tax" reformers[41]. [If it makes the IRS haters happy, perhaps we could change its name.] There will continue to be a need for an agency to implement the tax collections and to enforce the tax laws—whatever they might be.

Collecting and processing: The principal tasks of the IRS will continue to be to collect and administer taxes and enforce the tax laws. Among individuals, only those with very high incomes will be required to file an annual personal tax return, and the tax return and its calculation will be very simple compared to our present system. In the final year of the transition, when the annual exclusion reaches $1 million:

(total income - $1 million exclusion) * tax rate = taxes due

The tax rate will be the appropriate rate for the year of transition and the level of income (Exhibit 11-1).

Businesses will no longer need to file income tax returns with the IRS. Nor will they pay income or Social Security/Medicare taxes or to collect and remit the taxes of their employees.

The only businesses that will need to report to the IRS will be retailers—but they will only need to report about their sales and tax collection, not their incomes or expenditures. Those retail tax returns will not be very complicated. [Gone completely and forever will be the days when a General Electric submits a 57,000-page tax filing[42] to the government.] And, there will no longer be the massive seasonal surge of tax filings around April 15. Although each retailer will collect the FCT on its sales and remit the taxes weekly to the Treasury Department (or monthly for smaller businesses), at the end of a fiscal year of its own choosing, they will submit a simple report:

(total net sales) * (FCT tax rate) = taxes due

The FCT tax rate will be the FCT tax rate in effect for the previous year—6% in the first year, 12% in the second, rising to the full rate in the fifth year.

The IRS will immediately experience a significant change in its role. There will be one final tax filing by all individuals and businesses in the year in which the new tax rules go fully into effect—the income and profit taxes of the previous year, the final year of those taxes.

When that process is complete, the income-tax collection function will quickly fade within the agency. Tax receipts will change dramatically. Sales taxes will begin pouring in, but no more income taxes. [After five years, there will be no more tax withholding at all, not even for the very rich.]

Auditing: The auditing responsibility of the IRS will be no less important than now, but it also will be much simpler. Only retailers and the very rich will pay any taxes. They alone will be subject to audits, which will focus upon the individuals and retail industries or companies that are most suspect. [How very different from now when *the poor and lower-middle income groups are more likely to be audited than the wealthy* and where really complicated corporate returns are unlikely to ever receive careful scrutiny—after all, who could possibly understand GE's 57,000 pages of tax return?] Because of the nature of the ***STR*** tax laws and the simplicity of the filing process, tax audits will generally be relatively simple affairs.

Enforcement: Since the income of the rich will not be subject to the messy mass of regulations that exists now, the enforcing process for personal income taxes will be relatively simple. Similarly, enforcement of business taxes will focus upon ensuring that all retailers collect the FCT and transmit it honestly to the government. [See the tax-evasion section below.] The transitional period will involve a lot of adjustments as the IRS and retailers adapt to the new tax rules. However, it will become much simpler each year and the process should be quite smooth within a few years—certainly simpler and smoother than the burden that retailers now have with their income and Social Security/Medicare taxes.

Social Security and Medicare

Americans' concern about Social Security and Medicare are realistic. Social Security is underfunded. Medicare (including its *completely unfunded* prescription-drug program) is drastically underfunded. The new tax program will have a major impact upon these systems: the revenue for the systems will come from the general revenues of the U.S. Government instead of directly from workers and their employers. The US Treasury will regularly pay an amount to the Social Security Administration from the revenues that it has received from the collection of the federal consumption tax to compensate for the payments that are no longer coming from workers and their employers.

There will be no changes in the currently existing Social Security and Medicare benefits from the system. In other words, *no one need fear that their benefits will be reduced in any way* as a result of the introduction of the new tax system. Both programs will have a much more solid footing because of the broader base for the system. The Social Security Administration will continue to draw upon the Social Security Trust Fund, but any shortfall will be guaranteed by the federal government. Medicare will be handled in a similar fashion.

Tax Evasion

Many critics of the federal consumption tax fear that tax evasion will be a huge issue. Specifically, they tend to fear such problems as (1) casual trade, (2) informal markets and (3) individuals using businesses fraudulently for personal purchases.

Casual trade: The casual trade of used or personally-made items will not be subject to the FCT. Garage and yard sales or other casual sales (or barter exchanges) of goods or services selling for less than $1000 (for example, high-school kids babysitting or cutting lawns or sales via the local newspaper or Craigslist) will not be subject to the tax. Such sellers need not have any worry about the Internal Revenue Service. However, if someone does a substantial amount of business (e.g., more than $5,000 per year or someone who organizes such sales as a business), their status would change and they would need to file as a retailer and be required to collect the FCT.

Informal markets: Farmers' markets, flea markets and art fairs are generally comprised of sellers for whom their sales are very clearly a business. They would need to file with the IRS as a retailer and collect the FCT. These retailers commonly collect state sales taxes now. ***STR*** would simply be extending that process to federal sales taxation.

Business purchases for personal use: This type of fraud by any type of business (whether producer, wholesaler or retailer) could be a serious issue—just as it is under our current federal tax systems. The IRS auditors will need to be well trained and very diligent. The financial penalties should be harsh—a substantial fine in addition to the taxes due. Those penalties should be coupled with the *guarantee* of annual IRS audits for the next several years. That penalty could well be the strongest deterrent against fraud. Consistency and firmness in enforcement should do wonders for honesty.

Tax cheats: There will always be tax cheats. However, because of the simplicity of the new tax rules, the opportunities for cheating will be much more limited than now. IRS audits and enforcement will need to be consistent, thorough, recurring and much simpler than now. Chances of being caught will be much greater. And, penalties will be serious. In any event, it is very unlikely that evasion could be anywhere near as great as it is now.

Organized crime: As was described above, anyone who is guilty of having failed to pay income taxes on previous income will find no respite under ***Sensible Tax Reform***. That includes organized crime, drug dealers and "disorganized" criminals, including tax cheats. Those who have evaded taxes on pre-***STR*** income will remain subject to the old tax system—even for future income. Until they have settled their past tax obligations with the government, they will neither qualify for the $1 million income exclusion nor the new lower income tax rates. Like Al Capone, they will be subject to taxes even on their illegal income.

Conclusions

Any major policy change will bring many transitional issues with it. Policy changes on the magnitude of the ***Sensible Tax Reform—Simple, Just and Effective*** will bring major transitional adjustments: for households, businesses, the overall economy, the financial markets and the government. However, as the Europeans have demonstrated three different times in the past generation, a large modern economy can absorb major changes. This tax plan takes a realistic, hard-nosed approach to the transitional difficulties—unlike some other tax-reform proposals, such as the "fair-tax" plan that proposes a very abrupt introduction of their system and assumes relatively little disruption.

As this chapter has shown, there will be many different types of adjustments that we will experience. Changeover will be inconvenient, but not more than we can reasonably handle.

Endnotes

39 William P. Barrett and Janet Novak, "52,000 Had Secret UBS Accounts," *Forbes*, February 19, 2009

40 Steven Pearlstein, "Marty Sullivan figured out how the biggest companies avoided billions in taxes," *Washington Post*, October 26, 2013

41 Neal Boortz and John Linder, *The Fair Tax Book*, Regan Books, 2005, p. 184

42 John McCormack, "GE Filed 57,000-Page Tax Return, Paid No Taxes on $14 Billion in Profits," *Weekly Standard*, November 11, 2011

CHAPTER 12

IS *SENSIBLE TAX REFORM* RIGHT FOR AMERICA?

What America needs is smarter taxes—taxes that are simple, just and effective!

The current federal tax code is not only ugly, deformed and not doing much good, but is also a core part of our basic economic problems. It is a serious impediment to America's continued economic and social progress. ***Sensible Tax Reform—Simple, Just and Effective*** is major tax reform. Indeed, in many ways it is a radical reform. Major changes are never easy—they require serious adjustments. The reader, and America, must decide whether the advantages justify the changes.

A World in Transition

The world has changed drastically in the past twenty-five years:

- The fall of communism in Europe;
- The opening of the markets of Russia, China and many others that had formerly been tightly controlled;

- The rise of developing countries in Asia to become major economic forces;
- A swelling of the European Union to include almost thirty countries;
- Soaring oil prices;
- The accumulation of hundreds of billions and even trillions of dollars in the hands of governments and private hedge and private-equity funds;
- The development of sophisticated financial markets with little regulation and the ability to threaten the world's economy.

The list can go on and on.

Living in the Past

The worldwide roster of economic players is changing. The rules of the game are changing. The United States, however, is still living in the past century—acting like the rules are the same, rules largely of its own design. We remain the world's largest economy but we long ago yielded our rightful position as the world's most successful international trader. Instead, like a developing country, we import far more than we export. We also long ago yielded our traditional role as the world's major creditor nation. Now we run the largest trade deficit in world history—a trade deficit larger than the GDP of all except a very small group of countries. We are the most indebted nation internationally that the world has ever seen.

America Is Falling Behind

The United States can no longer afford to passively allow our destiny to be determined by others. We must take steps to reinvigorate our economy and to reassume our role as the world's economic leader. Because of our perceived weaknesses, even the dollar is under assault. Countries are untying their currencies from the dollar.

We have lost international prestige. We have lost substantial influence. We are clearly vulnerable economically. Yet most of these flaws and the deterioration of our position on the world stage is the result of *our own actions and inactions*—including the monumental greed on Wall Street and the pathetic ineptitude in Washington, which has become completely dysfunctional. We are master of our own destiny—we are the prime reason that we have our current international and domestic weaknesses. Only we can take the steps that are necessary to remedy them.

America in Transition

America is also under assault at home. Here, just as internationally, most of our problems are of our own making—lack of vision; lack of resolve; lack of strategy; lack of cooperation; lack of leadership; and lack of courage.

We are assaulted by one crisis after another: the sub-prime mortgage crisis; housing crisis; healthcare crisis; education crisis; a yawning income and wealth gap between the very rich and the mass of the American people; inadequate savings; huge personal debt; a government debt that grows by more than $1 million per *minute* and has doubled since 2005; a pension and Social Security crisis; an under-funded Medicare crisis of huge proportions; a hallowing out of entire industries as they and their hundreds of thousands of jobs get "off-shored"; a huge illegal immigrant population that lives in the underground economy; a national infrastructure that is very outdated—highways, bridges, trains, air traffic control, electric power, underground utilities (especially water and sewer); etc., etc., etc.

How Did We Get Here?

How did things get so bad? Where are the leaders? When will the American people start demanding new direction from Washington? When will we bring an end to "politics as usual"? We can no longer afford it! Everyone likes to say: "Somebody needs to do something!" Well, we are somebody! We should do something. We bear much of the responsibility for our nation's problems. As long as we fail to demand that these crises be addressed, then WE are the biggest problem. Shame on the White House and Congress for not doing what is right for this country. Shame on us for not demanding that they do their jobs!

All of the great world powers of the past collapsed not because of determined foreign efforts to destroy them. No, they collapsed from within—the Greeks, the Romans, the Holy Roman Empire, the Spanish, the Ming Dynasty, the Ottomans, the French, the British, the Soviet Union. They all failed internally long before external pressure overwhelmed them. That is what will happen to the United States unless we acknowledge the crises that threaten us. That is what will happen here if we lack the wisdom, the courage, the strategic vision and the leadership to change the direction of this country.

Sensible Tax Reform

STR is visionary. It is ambitious. It is radical. It will not be easy to sell to millions of people who fear change. People generally do not like change. Even when they do not like what is currently done, the preference is typically for fine-tuning, for trimming around the edges—not for fundamental change. It is human nature to try to use home remedies, bandages and aspirin rather than take the doctor's advice to have the operation that will permanently relieve the malady. We can no longer afford that. Is ***STR*** right for America? It certainly is! Our economy and our government both need a major tax operation—as soon as possible.

Our Current Federal Tax System

There is not much that can be said favorably about our current Internal Revenue Code. It is an absolute disaster. No matter what form of tax modifications someone supports (and virtually everyone wants major modifications of one form or another), few will disagree with the assertion that our tax system is overly complex, conflicting, unjust and economically damaging to both businesses and individuals. It is difficult and expensive to comply with. It is cynically manipulated by the tax lobbyists who represent powerful and wealthy narrow-interest groups. In enforcing the laws, the government is felt to be intrusive and threatening.

STR is a tax system that will drastically alter that scenario. However, even the ugliness of the existing tax systems may not be sufficient to make such a dramatic change in our tax system palatable to most Americans. We need to re-examine and summarize the benefits for different major parts of the economy.

The Impact of *STR* upon Businesses

One of the most important results of the introduction of this new tax system will be how it will benefit American businesses—and how those benefits for businesses will accelerate benefits for the rest of the economy [Chapter 9]. Businesses do not pay taxes: they serve merely as a very inefficient intermediary between individuals and the government.

All of the money that businesses pay in income taxes or Social Security and Medicare taxes is ultimately paid by their customers in higher prices or their employees in lower benefits or shareholders in the form of lower profits. By removing these tax burdens from businesses, management can focus upon becoming more competitive and successful—lowering prices, increasing compensation to workers, increasing investment, increasing dividends, reducing debt, etc. All of these results benefit the American people and our overall economy as well.

More competitive businesses will:

- Increase our exports,
- Reduce our imports,
- Restrain our obscene pace of international borrowing,
- Create companies,
- Create jobs,
- Diversify the economy and
- Broaden the government's tax base.

These and other economic benefits that ***STR*** will bring (e.g., lower interest rates) will greatly strengthen our economy.

The Impact of *STR* upon Individuals and Families

The innovative new tax plan will change numerous things for individuals and their families:

- No Social Security taxes;
- No Medicare taxes;
- No estate taxes;
- No alternative minimum tax;
- No income taxes for 99% of all Americans;
- No tax-compliance burden;
- Minimal record keeping; and
- No government tax agency looking over your shoulder, inquiring about what you earn, what you do with it and threatening you with penalties.

Sensible Tax Reform will bring:

- Increased real income and standard of living;
- Increased savings—not only for retirement but also for education, healthcare, buying a home or starting a business;
- A strong job market;
- Healthier employers;
- A strong economy;
- Greater opportunity to start new businesses; and
- More secure Social Security, Medicare and business retirement programs

***STR** will bring dramatic benefits to the American people.*

Obstacles to Implementation of the *Sensible Tax Reform*

When people fully understand the advantages of the wonderful new tax system, there will be very strong advocacy to see it implemented. However, the passage will not be easy. There will be strong opposition from various sectors.

The Public

Most people fear change. Most people tend to support the status quo. [Consider how few congressmen and senators are ever defeated.] This inertia by the general public will be a very major hurdle.

Some Businesses

Businesses in general will be obvious beneficiaries of ***STR***: no income taxes, no Social Security or Medicare taxes, no tax compliance costs, and no need to expend expensive effort gaming our old tax system when planning the financing of major projects. While most management should readily recognize the attractions of the new tax program and strongly support it, some managers will undoubtedly be reluctant to leave their comfort zone—even if doing so would be to the benefit of their companies and families. However, a few business groups have legitimate concerns.

Retailers: The retail industry will be significantly affected by the new tax system. Those that have never before been required to collect taxes will have an adjustment and added expense. Also, the inventory transition problem likely will worry many. However, if they remember the savings that ***STR*** will bring (no Social Security or profit taxes; lower supply and capital costs; much simpler compliance; and lower interest rates) and the increase in consumer income, they will realize how much better off they will be under the new tax system.

Some retail organizations are also concerned about the possibly disruptive impact upon sales. We have seen that, even with the increase in real income, consumers will experience some degree of "sticker shock." Until they become accustomed to the new prices and become convinced of their truly increased income, some discretionary consumption may be deferred. Some retail industries will understandably be somewhat antsy.

Financial planning: Nobody actually reads the entire tax code. Even if they did, few could understand it. [Indeed, it is doubtful whether *anyone* understands it all.] That has created the opportunity for tax experts to cut through the webs of tax complexity. *Those who benefit from the complexity and loopholes of the current system* will clearly face major changes in their careers. Some tax planners make a very good living "gaming" the tax system by finding loopholes to help their wealthy and influential clients. Indeed, most of their success is the direct result of the burden, the complexity, the constant changes and the loopholes of the current system.

Financial planners will be affected by the transition to the new tax system. After all, they have invested a lot of time and effort in understanding the old tax system. They should remain in high demand and do very well during the five-year transition period of ***STR*** as both businesses and individuals adjust to the new tax environment. The tax-advising aspect of their services will decline significantly, but their clients will still need investment and retirement advice. And, because the magnitude of investable funds will grow rapidly, the overall demand for their services will rise. Most accountants and financial planners will likely do well.

Tax lobbyists: Another group that benefits from the flaws of the current system is the tax lobbyists. Because the tax code is so full of loopholes and susceptible to hidden changes, the lobbyists have become one of the biggest industries in Washington. They make very little contribution to the betterment of our country but they are paid very well for twisting the tax system to benefit their clients. Tax lobbyists will be bitter opponents of the ***Sensible Tax Reform***.

Congress and the White House

The biggest hurdle, other than public inertia and fear, to the passage and implementation of ***STR*** is political. Numerous Washington insiders have stated, when earlier tax-reform proposals have been offered, that the tax-relief side of the "power of the purse" is one of a politician's most attractive and powerful tools. Many politicians will be very reluctant to give that up—no matter how good the proposal might be for the country.

Political inertia: I have no illusions that getting strong congressional and White House support will be easy. There are many things wrong with politics in Washington that Americans need to root out and correct—the earmarks; the soft treatment by Congress of ethical violations by its members; the corrupting influence of tax lobbyist; endless budget deficits and skyrocketing national debt; the constantly recurring debt-ceiling crises; the failure to seriously address the energy crisis; the weaknesses of Social Security and the Medicare time bomb; and the healthcare crisis. "Politics as usual" has been the trademark of our political leaders in Washington with little interest in seriously addressing the major problems of our country.

Radical and Simple

A Critical Juncture

The United States is at a critical juncture in its history—economically, socially and politically. It must implement serious, fundamental reforms. The world has changed, both internationally and domestically. What worked in the past will no longer be adequate in the future. The longer that we postpone facing up to our critical problems then the more difficult it will be to resolve them. Tough decisions must be made.

"Ask What You Can Do for Your Country!"

In his first inaugural address, President Kennedy made that famous request. It is the embodiment of what has always made America great. Whenever times have been difficult, that spirit has always been what has moved this country ahead. It is what we need now.

This book has been about many problems—but only one solution. This book has focused upon how our federal tax system evolved and deteriorated over the past three generations. The system badly needs an overhaul. However, until a critical mass of the American people recognizes just how serious our national problems are, little will be done. I am asking that the United States institute a very substantial change in its method of taxation. It will not be easy—no fundamental change ever is. The greater the problems that must be surmounted and the greater the benefits that we seek then the greater the difficulty will be to reach those goals.

What I have proposed in this book is a new direction for the American economy—based upon a change to a very different tax system. ***Sensible Tax Reform—Simple, Just and Effective*** is only one of many steps that the United States must take in order to move out of the twentieth-century mentality into the twenty-first. However, it is one of the most important. And it is one that will favorably affect many of our problems—weak exports, excessive imports, lost industries, lost jobs, massive foreign debt, huge federal budget deficit, falling dollar, a convoluted tax system which hurts our economy and inadequate savings.

Our current federal tax system is a very serious problem. The fundamental change that this book has introduced will directly improve many aspects of those problems. It will not resolve all of them—there is no magic wand. However, the problems have become very serious. They continue to rapidly worsen. We need to act. We need to act now.

It is the right and the responsibility of the American people to take the efforts to force our politicians to make the decisions that are necessary to address our critical problems. The passage of the new tax proposal will not be easy. Like these other very important issues, its passage will need to be the result of a demand from the American people that our government give to their constituents the type of government that we deserve. We need a drastically different federal tax system. We need ***Sensible Tax Reform—Simple, Just and Effective***! We will need to force our politicians to give it to us if they will not take the lead and do it on their own.

The reform journey begins here. If you recognize just how badly deformed our current federal tax system is and if you acknowledge the need for truly serious reform of our taxes now, it is time to take action. Get involved. The American Revolution was ignited by the demand for tax reform—"taxation without representation." The time for the next tax revolution is now—a peaceful tax revolution. Please check the STR website: www.sensibletaxreform.org. Also, follow the revolution on Facebook and Twitter.

BIBLIOGRAPHY

Bartlett, Bruce. *The Benefit and the Burden: Tax Reform: Why We Need It and What It Will Take.* Simon & Schuster, 2012.

Bartlett, Donald L. and James B. Steele. *The Great American Tax Dodge.* University of California Press, 2000.

Barrett, William P. and Janet Novak. "52,000 Had Secret UBS Accounts," *Forbes*, February 19, 2009.

Boortz, Neal and John Linder. *The Fair Tax Book*, Regan Books, 2005.

Burman, Leonard E. and Joel Slemrod, *Taxes in America: What Everyone Needs to Know. Oxford University Press, 2012.*

Center for Tax Justice. "The US Has a Low Corporate Tax." (April 5, 2012).

CBSNews. "How Merck Lost $2.3 Billion in the Bermuda Triangle." (November 17, 2009).

Department of Treasury. *Major Foreign Holdings of Treasury Securities* (June 2013).

Drawbaugh, Kevin. "Twin Rebukes Jolt Business Tax Holiday Campaign." *Reuters*, (October 4, 2011).

Forbes. "The World's Billionaires." (March 4, 2013).

Forbes, Steve. *The Flat Tax Revolution.* Regnery Publishing, 2005

Fox, John O. *If Americans Really Understood Income Taxes.* Westview, 200-1

Graetz, Michael. *Death By 1000 Cuts*, Princeton University Press, 2006.

Hall, Robert E. and Alvin Rabushka. *The Flat Tax* (2d). Hoover Institution Press, 2007.

Internal Revenue Service, Statistics of Income Division. *Estate Tax Returns Filed in 2011*, Table 1. (August 2012).

Johnston, David Cay. *Perfectly Legal*, Portfolio, 2003.

McCaffery, Edward J. *Fair Not Flat.* University of Chicago Press,2002.

McCormack, John. "GE Filed 57,000-Page Tax Return, Paid No Taxes on $14 Billion in Profits." *Weekly Standard*, (November 11, 2011).

Moody, J. Scott et al. *The Rising Cost of Complying with the Federal Income Tax.* The Tax Foundation. (December 2005); Special Report #138.

Office of Management and Budget,. *The Budget for the Fiscal Year 2014*, February 2013; Table 2.1 and 2.5.

Ohlemacher, Stephen. "Tax Cheats Pony Up $5.5 billion in Amnesty Program." *Huffington Post*, (April 26, 2013).

Organization of Economic Cooperation & Development. *OECD Factbook: 2013.*

Pearlstein, Steven. "Marty Sullivan figured out how the biggest companies avoided billions in taxes." *Washington Post* (October 26, 2013).

President's Advisory Panel on Federal Tax Reform. *America Needs a Better Tax System.* (April 13, 2005).

Santoli, Michael. "Rich America, Poor America." *Barron's* (January 23, 2007).

Slemrod, Joel and Jon Bakija. *Taxing Ourselves* (4th). MIT Press, 2008.

Steuerle, C. Eugene. *Contemporary U.S. Tax Policy.* Urban Institute Press, 2004.

Thurm, Scott and Kate Linebaugh. "More U.S. Profits Parked Abroad, Saving on Taxes." *Wall Street Journal* (March 10, 2013).

VAT Reader, Tax Analysts, 2011

INDEX

A

Abbott Laboratories, 163
ABCITS (Any But the Current Income Tax System), 44
Abramoff, Jack, 48
Accountants and Lawyers Employment Act of 1986, 44
Acton, Lord, 47
Adams, Charles, 61
adoption credit, 51
Advisory Panel on Federal Tax Reform, 5–6, 7, 9, 43
alcohol tax, 32, 39, 41, 142
alternative minimum tax (AMT), 34, 35, 79, 137, 195
American Institute of Certified Public Accountants (AICPA), 8, 53, 106
American International Group (AIG), 75
American Revolution, 218
Americans for Fair Taxation, 44
annuities, tax sheltered, 17, 22, 115
Any But the Current Income Tax System (ABCITS), 44
Apple, Inc., 159, 162, 163
Armey, Richard, 112
asset taxation, 36–38
audits by Internal Revenue Service, 9, 11, 205
Australia tax revenue, 33
automobile purchase taxation, 38, 146–47, 166–67

B

balance of trade in United States
    current, 12–14, 24–25, 27–28, 74–76, 162, 178–80
    impact of ***Sensible Tax Reform*** on, 176–77
Barron's newspaper, 110, 111

Bartlett, Bruce, 152
Belgium, U.S. debt to, 12, 180
bequest taxation, 72, 112, 121–22
Bezos, Jeff, 118
Bismarck, Otto von, 46, 48
Blackstone Group, 182
Boeing, 159
bonds, investment (*see* investment activities)
Brazil
  balance of trade in, 25
  U.S. debt to, 12, 180
Brown, Jerry, 43
Buffett, Warren, 18, 41, 77–78, 109
Bush, George W., 3, 4, 5, 9, 43, 171
business operations
  financing and, 155–56, 197–99
  impact of ***Sensible Tax Reform*** on, 156–59, 204, 212–13, 214–15
  offshore profit holding, 162–63, 182–83
  personal use purchases, 206–7
business taxation
  burden, 9–10, 19–21, 42, 151
  compliance expenses, 21, 23–24, 154–55
  core elements of ***Sensible Tax Reform*** on, 149–52
  gaming the system and, 55, 73, 150
  impact of ***Sensible Tax Reform*** on, 66, 73–76, 98–99, 152–54
  transition to ***Sensible Tax Reform,*** 195–201

C

Canada
  balance of trade in, 25, 179
  tax revenue, 33
capital gains taxation
  current, 50–52
  gaming the system and, 53–56
  impact of ***Sensible Tax Reform*** on, 79, 115, 119, 121, 136, 139, 140, 184
  regressiveness of, 42, 77
  as unearned income, 17–18, 29, 36, 41, 43, 113–14, 173
Capone, Al, 207
carbon tax, 40, 62
care for elderly or disabled credit, 51
Caribbean
  as tax haven, 184
  U.S. debt to, 12, 180
car purchase taxation, 38, 146–47, 166–67
carried interest, 52, 77, 102, 113, 114 (*see also* investment activities)
casual trade and ***Sensible Tax Reform,*** 206
certified public accountants, 7, 8, 21, 53, 54, 73, 106, 154, 215
charitable donations, 72, 88, 89, 143, 173
child and dependent care credit, 51, 173

China
balance of trade in, 25, 178, 179
international reserves, 181
sovereign wealth funds, 182
U.S. debt to, 12, 13, 25, 27, 180
Chrysler, 75
cigarette tax, 32, 39, 41, 89, 142, 191
Cisco Systems, Inc.
Citibank, 75
Citicorp, 23, 34, 154
Citigroup, Inc., 163
Citizens for Tax Justice, 44
Coca-Cola, 159
compliance expenses, 9, 21–24, 73, 91, 138
congressional politics
lobbyists and, 47–49
Sensible Tax Reform and, 80, 81, 112, 216
Constitution, United States, 27, 47
consumer price index, 201
consumption tax (*see* federal consumption tax (FCT))
copyrights shifted abroad, 164, 183, 200
corporate tax (*see* business tax)
cost of living index, 201
credit crunch of 2007-2010 (*see* economic history of United States)
credits
income tax, 36–37, 113
types of, 51, 153
crises, economic (*see* economic history of United States)

D

death tax, 42, 119
(*see also* estate tax)
debt financing
business and, 11, 73, 75, 152, 155–56
transition to ***Sensible Tax Reform,*** 197–99
deductions, income tax, 36–37, 50–51, 113
diplomatic tensions of United States, 182
dividends tax rate, 51–52, 75, 135, 155, 199
dollar reputation, U.S., 160, 210, 217
Domenici-Rivlin Task Force, 44
donation taxation, 121–22, 143

E

earmarks, 53
earned *vs.* unearned income tax, 17, 29, 36, 41, 51, 113, 173
economic history of United States
21st century, 171–72
diversity and, 13–14
global reputation, 210–12
Great Recession of 2007-2010, 11, 14, 75, 156, 194, 198
Economic Recovery Advisory Board (PERAB), 44
educational provisions, 51, 141–42

Einstein, Albert, 63, 189
Ellison, Larry, 118
embedded taxation
- burden on domestic goods, 9–10
- burden on exports, 27, 75
- eliminating, 98–99
- transition to ***Sensible Tax Reform,*** 196

equity financing and business, 152, 155–56, 197–99
estate planning, 69, 101, 120
estate tax
- current system of, 16–17, 19, 20, 32, 38, 68–69, 119–21
- impact of ***Sensible Tax Reform*** on, 67, 72, 121–23
- individual and, 10, 36, 54
- progressiveness of, 42
- provisions, 173
- revenue from, 65

Europe
- aristocracy of, 28
- transaction tax in, 38–39, 180
- (*see also specific countries*)

excise tax, 20, 32, 38, 39, 41, 89, 142
exclusions from taxable income, 50, 114–15
export and import trade (*see* foreign trade)
Exxon Mobil Corporation, 153, 163

F

fair tax plan, 78, 143, 174, 207
Fannie Mae, 75
federal consumption tax (FCT)
- business obligation with, 164–65, 197
- core elements of proposed, 86–90
- exceptions to rule, 141–48
- foreign countries and, 74
- impact of proposed, 77–78, 130–41
- transition to ***Sensible Tax Reform,*** 190–91, 193–94, 201–2, 204, 206

financial crises (*see* economic history of United States)
financial planning
- of high income individuals, 137–38
- obstacles of ***Sensible Tax Reform,*** 215
- (*see also* estate planning)

529 College Savings Plans, 50
flat tax proposals
- estate tax, 42, 121
- excise tax, 39
- income tax, 43, 44, 78, 80, 112
- sales tax, 78, 91, 112
- (*see also* federal consumption tax (FCT))

Forbes, Steve, 43, 78, 112
Forbes Magazine, 118
foreign competitiveness, 4, 6, 10, 12–14, 55, 74–75, 139
foreign debt of United States, 12–14, 27–28, 176–77, 180–82, 199–201, 210

foreign income tax, 19, 51, 139
foreign profits and U.S. business, 159–60
  job migration, 13, 26, 73, 211
  profit holding, 162–64, 176, 182–83, 199–201
foreign trade
  about, 12–14, 24–28
  current tax system and, 74–75
  deficits, 162
  duties, 20, 32, 38, 39, 41
  impact of ***Sensible Tax Reform*** on, 159–63, 176–82
  tax variables, 74–75
  (*see also* balance of trade in United States)
401(k) retirement savings, 22, 50, 89, 138, 193
403(b) retirement savings, 22, 138, 193
457(b) retirement savings, 193
France
  balance of trade in, 25
  tax revenue, 33
Franklin, Benjamin, 4, 172
free enterprise system of United States, 111
Friedman, Milton, 31, 85

G

gaming the tax system
  business and, 73
  current use of, 3, 4, 14, 17–18, 21, 29, 36, 46, 53–56
  eliminating, 70, 79, 80–81
  estate tax and, 68
  high income individuals and, 113–14
  impact of ***Sensible Tax Reform*** on, 215
  patents for, 120–21
gasoline tax, 39, 41, 142
General Electric (GE), 23, 73, 154, 158–59, 163, 204
General Motors, 75
Germany
  balance of trade, 25, 162, 178, 179
  tax revenue, 33
gift tax, 10, 19, 20, 38
(*see also* estate tax)
governmental misfeasance, 152–53
grandfather clause of mortgages, 194
Great Recession of 2007-2010, 11, 14, 75, 156, 194, 198

H

Hand, Learned, 54
head tax, 40
healthcare expenditures provision to federal consumption tax, 147–48
health savings accounts, 50, 88
Helmsley, Leona, 53, 103
high income taxation
  case for, 109–13
  core elements of proposed, 123–24
  current tax burden, 107–9

estate and gift taxes, 119
impact of ***Sensible Tax Reform*** on, 102, 109–13, 135–38
IRS Tax Form 1040 HI, 114–15
proposed, 79, 91–94
rates, 116–18, 136–38
(*see also* estate tax; income and wealth disparity)
Hill, Lauryn, 103
history of federal tax system, 34, 47–48, 115
(*see also* economic history of United States)
Holmes, Oliver Wendell, Jr., 16
home purchase taxation, 143–46, 166
Hong Kong
international reserves, 181
U.S. debt to, 12
House Ways and Means Committee, 49
hybrid-electric car credit, 51

I

IBM (International Business Machines Corporation), 163
import and export trade (*see* foreign trade)
income and wealth disparity, 117–19
current *vs.* reformed tax systems and, 96–101, 109–12
gaming the system and, 46–48, 50
history of tax system and, 34–35, 42–43
tax rates and, 17–18, 19, 41, 51, 53, 69
income tax
about, 36
business and, 9, 19, 73
development of, 47–48
impact of ***Sensible Tax Reform*** on, 70–72
individual and, 10, 17–19, 68
transition to ***Sensible Tax Reform,*** 190–91
U.S. revenue from, 20
variations due to wealth, 79
(*see also* tax system, United States)
indexing for inflation, 35, 201–2
India
balance of trade in, 179
international reserves, 181
individual retirement accounts (IRA), 22, 50, 89, 138, 193
individual taxation
burden, 10–11, 16–19
compliance expenses, 21–22
current federal tax system and, 67–69
gaming, 54
impact of ***Sensible Tax Reform*** on, 70–72, 190–94, 213–14
income differences and, 78–79
inflation index, 35, 201–3
informal markets and ***Sensible Tax Reform,*** 206
inheritance tax, 32, 54, 72, 122–23
(*see also* estate tax)

insurance, 88, 89, 142
intangible asset tax, 38, 200
"intaxification," 21, 72
intellectual property tax evasion, 54, 164, 183, 200
interest rates and payments
  current tax system and, 11, 75
  impact of ***Sensible Tax Reform*** on, 139, 142, 155–56
  transition to ***Sensible Tax Reform,*** 193–94, 198
Internal Revenue Code
  history of, 66
  revisions to, 34–36, 68, 113, 171
  state of current, 7, 212
Internal Revenue Service (IRS)
  2013 report by, 41
  audits, 9, 11
  budget of, 11
  foreign earnings and, 183
  impact of ***Sensible Tax Reform*** on, 174–75, 203–7
  IRS Tax Form 1040 HI, 114–15
  taxpayer support by, 8
international business and trade (*see* foreign trade)
International Harvester, 159
international reserves, 181
internet retail obligations, 165
inventory transition to ***Sensible Tax Reform,*** retail, 196–97
investment activities
  bonds, 50, 155, 198
  foreign investments in U.S., 164
  foreign repatriation scandal, 162–64
  impact of ***Sensible Tax Reform*** on, 88, 138–39, 141
  transition to ***Sensible Tax Reform,*** 192–93, 198–99
invisible *vs.* visible taxes, 31–32
IRA (individual retirement accounts), 22, 50, 89, 138, 193
Ireland, U.S. debt to, 12
IRS (*see* Internal Revenue Service (IRS))
Italy
  balance of trade in, 25
  tax revenue, 33
Iwry, J. Mark, 46

J

Japan
  balance of trade in, 25, 179
  international reserves, 181
  tax revenue, 33
  U.S. debt to, 12, 25, 27, 180
Jefferson, Thomas, 111
Jobs, Steve, 118
Johnson & Johnson, 163

K

Kennedy, John F., 217
Keogh investments, 22, 138
Koch brothers, 118
Korea
  international reserves, 181
  tax revenue, 33

K Street tax lobbyists, 175
Kuwait balance of trade, 25

L

Linder, John, 49
lobbyists, tax
impact of ***Sensible Tax Reform*** on, 66, 85, 175, 215–16
power of, 47–49, 81, 114
loopholes in tax system (*see* gaming the tax system)
Lott, Trent, 49
low income taxation
impact of ***Sensible Tax Reform*** on, 130–32
proposed rebate for, 93–94
Luxembourg, U.S. debt to, 12

M

Malaysia balance of trade, 25
manipulation of tax system (*see* gaming the tax system)
marriage tax, 133
Mars, Inc., 118
McCaffery, Edward J., 149
Medicare tax
business and, 9, 19, 21, 74–75, 154
impact of ***Sensible Tax Reform*** on, 70, 140, 172–73
individual and, 10, 16–17, 29, 67–68, 70
transition to ***Sensible Tax Reform,*** 190, 195–96, 205–6
U.S. revenue from, 20
Merck & Company, 159, 162, 163
meritocracy of United States, 18, 28
Microsoft Corporation, 163
Middle East and U.S. relations, 28
middle income taxation
impact of ***Sensible Tax Reform*** on, 57, 70–72, 132–35
savings rate of, 97, 99–101, 134–35, 138
tax burden on, 10, 17–18, 41, 43, 67–69, 77, 91, 102
transition to ***Sensible Tax Reform,*** 192
mineral tax, 40
Money Magazine, 8
Morgan, J. Pierpont, 111
mortgage crisis (*see* economic history of United States)
mortgage interest, 173, 193–94, 198
municipal bonds (*see* investment activities)
municipal income tax, 142
mutual fund investments (*see* investment activities)

N

National Taxpayers Union, 44
Netherlands
balance of trade in, 25
tax revenue, 33
neutrality, tax, 42–43, 64, 107
non-sheltered accounts, 140
Norway balance of trade, 25

O

Obama, Barack, 44
occupancy tax, 40
occupation tax, 40
offshore business operations (*see* foreign profits and U.S. business)
oil industry, 12, 152–53, 180
O'Neill, Paul H., 3, 4
Organization of Economic Cooperation and Development (OECD), 32–33
organized crime and ***Sensible Tax Reform,*** 207

P

patents
  shifted abroad, 164, 183, 200
  on tax-avoidance schemes, 54, 120–21
payroll tax (*see* Medicare tax; Social Security tax)
PERAB (Economic Recovery Advisory Board), 44
per capita tax, 40
Peterson, Shirley, 8
Pfizer, Inc., 55, 162, 163
pharmaceutical industry, 152–53, 157, 162, 175, 200, 202 (*see also specific companies*)
plutocracy of United States, 111
political appeal for tax ***Sensible Tax Reform,*** 79–81, 112–13, 216
poll tax, 40
poverty-level individuals (*see* low income taxation)
presidential politics
  lobbyists and, 48–49
  reform and, 18, 41, 43–44, 216
privacy of individuals, 104
Proctor & Gamble, 163
production tax, 40
profit repatriation scandal, 162–64
profit tax, 55
progressive taxes, 18, 19, 20, 42, 77
property tax, 32, 37, 89, 173, 198–99

R

Reagan, Ronald, 44, 47, 80
real estate tax, 37
rebate for poverty level consumption, proposed, 93–94, 133
regressive taxes
  about, 17, 18, 22, 40, 41, 77–80
  creating, 136–37
  reducing, 78, 91–93, 172–73
renewable energy credit, 51
repatriation scandal, profit, 162–64
retail industry transition to ***Sensible Tax Reform,*** 191–92, 195–97, 215
retail tax (*see* federal consumption tax (FCT))
retirees benefits of ***Sensible Tax Reform,*** 139
retirement savings, 22, 50, 51, 88–89
revisions to Internal Revenue Code, 34–36, 68, 113, 171

Ricardo, David, 62
Rogers, Will, 129
Romney, Mitt, 41, 77, 109
Roth IRA, 22, 138, 193
Russia
  balance of trade in, 25, 179
  international reserves, 181
  U.S. debt to, 12

S

sales tax, 32, 38–39, 164–65
  (*see also* federal consumption tax (FCT))
Santoli, Michael, 110, 111
Saudi Arabia
  balance of trade in, 25, 179
  international reserves, 181
savings
  rates, 99–101, 134, 138
  transition to ***Sensible Tax Reform,*** 193
scandals, tax, 48, 53, 54, 55, 162–64, 183, 200
Schaeffer-Tauzin National Retail Sales Tax Act of 1997, 78, 112
self-employment tax, 74, 165–66
Senate Finance Committee, 49
shopping and ***Sensible Tax Reform,*** 191–92
Simpson-Bowles Commission, 44
Singapore international reserves, 181
16th Amendment (1913), 47
small business taxation
  burden, 74, 165–66
  compliance, 23–24
  (*see also* business tax)
Snipes, Wesley, 103
social engineering of tax system, 10, 19, 114, 152–53, 172, 173–74
Social Security Administration, 154, 206
Social Security tax
  business and, 9, 19, 21, 74–75, 154
  impact of ***Sensible Tax Reform*** on, 70, 140, 172–73
  individual and, 10, 16–17, 29, 67–68, 70
  transition to ***Sensible Tax Reform,*** 190, 195–96, 205–6
  U.S. revenue from, 20
South Africa balance of trade, 25
South Korea balance of trade, 25
sovereign wealth funds, 182
Spain
  balance of trade in, 25
  tax revenue, 33
Spielberg, Steven, 118
standards of good taxation, 50
state income tax reform, 34–35, 50–51, 87, 89, 158, 164–65, 175–76
  (*see also* tax system, United States)
stock and bond trading tax, 38–39, 88, 135, 155
  (*see also* investment activities)
subsidies (*see* credits)

sunset provisions on non-tax goals, 114
Switzerland
- balance of trade in, 25, 162, 178–79
- international reserves, 181
- U.S. debt to, 12, 180

T

Taiwan, U.S. debt to, 12, 180
Targowski, Andrew, 83
tax arbitrage, 200
- (*see also* foreign trade)

tax evasion
- examples, 53, 102–3, 183, 194, 200
- ***Sensible Tax Reform*** and, 206–7

tax favored incentives, 50–52
Tax Foundation, 11, 22, 23, 44, 76
tax haven, United States as, 13, 159, 164, 176, 178, 183–84
tax-loss harvesting, 192
tax neutrality, 19, 43, 107, 124, 169, 171–72
Tax Reform Act of 1986, 44
tax sheltered accounts, 140, 193
tax system, United States
- advantages of, 32–33, 50
- comparison of current and reformed, 96–101
- core elements of proposed, 62–66, 82–84, 95, 169–70
- disadvantages of, 34–36, 43, 53–56, 212
- gaming the (*see* gaming the tax system)
- history of, 34, 47–48, 115
- impact of ***Sensible Tax Reform*** on individuals, 70–72
- legal crimes, 55
- problems with current, 3–15
- reform history, 43–44
- social engineering of, 10, 19, 114, 172, 173–74
- transition for business, 195–99
- transition for individuals, 189–94
- transition for U.S. economy, 199–203
- transition for U.S. government, 203–7
- transparency of, 7, 10–11, 80–81

tax writing committees in Congress, 49
tobacco tax, 32, 39, 41, 89, 142, 191
Tobin, James, 38
Tobin tax, 38
tourist tax, 38, 39, 40
trade deficit (*see* balance of trade in United States)
transaction tax, 38–39
transfer of wealth taxation, 121–23
transfer pricing, 183, 200
transition to ***Sensible Tax Reform***
- for business, 195–99
- for individuals, 189–94
- obstacles, 214–18
- for U.S. economy, 199–203
- for U.S. government, 203–7

transparency of tax system
current level of, 7
increasing, 10–11, 80–81
Treasury (*see* United States Treasury)
Trump, Donald, 131
Turkey balance of trade, 25

U

unearned *vs.* earned income taxation, 17, 29, 36, 41, 113
Union Bank of Switzerland (UBS), 194
United Kingdom
balance of trade in, 25, 179
tax revenue, 33
U.S. debt to, 12, 180
United States
balance of trade (*see* balance of trade in United States)
budget development, 47
diplomatic tensions, 182
domestic impact of ***Sensible Tax Reform*** and, 172–76, 203–7
economic history (*see* economic history of United States)
economic reputation, 160, 210–12, 217
foreign competitiveness, 4, 6, 10, 12–14, 55, 74–75, 139
foreign debt, 12–14, 27–28, 176–77, 180–82, 199–201, 210
foreign impact of ***Sensible Tax Reform*** and, 176–84
foreign trade (*see* foreign trade)
governmental misfeasance, 152–53
international reserves, 181
Middle East relations with, 28
revenue sources, 20, 170–71, 203–5
tax revenue, 19, 20, 33, 36, 64–65, 68, 107–8
values (*see* values of United States)
United States Congress, xii, 4, 5, 6, 8, 17, 18, 20, 22, 47
United States Department of Health and Human Services (HHS), 93
United States Department of Justice, 183, 194
United States Treasury, 155, 174, 205–6
(*see also* Internal Revenue Service (IRS))
University of Notre Dame, 142

V

value-added tax (VAT), 27, 38, 39, 44, 74, 76, 152
values of United States, 10–11, 18, 28–29, 33, 111, 117–19, 142–43
visible *vs.* invisible taxes, 31–32
von Bismarck, Otto, 46, 48

W

Wall Street Journal, 162
Wal-Mart, 51, 54, 192
Walton, Sam, 51, 54, 118

wealth transfer taxation, 121–23
welfare system, 103–4
window tax, 38
Winfrey, Oprah, 118
withholdings, income tax, 68, 70
World Trade Organization, 177
Wriston, Walter B., 34

Y

Yom Kippur War, 28

ABOUT THE AUTHOR

Christopher Korth is Professor of Finance and International Business at the Haworth College of Business of Western Michigan University.

Professor Korth received his doctorate in International Business and Finance from Indiana University. He joined the Western Michigan University faculty in 1994 after serving seventeen years as Professor of International Business and Finance and also the Director of the Faculty Development in International Business Program at the University of South Carolina.

Prior to that, Dr. Korth was the Chief International Economist with the First National Bank of Chicago after previously serving as the Director of Research at the Institute of International Commerce and Assistant Professor of International Business, both at the University of Michigan, and as Assistant Professor of International Business and Economics at the Pennsylvania State University. He has also taught graduate and undergraduate courses in Europe, Latin America and Asia.

In addition to writing ***Sensible Tax Reform--Simple, Just and Effective***, Dr. Korth is the author of ***International Business: Environment and Management*** (Prentice-Hall) and ***International Countertrade*** (Quorum Books). He has also authored articles which have appeared in many management and scholarly journals on such topics as tax reform, management of foreign exchange risk, international banking, the impact of foreign investments upon host countries and American depositary receipts.

Printed in the USA
CPSIA information can be obtained
at www.ICGtesting.com
JSHW022321140824
68134JS00019B/1227

9 781630 470869